Holding a Cat
by the Tail

Steve Blank

First Edition Copyright ©2014 Steve Blank

All rights reserve. No part of this book may be reproduced in any form whatsoever without permission, except in case of brief quotations embodied in critical articles or reviews.

Published 2014
K&S Ranch

ISBN 0 989200 5 58
$19.99

Table of Contents

7   Entrepreneurship Is an Art

Entrepreneurs as Dissidents

Too Young to Know It Can't Be Done

Entrepreneurship Is an Art, Not a Job

Tenacious

You're Not a Real Entrepreneur

Founders and Dysfunctional Families

Incentives and Legends

Emulating Empathy

Entrepreneurial Finishing School—Should I Get an MBA?

Napkin Entrepreneurs

Mentors, Coaches and Teachers

The Apprentice—Entrepreneur Version

Killing Your Startup By Listening to Customers

Blinded by the Light—The Epiphany

59 Startups Are Not Small Versions of Large Companies

A Startup Is Not a Smaller Version of a Large Company

What's A Startup? First Principles

Touching the Hot Stove—Experiential Versus Theoretical Learning

Search Versus Execute

Make No Little Plans—Defining the Scalable Startup

Lean Startups Aren't Cheap Startups

How to Build a Billion Dollar Startup

9 Deadliest Startup Sins

Why Too Many Startups (er) Suck

Startup Suicide—Rewriting the Code

Open Source Entrepreneurship

105 The Customer Development Manifesto— A Startup's Guiding Light

The Product Development Model

The Customer Development Manifesto: Reasons for the Revolution (part 1)

The Customer Development Manifesto: Reasons for the Revolution (part 2)

The Customer Development Manifesto: The Startup Death Spiral (part 3)

Customer Development Manifesto: Market Type (part 4)

Customer Development Manifesto: The Path of Warriors and Winners (part 5)

Building a Company with Customer Data—Why Metrics Are Not Enough
Why Startups are Agile and Opportunistic—Pivoting the Business Model
The Phantom Sales Forecast—Failing at Customer Validation
Entrepreneurship as a Science—The Business Model/Customer Development Stack
Crisis Management by Firing Executives—There's A Better Way
Consultants Don't Pivot, Founders Do
Death By Revenue Plan
It Must Be A Marketing Problem
Nail the Customer Development Manifesto to the Wall

165 Corporate Innovation—Making Elephants Dance

The Future of Corporate Innovation and Entrepreneurship
Durant Versus Sloan
When Big Companies Are Dead But Don't Know It
Solving the Innovator's Dilemma—Customer Development in a Big Company
Why Innovation Dies
No Accounting For Startups
The Search For the Fountain of Youth—Innovation and Entrepreneurship in the Enterprise
Job Titles That Can Sink Your Startup
Why Board Meetings Suck—Part 1 of 2
Reinventing the Board Meeting—Part 2 of 2—Virtual Valley Ventures
Why Governments Don't Get Startups
How the iPhone Got Tail Fins—Part 1 of 2
How the iPhone Got Tail Fins—Part 2 of 2

231 Startup Culture

Preparing for Chaos—the Life of a Startup

Faith-Based Versus Fact-Based Decision Making

The Startup Team

The Road Not Taken

The End of Innocence

Relentless—The Difference Between Motion And Action

Closure

The Elves Leave Middle Earth—Sodas Are No Longer Free

No Plan Survives First Contact With Customers—Business Plans versus Business Models

The Cover-Up Culture

Burnout

I've seen the Promised Land. And I might not get there with you.

The Peter Pan Syndrome–The Startup to Company Transition

You'll Be Dead Soon—Carpe Diem

281 On-the-Job Training—The Best Way to Learn

Entrepreneurship Is Hard But You Can't Die

Careers Start by Peeling Potatoes

SuperMac War Story 6: Building The Killer Team—Mission, Intent and Values

Supermac War Story 8: Cats and Dogs—Admitting a Mistake

When Microsoft Threatened to Sue Us Over the Letter "E"

Nuke'em 'Till They Glow— Quitting My First Job

Lying on Your Resume

311 An Entrepreneur in the Family

Lies Entrepreneurs Tell Themselves

Epitaph for an Entrepreneur

Unintended Lessons

Thanksgiving Day

The Seven Days of Christmas

327 VC Confidential

Is Your VC Founder Friendly?

"Lessons Learned"—A New Type of Venture Capital Pitch

Steel In Their Eyes—Why VCs Should Be Startup CEOs

Raising Money Using Customer Development

How Scientists and Engineers Got It Right, and VCs Got It Wrong

The $10 Million Photo and Other VC Stories

353 Steve's Favorite Posts

When It's Darkest Men See the Stars

Philadelphia University Commencement Speech

Requiem For A Roommate

I.

Entrepreneurship Is an Art

Entrepreneurs as Dissidents

November 6, 2012 (Steve Blank)

Here's to the crazy ones. The misfits. The rebels. The troublemakers. The round pegs in the square holes. The ones who see things differently. They're not fond of rules. And they have no respect for the status quo. You can quote them, disagree with them, glorify, or vilify them. About the only thing you can't do is ignore them. Because they change things. They push the human race forward. While some may see them as the crazy ones, we see genius. Because the people who are crazy enough to think they can change the world, are the ones who do.

Countries that put their artists and protesters in jail will never succeed in building a successful culture of entrepreneurship. They will be relegated to creating better mousetraps or cloning other countries' business models.

Entrepreneurs as Dissidents

When Steve Jobs returned to Apple, he ran the Think Different ads, a brilliant marketing campaign to make Apple's core customers believe that Apple was still fighting for the brand.

But in hindsight, the ad captured something much more profound.

The crazy ones? The misfits? The rebels? The troublemakers? To celebrate those people as heroes requires a country and culture that tolerates and encourages dissent.

Because without dissent there is no creativity.

Countries that stifle dissent while attempting to encourage entrepreneurship will end up at a competitive disadvantage.

Pushing the Boundaries

Most startups solve problems in existing markets—making something better than what existed before. Some startups choose to resegment a market—finding an underserved niche in an existing market or providing a good-enough low-cost solution. These are all good businesses, and there's nothing wrong with founding one of these.

But some small segment of founders are truly artists—they see something no one else does. These entrepreneurs are the ones who want to change "what is" and turn it into "what can be." These founders create new ideas and new markets by pushing the boundaries. This concept of creating something that few others see—and the reality distortion field necessary to recruit the team to build it—is at the heart of what these founders do.

The founders that make a dent in the universe are dissidents. They are not afraid to tell their bosses they are idiots or tell their schools they been teaching the wrong thing or to tell an entire industry to think differently. And more importantly, they are not afraid to tell their country it is mistaken.

Freedom of Speech, Expression, and Thought

Entrepreneurs in the United States take for granted our freedom of speech, freedom of expression and freedom of thought. It's enshrined in our constitution as the first amendment.

In the last few years I've traveled to lots of countries that understand that the rise of entrepreneurship will be an economic engine for the 21st century. In several of these countries, the government is pouring enormous sums into building entrepreneurship programs, faculties, and even cities. Yet time and again when I ask the local entrepreneurs themselves what questions they have, most often the first question is: "How do I get a visa to the United States?"

For years I thought the reason hands were raised was simply an economic one. The same countries that repress dissent tend to have institutionalized corruption, meaning the quality of your idea isn't sufficient enough to succeed by itself, you now need new "friends in the right places." But I now see that these are all part of the same package. It's hard to focus on being creative when a good part of your creative energies are spent trying to figure out how to work within a system that doesn't tolerate dissent.

Lessons Learned

- Entrepreneurs require the same creative freedom as artists and dissidents.

- Without that freedom, countries will be relegated to cloning others' business models or creating better versions of existing products.

- History has shown that the most creative people leave repressive regimes and create elsewhere.

Too Young to Know It Can't Be Done

October 13, 2010 (Steve Blank)

"The young do not know enough to be prudent, and therefore they attempt the impossible—and achieve it, generation after generation."
— Pearl S. Buck

Ask people what makes entrepreneurs successful and you'll hear a familiar list of adjectives: agile, tenacious, resilient, opportunistic, etc.

What you don't hear often: they didn't know any better.

It Can't Be Done

I was just rereading Jessica Livingston's book "Founders at Work," and a common thread through the stories reminded me that there is a type of technology innovation that occurs in startups when a founder/team simply doesn't know what they're attempting is impossible.

Steve Wozniak at Apple building the AppleII floppy disk controller without ever seeing one. The original Fairchild Semiconductor team of Moore and Hoerni racing to build the first silicon diffused PNP and NPN transistors and ending up with Planar transistors and integrated circuits. The list of "I just did it without knowing it was impossible" appears time and again as a common thread in stories about technology innovation.

I got to see this firsthand when I was lucky enough to be present as an incredibly small team designed and built the Zilog and MIPS microprocessors. And at Ardent, I watched an equally minuscule company tackle building a supercomputer and again at E.piphany building a data warehouse.

Almost all these innovations were built by people in their 20s with a few of old-timers in their 30s. (One of the common themes was the physical effort to get these projects completed—entrepreneurs staying up for days to finish a project and/or sleeping at work until it shipped.) I flew more red-eyes than I can remember, and also had days where I just slept in the office with the engineers.

Age Means Wisdom

It's not that older entrepreneurs can't start or build innovative companies—of course they can. Older entrepreneurs just work smarter and strategically. (Though my hypothesis is that funding from risk capital sources—angels and VCs, don't follow a normal distribution curve for older founders.)

And if they're really strategic older founders hire engineers in their 20s and 30s who don't know what they've been asked to do is impossible (exactly the strategy of my partner Ben at E.piphany).

Older Means You Know Too Much

However, as I've gotten older I've observed that it's not just that stamina changes for entrepreneurs. One of the traps of age is growing to accept the common wisdom of what's possible and not. Accumulated experience can at times become an obstacle in thinking creatively. Knowing that "it can't be done" because you can recount each of the failed attempts in the last 20 years to solve the problem can be a boat anchor on insight and imagination. This not only affects individuals, but happens to companies as they age.

When you're young anything seems possible. And at times it is.

Entrepreneurship Is an Art, Not a Job

March 31, 2011 (Steve Blank)

> "Some men see things as they are and ask why.
> Others dream things that never were and ask why not."
> — George Bernard Shaw

Over the last decade we assumed that once we found repeatable methodologies (Agile and Customer Development, Business Model Design) to build early stage ventures, entrepreneurship would become a "science," and anyone could do it.

I'm beginning to suspect this assumption may be wrong.

Where Did We Go Wrong?

It's not that the tools are wrong, I think the entrepreneurship management stack is correct and has made a major contribution to reducing startup failures. Where I think we have gone wrong is the belief that anyone can use these tools equally well.

Entrepreneurship Is an Art, Not a Job

For the sake of this analogy, think of two types of artists: composers and performers (think music composer versus members of the orchestra, playwright versus actor, etc.).

Founders fit the definition of a composer: they see something no one else does. And to help them create it from nothing, they surround themselves with world-class performers. This concept of creating something that few others see—and the reality distortion field necessary to recruit the team to build it—is at the heart of what startup founders do. It is a very different skill than science, engineering, or management.

ART

**Search for a
Business Model**

Founders
Artists/Composers

*Entrepreneurial
Employees*
Artists/Performers

Customer Discovery → Customer Validation

Pivot

Entrepreneurial employees are the talented performers who hear the siren song of a founder's vision. Joining a startup while it is still searching for a business model, they too see the promise of what can be and join the founder to bring the vision to life.

Founders then put in play every skill that makes them unique—tenacity, passion, agility, rapid pivots, curiosity, learning and discovery, improvisation, ability to bring order out of chaos, resilience, leadership, a reality distortion field, and a relentless focus on execution—to lead the relentless process of refining their vision and making it a reality.

Both founders and entrepreneurial employees prefer to build something from the ground up rather than join an existing company. Like jazz musicians or improv actors, they prefer to operate in a chaotic environment with multiple unknowns. They sense the general direction they're headed in, okay with uncertainty and surprises, using the tools at hand, along with their instinct to achieve their vision. These types of people are rare, unique, and crazy. They're artists.

Tools Do Not Make the Artist

When page-layout programs came out with the Macintosh in 1984, everyone thought it was going to be the end of graphic artists and designers. "Now everyone can do design" was the mantra. Users quickly learned how hard it was to design well (yes, it is an art) and again hired professionals. The same thing happened with the first bit-mapped word processors. We didn't get more or better authors. Instead we ended up with poorly written documents that looked like ransom notes. Today's equivalent is Apple's Garageband. Not everyone who uses composition tools can actually write music that anyone wants to listen to.

"Well If It's Not the Tools, Then It Must Be…"

The argument goes, "Well if it's not tools, then it must be…" But examples from teaching other creative arts are not promising. Music composition has been around since the dawn of civilization yet even today the argument of what "makes" a great composer is still unsettled. Is it the process (the compositional strategies used in the compositional process)? Is it the person (achievement, musical aptitude, informal musical experiences, formal musical experiences, music self-esteem, academic grades, IQ, and gender)? Is it the environment (parents, teachers, friends, siblings, school, society, or cultural values)? Or is it constant practice (apprenticeship, 10,000 hours of practice)?

It may be we can increase the number of founders and entrepreneurial employees, with better tools, more money, and greater education. But it's more likely that until we truly understand how to teach creativity, their numbers are limited.

Lessons Learned

- Founders fit the definition of an artist: they see—and create—something that no one else does.

- To help them move their vision to reality, they surround themselves with world-class performers.

- Founders and entrepreneurial employees prefer operating in a chaotic environment with multiple unknowns.

- These type of people are rare, unique, and crazy.

- Not everyone is an artist.

Tenacious

July 19, 2012 (Steve Blank)

TE·NA·CIOUS/TƏ'NĀSHƏS/ Adjective:

1. Not readily letting go of, giving up, or separated from an object that one holds, a position, or a principle: "a tenacious grip."

2. Not easily dispelled or discouraged; persisting in existence or in a course of action.

When I was an entrepreneur, I'd pursue a goal relentlessly. Everything in between me and my goal was simply an obstacle that needed to be removed.

This week I had another reminder of what it was like.

Plenty of Time

I was speaking at the National Governors Conference in Williamsburg, Virginia and my talk ended Sunday at noon. I knew I had to be in Chicago at 9:30 A.M. Monday for a Congressional hearing (I was the lead witness) so I made sure I was on the next to last plane out of Richmond (just in case the last one got cancelled).

My wife and I got to the airport for our 4:45 P.M. plane and found it was delayed to 6 P.M. Okay, no problem. Oops, now it's delayed until 7:30 P.M. Hmm, the last plane out looks like it's leaving on-time at 8 P.M.—can I get on that? No, sold out. So we sit around and watch our plane get delayed to 8 P.M., then 9 P.M. then 10 P.M., then cancelled.

This is looking a bit tight, but there's a 6 A.M. from Richmond to Chicago. No problem. If we can get on that, I can still make the hearing. The nice, smiling United agent says "oh that's sold out as well." Now I'm getting a bit concerned. "Well, how about the American Airlines 6 A.M.?" "Sold out," she replied. "The next flight is at 8 A.M." Okay, put me on that one. "Oh, that's sold out as well."

We Have a Problem

I need to be in downtown Chicago by 9:30 A.M. Period.

So I ask, "where's the nearest airport that has a 6 A.M. flight to Chicago?" Oh, that's Dulles airport in Washington. "Okay, how far is that?" 120 miles.

We head back to the car rental booth, rent our second car of the day, and head to Washington in pouring rain and drive in bumper to bumper traffic, crawling to our next airport. Three hours later, we check into the airport hotel at 1:30 A.M. assured that all we needed to do is get three hours sleep and United would whisk us on the way to Chicago.

Tenacious

Waking up at 4:15 A.M., I glance at my email and couldn't believe it—United canceled our 6 A.M. from Dulles. The next flight they had would get us into Chicago at 10 A.M.—too late to testify in front of Congress. It looked like there was simply no way to get where we needed to go.

My first instinct was to give up. Screw it. I tried hard, failed due to circumstances beyond my control. Why don't we just go back to bed and get a good night's sleep.

That thought lasted all of 30 seconds.

We quickly realized that Washington has two airports—the other one, National was 30 miles away. I looked up the flight schedule and realized that there was a 6 A.M. and 7 A.M. leaving from National. I booked the 7 A.M. online, not believing we could make the earlier 6 A.M. flight.

The only problem was there weren't any taxis to be found at 4:30 in the morning—in front of the hotel or on Uber. So I hiked over to the main road, flagged one down and had him drive me back to the hotel, pick up my wife and luggage and continue our adventure.

We got to Washington National Airport at 5 A.M. and walked directly into the longest security line I've seen in 10 years. Well, at least we can make the 7 A.M. plane (the one we're ticketed on) and barely make the congressional hearing.

After getting through security, the first gate we pass is the 6 A.M. for Chicago and they're in the process of closing the door. "Any chance you have any seats left?" Oh, we have two seats in the back of the plane but we don't have time to re-ticket you.

Trying to remember my reality distortion field skills from my entrepreneurial days, I convinced her to let us on.

We made it to Chicago. I actually got to sleep in our hotel for 45 minutes before the Congressional Field hearing.

Then I got to share my presentation, "Innovation Corps: A Review of a New National Science Foundation Program to Leverage Research Investments." You can read it at http://www.slideshare.net/sblank/house-subcommittee-testimony-of-steve-blank.

Lessons Learned

- Your personal life and career will be full of things that block your way or hinder progress.

- Keep your eyes on the prize, not the obstacles.

- Remove obstacles one at a time.

- There's almost always a path to your goal.

- Never, never, never give up.

You're Not a Real Entrepreneur

June 10, 2010 (Steve Blank)

Who is an entrepreneur really? It turns out that there are four distinct types of entrepreneurial organizations: small businesses, scalable startups, large companies, and social entrepreneurs. They all engage in entrepreneurship. Yet entrepreneurs in one class think that the others aren't the "real" entrepreneurs. This post looks at the differences and similarities and explains why there's such confusion.

Small Business Entrepreneurship

My parents came to the United States through Ellis Island in steerage in sight of the Statue of Liberty. As immigrants, their biggest dream was opening a small grocery store on the Lower East Side of New York City, which they did in 1939. They didn't aspire to open a chain of grocery stores, just to feed their family.

My parents were no less of an entrepreneur than I was. They went on an uncharted course, took entrepreneurial risk and only made money if the business succeeded. The only capital available to them was their own savings and what they could borrow from relatives. Both my parents worked as hard as any Silicon Valley entrepreneur but with a different definition of a successful business model; when they made a profit, they could feed our family. When business was bad, they figured out why, adapted and worked harder still. They were only accountable to one and other.

Startup → Small Business

Today, the overwhelming number of entrepreneurs and startups in the United States are still small businesses.

Scalable Startup Entrepreneurship

Unlike my parents, Fred Durham and his partner Maheesh Jain started the now $100+ million CafePress, knowing they wanted to build a large company. Founded in offices smaller than my parents' grocery store, Fred and Maheesh's vision was to provide a home for artists who made personalized products assembled in a just-in-time factory that today delivers a customized gift each second. Once they found a profitable business model, they realized that scale required external venture capital to fuel rapid expansion. With venture capital came accountability to board members, forecasts, and other people's agendas. Success for a scalable startup is a three-times (or more) return on the investor's money—either by a public offering of stock or by selling the company.

Scalable Startup → Transition → Large Company >$100M/year

Scalable startups in technology centers (Silicon Valley, Shanghai, New York, Bangalore, Israel, etc.) make up a small percentage of entrepreneurs and startups but because of the outsize returns attract almost all the risk capital (and press).

Large Company Entrepreneurship

At the end of 1980, IBM decided to compete in the rapidly growing personal computer market. They were smart enough to realize that IBM's existing processes and procedures wouldn't be agile enough to innovate in this new market. The company established their new PC division (called Entry Systems), as a Skunk Works in Boca Raton Florida, 1000 miles from IBM headquarters. This small group consisted of 12 engineers and designers under the direction of Don Estridge. Success for this new division meant generating substantial revenue and profit for company.

Disruptive Innovation

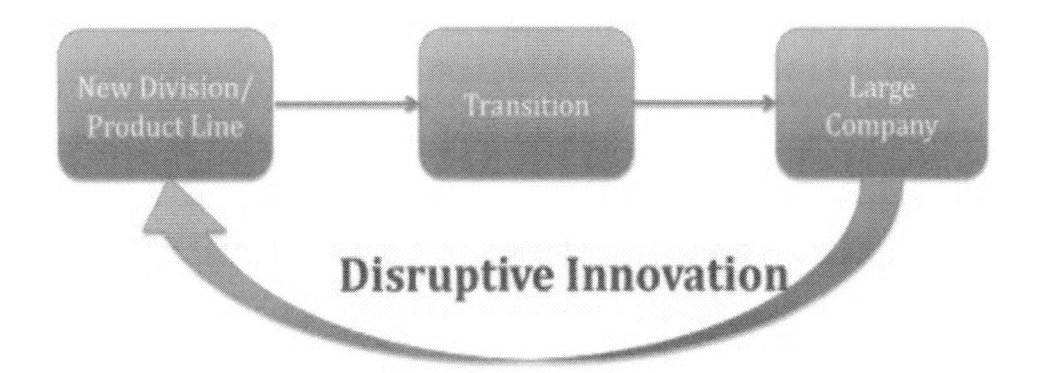

The division developed the IBM PC and announced it in less than a year. Three years later, the division had sold one million PCs, had 9500 people, and a billion dollars in sales.

Don Estridge's paycheck and funding for the division came from IBM, and he reported up the organization, but in his own division he was no less entrepreneurial than Michael Dell or Steve Jobs—or Fred Durham or my parents.

Social Entrepreneurship

Irfan Alam, a 27-year-old from the Indian state of Bihar, started the Sammaan Foundation to transform the lives of 10 million rickshaw-pullers in India. Irfan got banks to finance rickshaw-pullers and designed rickshaws that can shelve newspapers, mineral water bottles, and other essentials for rickshaw passengers. These rickshaws carry ads and the pullers get 50-percent of the ad revenue, the remainder going to Sammaan. The rickshaw-pullers end up as owners after repaying the bank loan in installments. Irfan started off with 100 such rickshaws in 2007 and has 300,000 today.

Irfan doesn't take a salary, but he is as focused on scalability, asset leverage, return on investment and growth metrics as any Silicon Valley entrepreneur ever was.

Summary

If you put the four types of entrepreneurs in a room you would understand what they had in common. They were resilient, agile, tenacious, and passionate—the four most common traits of any class of entrepreneur.

Also in common, each of their businesses initially were searching for a business model, and each was instinctively executing a customer discovery and validation process.

Yet there are obvious differences in each type: personal risk, size of vision, and goal.

	Personal Risk	**Financial Goal**
Small Business	High	Feed the Family
Scalable Startup	High	Get Rich/Implement Vision
Large Company	Low	Feed The Family/Get Promoted
Social	Moderate	Save the World

Lessons Learned

- Four different types of entrepreneurship: Small Business, Scalable, Large Company, Social.

- All searching for a sustainable business model.

- Regardless of type, entrepreneurs have common characteristics: resilient, agile, tenacious, and passionate.

- Differences include level of tolerance of personal risk, size and scale of the vision, and their personal financial goal.

Founders and Dysfunctional Families

May 18, 2009 (Steve Blank) Startup CEO Traits

I was having lunch with a friend who is a retired venture capitalist and we drifted into a discussion of the startups she funded. We agreed that all her founding CEOs seemed to have the same set of personality traits—tenacious, passionate, relentless, resilient, agile, and comfortable operating in chaos. I said, "Well, for me you'd have to add coming from a dysfunctional family." Her response was surprising, "Steve, almost all my CEOs came from very tough childhoods. It was one of the characteristics I specifically looked for. It's why all of you operated so well in the unpredictable environment that all startups face."

I couldn't figure out if I was more perturbed about how casual the comment was or how insightful it was. What makes an individual a great startup founder (versus an employee) has been something I had been thinking about since I retired. My comfort in operating in chaos was something I first recognized when I was working in the Midwest.

The Rust Belt—(Skip this Section if I'm Boring You)

Out of the Air Force, my first job out of school was in Ann Arbor, Michigan, in the mid-1970s, installing broadband process control systems in automotive and manufacturing plants throughout the Midwest. I got to travel and see almost every type of Rust Belt factory—at the time, the heart and muscle of American manufacturing—GM, American Motors, Ford, U.S. Steel, Whirlpool. Our equipment was installed in the manufacturing lines of these companies, and if it went down, sometimes it brought the entire manufacturing line down.

I always made a habit of getting a tour of whatever manufacturing plant I was visiting. Most plant foremen were more than accommodating and flattered that someone was actually interested. I was fascinated to learn how everyday objects (cars, washing machines, structural steel, etc.) that ended up on our shelves or driveways were assembled.

My favorite factory was the massive U.S. Steel plant by Lake Erie. On my first visit, the foreman walked through this enormous building, not much more than a giant steel shed, where they had an open-hearth furnace. We came in time to see the furnace being tapped, pouring steel out into giant buckets. (Years later, I realized I watched the end of an era. The last open-hearth furnaces closed in the 1980s.)

We stood on a platform several stories up, and light streamed diagonally through windows set high on top of the building cutting through the black soot particles created when the incandescent steel hit the bucket.

It was too loud to talk so I just watched the steel pour through the clouds of soot backlit by the blinding bright liquid metal. It looked like an update of the iconic image of Penn Station writ large.

And as I stared the billowing clouds of soot flashing between black and white took on fantastical shapes as tiny figures on the factory floor scurried around the bucket. I could have stayed there all day.

Automobile plants were equally fascinating. They were like being inside a pinball machine. At the Ford plant in Milpitas, the plant foreman proudly took me down the line. I remember stopping at one station a little confused about its purpose. All the other stations on the assembly line had groups of workers with power tools adding something to the car.

This station just had one guy with a 2x4 piece of lumber, a large rubber mallet and a folded blanket. His spot was right after the station where they had dropped the hoods down on the cars, and had bolted them in. As I was watched, the next car rolled down the line, the station before attached the hood, and as the car approached this station, the worker took the 2×4, shoved it under one corner of the hood and put the blanket over the top of the hood and started pounding it with the rubber mallet while prying with the lumber. "It's our hood alignment station," the plant manager said proudly. "These damn models weren't designed right so we're fixing them on the line."

I had a queasy feeling that perhaps this wasn't the way to solve the car quality problem. Little did I know that I was watching the demise of the auto industry in front of my eyes.

Operating in Chaos

Repairing our equipment could be time critical. One day, I was at the Ford Wixom auto assembly plant training my replacement, and I was at met at the door by an irate plant manager. He welcomed us by screaming, "Do you know how much it costs every minute this line is down." As I'm troubleshooting our equipment scattered across the plant (in the computer room, above the steel, in NEMA cabinets next to line, etc.), the manager followed us still yelling. My understudy looked at me and said, "How can you deal with this chaos and still focus?" And until that moment I had never thought about it before. I realized that what others heard as chaos, I just shut it out.

A Day in the Life of a Founder

For those of you who've never started a company, let me assure you that it never happens like the pleasant articles you read in business magazines or in case studies. Founding a company is a sheer act of will and tenacity in the face of immense skepticism from everyone—investors, customers, friends, etc. You literally have to take your vision of the opportunity and against all rational odds assemble financing, and a team to help you execute. And that's just to get started.

Next, you have to deal with the daily crisis of product development and acquiring early customers. And here's where life gets really interesting, as the reality of product development and customer input collide, the facts change so rapidly that the original well-thought-out business plan becomes irrelevant.

If you can't manage chaos and uncertainty, if you can't bias yourself for action, and if you wait around for someone else to tell you what to do, then your investors and competitors will make your decisions for you and you will run out of money and your company will die.

Great founders live for these moments.

Creating the Entrepreneurial Personality—A Thought Experiment

Fast forward three decades back to today. The lunch conversation was an interesting data point to add to a hypothesis I've had.

I've wondered, just as a thought experiment, how would we go about creating individuals who operate serenely in chaos, and have the skills we associate with one type of entrepreneurial founder/leader?

One possible path might be to raise children in an environment where parents are struggling in their own lives, and they create an environment where fighting, abusive, or drug/alcohol-related behavior is the norm.

In this household, nothing would be the same from day to day, the parents would constantly bombard their kids with dogmatic parenting (harsh and inflexible discipline), and they would control them by withholding love, praise, and attention. Finally, we could make sure no child is allowed to express the "wrong" emotion. Children in these families would grow up thinking that this behavior is normal.

(If this seems unimaginably cruel to you, congratulations, you had a great set of parents. On the other hand, if the description is making you uncomfortable remembering some of how you were raised—welcome to a fairly wide club.)

Over the last five years, I've asked over 500 of my students how many of them grew up in a dysfunctional family (participation was voluntary). I've been surprised at the data. In this admittedly very unscientific survey, I've found that between a quarter and half of the students I consider "hard-core" entrepreneurs/founders (working passionately to found a company) self-identified as coming from a less-than benign upbringing.

Founders as Survivors

My hypothesis is that most children are emotionally damaged by this upbringing. But a small percentage, whose brain chemistry and wiring is set for resilience, come out of this with a compulsive, relentless and tenacious drive to succeed. They have learned to function in a permanent state of chaos. And they have channeled all this into whatever activity they could find outside of their home—sports, business, or… entrepreneurship.

Therefore, I'll posit one possible path for a startup founder: the dysfunctional family theory.

Throwing Hand Grenades in Your Own Company

One last thought. The dysfunctional family theory may explain why founders who excel in the chaotic early phases of a company throw organizational hand grenades into their own companies after they find a repeatable and scalable business model and need to switch gears into execution.

The problem, I believe, is that repeatability represents the extreme discomfort zone of this class of entrepreneur. And I have seen entrepreneurs emotionally or organizationally try to create chaos—it's too calm around here—and actually self-destruct.

So What?

Let's be clear, in no way am I suggesting that growing up in a dysfunctional family is the only path to becoming a founder of a startup. Nor am I suggesting that everyone who does so turns out well. And in particular, I'm not suggesting that every employee who joins a startup fits this profile, it just seems more prevalent in the founder(s).

And this hypothesis might be a good example of confusing cause and effect. Yet I am surprised given how much is written about the attributes of a startup founder, how little has been written about what "makes" a founder.

Incentives and Legends

February 1, 2010 (Steve Blank)

Entrepreneurs and the early startup team all need to be motivated by a shared vision, passion and desire to build a large company. Yet it's the company legends that live on.

Fund Raising

Our little startup was less than a year old. We had been busy assembling our team and had just hired the last member of our exec staff. We had also just closed our Series B financing with a major overseas partner. The financing felt like a real validation of our strategy. In truth, it was only proof that our reality distortion field worked in Asia as well.

My Wife Thinks I Deserve a Bonus

One of the new hires was Bob, my VP of Business Development. He knew so little about technology that I used to say he needed a manual to operate a light switch, but I hired him because a small voice said, "He'll do extraordinary things."

He did. And still does.

Bob, among other things ran the fundraising for us in Asia and worked with an outside firm that had great connections in Japan to drag us around Tokyo and get the deal closed. As in, "raising $10 million" kind of closed.

Everyone at our startup was working on startup starvation salaries, and Bob had taken a large pay cut to join us. When the Japanese partner deal was done, Bob said, "Steve, I deserve at least a $10,000 bonus. I haven't been home in weeks, and I pulled off a financing even you admit was unbelievable."

I patiently explained that this type of miraculous event was the norm for startups. The engineers were pulling off miracles on a daily basis, and we were all taking fumes for salaries, but our payoff will be when our stock is worth something. Until then, tell your wife you'll get $10,000 when hell freezes over. No bonuses in a startup. To his credit, Bob said while he understood, he was going to hear about it at home for not being appreciated.

Dinner

Since our management team hadn't met each others' spouses, I thought the financing would be a great reason to get everyone together for a low key celebratory dinner. We picked a restaurant in Palo Alto down the street from the company and got a private room.

We drank lots of wine, had a nice dinner, and (after the dinner plates had been cleared) I made a speech about teamwork, startup, passion, commitment, blah, blah.

I then congratulated the outside firm that Bob had used in Japan. I had invited their CEO and his wife and handed him a check for their retainer bonus for their help in the deal. Bob kept glancing at his wife who was giving him frosty looks and was very clearly not happy.

The New Briefcase

I then announced that it was unfair that Bob shouldn't go unrecognized for his hard work so I had an award for him as well. The atmosphere around Bob's wife began to thaw. I said, "Bob had carried the same old beat up leather briefcase he had since law school, and I knew he wouldn't trade it for anything, but I think it's time he had something more professional-looking. So Bob, on behalf of the company, we bought you a new briefcase."

The look on both Bob's face and his wife's went from happy to disbelief, to "I can't believe you're working for this idiot" on his wife's face to "I can't believe I work for this idiot" on Bob's face.

I said, "Your new briefcase is under the table by your feet. Why don't you just put it on the table." Bob rooted around a bit and found the briefcase and put it on the table. It was the ugliest and cheapest briefcase you will ever see.

Everyone was now looking slightly embarrassed, all thinking that perhaps they had the most obtuse CEO in Silicon Valley. I thought Bob's wife was going to throw a steak knife across the table. I made another speech about how great Bob was and then sat down and said, "Let's get the waiter for coffee and dessert."

The ugly briefcase with its implicit statement sat on the table virtually steaming.

Legend

"Oh, one more thing," I said. "Bob, can you open up the briefcase and dump the papers on the table. We should clear out the stuffing, so you can put your papers from your old briefcase in it."

With almost an audible sigh, Bob unlatched the briefcase, held it upside down over the table and dumped out the contents.

In slow motion, dollar bills began to tumble out of the new briefcase. And they kept coming out. And they started making a pile of bills in front of Bob and his wife and the rest of the executive staff.

15,000 dollars in dollar bills.

Bob's wife started crying.

I said, "Extraordinary work in a startup is the norm, but you performed even beyond my expectations. In my startups, that's worth recognizing."

Rewards for extraordinary effort became part of the company's legend.

Epilogue

Lest you think only salespeople are motivated by cash in a startup, over the life of the company we sprung the same surprise on engineers who delivered the impossible. And at Christmas we gave out hundred dollar bills to each employee. While this small token of appreciation would have been dismissed if it had been a check, it had our engineers showing these bills to their friends in other companies.

In three or so years, these cash incentives added up to no more than $50K. While everyone understood the theory that we were working to make the stock valuable (and we did), the cash reminded them that we cared and noticed.

Lessons Learned

- Cash has a much greater effect than a check.
- Awards for critical contributions can make a lasting impact.
- Small amounts spread through the company can be a great motivator.
- Done correctly it turns incentives into legends.

Emulating Empathy

February 8, 2010 (Steve Blank)

One of the hardest problems for engineers in founding roles in a startup is interacting with customers up close and personal. Over the years I've found the best way to learn to do this is by emulating empathy.

The Problem

I was having dinner in Palo Alto with some of my Stanford engineering students, and one of the subjects they were most interested in talking about was "how do you really get out of the building and talk to customers." Listening to them reminded me how terribly painful it had been for me.

Data Driven

I was always curious about technology and how things worked, but early in my career, this curiosity didn't extend to people. I was more comfortable with data.

In my first company, ESL, I sat in secure locations and taught complex intelligence gathering systems to a classroom of maintenance and/or operations students. I was essentially responsible for imparting a fire hose of technical information efficiently. At my next company, Zilog, it was the same—I taught microprocessor system design to engineers. It was all about the efficient transfer of knowledge. High bandwidth, low noise.

But later at Zilog I moved into marketing. While I learned how to write data sheets, product marketing at Zilog was very little "listen to customers" and much more "talk at customers." It wasn't until my next company, Convergent Technologies, that I began to understand the value of customer interaction. As a product marketing manager, I traveled to customers at the behest of our salespeople to impart the latest technical wisdom from the factory.

Traveling with these salesmen was eye-opening -- they were comfortable having conversations with strangers and knew how to build rapport, relationships, and trust. These guys explained to me that most people were happy to talk about themselves. My job was just to get the conversation started. Our products improved as our salesmen made customers comfortable enough to share their needs and issues. (As I would find out, every one of these salesmen had been design engineers in their past. Yet most of the time, they artfully hid how much they knew.)

Emulation

I began to understand that while my brain was wired to dive into technical minutia and exchange product information at high speed, this wasn't what most potential customers (and most people who had a modicum of social skills) wanted to do. In fact, unbelievably (to me) most people would trade valuable time in a meeting for social niceties.

Although these social cues were something that still didn't come naturally to me, I concluded that to get much further in my career, I was going to have to have to learn. Over time, I watched how the best salespeople did it and emulated their behavior. I learned how to smile, shake hands, make eye contact rather than stare at my shoes, talk about sports, ask customers about their jobs, their families, etc., and evidence apparent interest in people I didn't know way before we got to chat about products. I'd even go out to lunch or dinner and manage to hold a conversation. The two hardest things to learn were: how to speak in front of a group and to make "cold calls" by myself. (Every once in a while I'd run into a customer wired like me who'd say, "Can we cut the chatter and get down to business?" I'd laugh, and we'd do a high-speed data transfer.)

Surprisingly, I learned that listening to customers and others made me more creative. My best ideas started coming from brainstorming with others, something just not possible when communication was a one-way street.

Fast forward a few companies— MIPS and Ardent —I was still learning (at times painfully) to appreciate that facts were outside the building and not between my ears. After a decade in Silicon Valley, I had finally learned to emulate empathy.

Emulating Empathy

By the time I got to SuperMac, the transformation had taken hold. It was here that I began to teach others what I had learned.

I had inherited a manager of technical marketing, much smarter than me but with zero instinct or feel for customers. He was completely data driven, and our sales department wanted him nowhere near customers. I felt like I had just met my doppelganger from ten years ago. We established that his worldview was not shared by most customers. And he understood that if he wanted a bigger role in marketing, he was going to have to change. So I ran the first of what would be many "how to emulate empathy" classes.

I described how getting closer to customers was at first going to be a cerebral rather than gut activity. With no instinct to guide him, he would have to consciously precompute what kind of response each situation called for and play them back when appropriate. He was going to have to sign up for public speaking classes. He was going to go on the road with our salespeople, but this time he was going to have to watch what they do and start to copy them. I found him a mentor in a salesman who appreciated his technical skill and was willing to let him tag along.

As expected, the first couple of months were tough—on him, sales, and customers. We'd debrief after many of his road trips and calls and course correct as necessary. (At times, I'd feel like I was talking to some earlier version of myself.) But by the end of the year, he had learned enough that the VP of Sales asked whether he could move permanently into a pre-sales support role.

Repeatability

Over the next ten years in startups, I repeated this process with others. Today I remind my engineering students that empathy, while seemingly a foreign language, is possible to learn.

As for me, what I had emulated became second nature. Most of the time I can't tell which mode is running.

Lessons Learned

- Customer metrics are not the same as customer interaction.

- Customer interaction is necessary for startup founders.

- For some it is extremely difficult.

- If it's not instinctual customer empathy is a skill that can be taught and learned.

Entrepreneurial Finishing School— Should I Get an MBA?

May 10, 2010 (Steve Blank)

I usually hear the "Should I get my MBA?" question at least once a month.

If you're an entrepreneur, the glib answer is "no." It's also the wrong answer.

Should I Get My MBA?

Last week I was having coffee with an ex-engineering student of mine, now on his second startup (and for a change it wasn't a Web 2.0 startup) who wanted to chat about career choices. "I'm thinking of going back to school to get my MBA." It was said less as a clear declaration than a question. It was six years since he had left school and three and a half years ago he had joined an eight-person startup as a product manager. The company was now four-years old, had over 70 people, and was profitable and growing fast.

I didn't say anything as he continued, "I'm now director of product management, but I think I'm missing stuff I ought to know; finance, marketing, and operations management. We're starting to hire senior execs as VP's and all the jobs specs have 'MBA' as a requirement. What should I do?"

The easy answer would have been, "Yes, go back and get an MBA. You fit the perfect profile; you have an engineering background, work experience in two startups, and you'll be limited in your career growth without one." But the answer I gave him was a bit different.

Where Do You Fit?

In between the coffee and breakfast I drew this diagram:

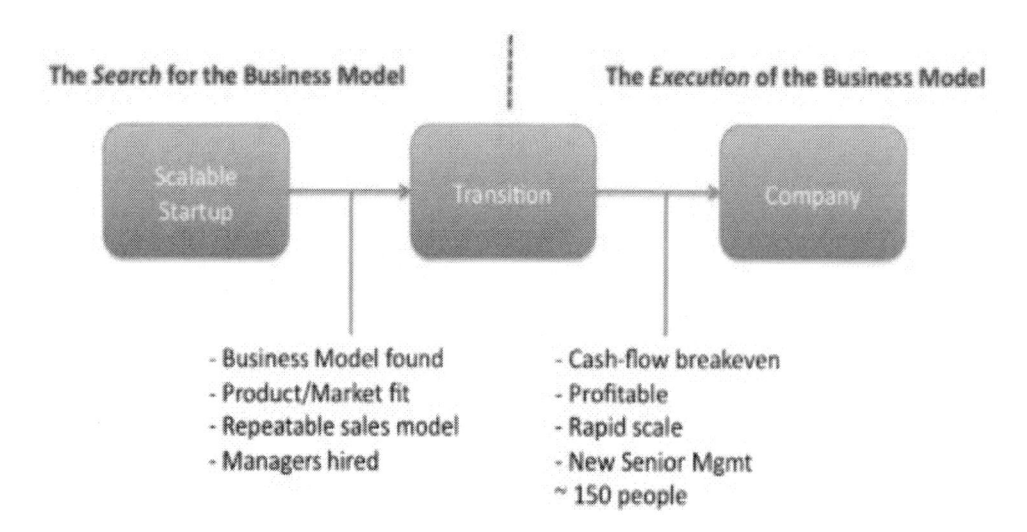

The *Search* for the Business Model | **The *Execution* of the Business Model**

Scalable Startup → Transition → Company

- Business Model found
- Product/Market fit
- Repeatable sales model
- Managers hired

- Cash-flow breakeven
- Profitable
- Rapid scale
- New Senior Mgmt
- ~150 people

I explained that as startups grow, they go from the box on the left to the box on the right, and the skills people need at each step of a company's growth evolve and change. The skills required when they were an eight-person startup trying to "search for the business model" wasn't the same set of skills needed now that they were a 70-person company "executing the business model." I offered that it sounded to me as if his company was going through the transition (the box in the middle) where it was starting to put in place the processes needed to build and execute the business model.

Who Are You?

I suggested that perhaps his first question shouldn't be whether he needed an MBA. Rather the question he should be thinking of was: in which part of a company's lifecycle did he think he wanted to spend the rest of his career? Did he enjoy the early chaotic stage of the startup? Was he fondly telling stories of how much better it was when the company was smaller? After the rocketship ride of this successful startup, did he now want to be a founder of his own startup?

Or was he more comfortable now that there was more structure, repeatability, and he was managing a staff? Was his goal to be a large company executive managing large groups of people? And if a larger company was his destination, did he want to manage complex technology projects or did he see himself in more general management in sales, marketing, or finance?

His vision about the trajectory of his career would answer what type of education he should get—and where he might get it.

MBA or Engineering Management?

I pointed out that if he wanted to work in a larger company he actually had two choices—go to business school for an MBA degree or go back to a graduate school of engineering for an Engineering Management degree. (I find a disconcerting number of my MBA students with engineering backgrounds realized too late that they ought to have been in an engineering management program. They had picked the MBA route because it was trendy or they hadn't thought through that managing engineering projects was what really excited them.)

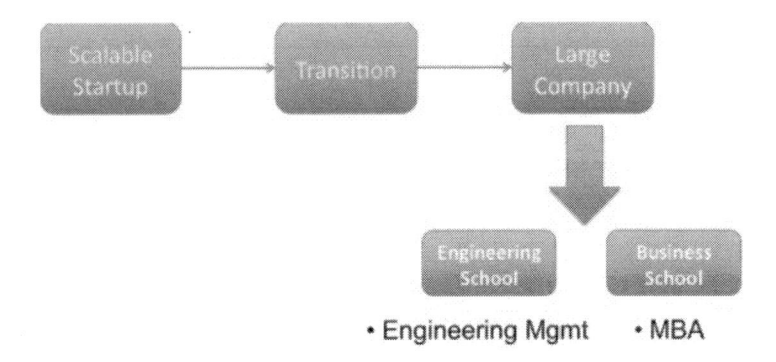

Scalable Startup → Transition → Large Company
↓
Engineering School • Engineering Mgmt   Business School • MBA

Why Yes! I am an Entrepreneur

I could see I was having an effect when he blurted out, "You know my happiest times in these startups were when we were a small team figuring out the business model. The chaos and camaraderie gave me an adrenalin rush and incredible satisfaction. While I'm really good at managing the process, this phase of the company feels like a job. I've been bouncing some ideas about a company with some fellow employees who feel the same way. Maybe I do want to do startups as a career."

Then he asked me the real hard question. "So what type of graduate school do I attend to get the skills to be a great entrepreneur?"

Entrepreneurial Apprenticeship

I congratulated him. "You already have started your apprenticeship. You have two startups under your belt as one of the first 10 employees. If you decide that you want to be a founder of a startup you've made a good start." "But where do I learn all the things a founder needs to know, not just an early employee?

Team building? Creativity and innovation? Entrepreneurial finance? Agile Development? This Lean Startup stuff? Where's the school for that?"

I said, "Welcome to the wonderful world of entrepreneurial education. It's everywhere and nowhere."

E-School versus B-School

Almost all business schools now have entrepreneurship programs or departments. (At U.C. Berkeley that's exactly the program I teach in. But you can also find entrepreneurship programs in most engineering schools. (At Stanford that's the program I teach in as well.)

And startup "accelerators" like Y-Combinator, Techstars, etc. also offer a crash course in Darwinian education. I also pointed out, "If your passion is starting your own company, learning by doing is an equally viable choice."

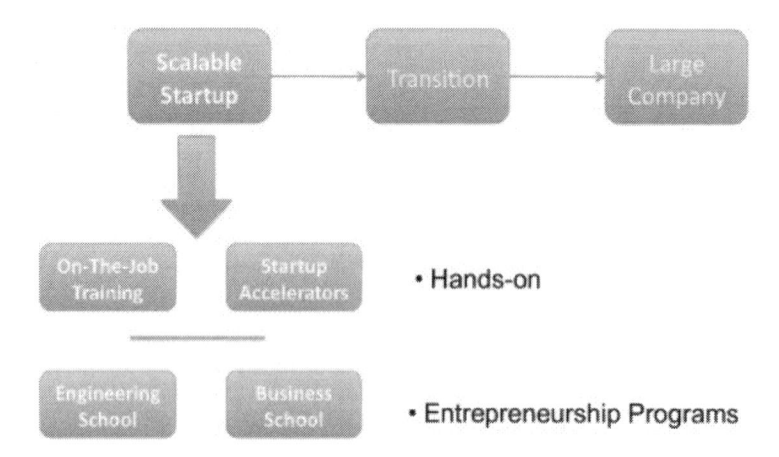

MBA? Engineering Management program? Startup accelerators? Just do it? He had more choices than most. But first…

Who was he? And who did he want to be?

Lessons Learned

- Where do you want to work: startups, mid-size, or large companies?

- If large companies, what do you want do: engineering management or corporate management?

- If you find yourself debating the "startup versus large company" choice you've already chosen the big company. Entrepreneurship isn't a career choice; it's a passion and obsession.

Napkin Entrepreneurs

March 29, 2011 (Steve Blank)

"Faith is taking the first step even when you don't see the whole staircase."

— Martin Luther King, Jr.

The barriers for starting a company have come down. Today the total available markets for new applications are hundreds of millions if not billion of users, while new classes of investors are popping up all over (angels, superangels, archangels, and even seraphim and cherubim have been spotted.)

Entrepreneurship departments are now the cool thing to have in colleges and universities, and classes on how to start a company are being taught over a weekend, a month, six weeks, and via correspondence course.

If the opportunity is so large, and the barriers to starting up so low, why haven't the number of scalable startups exploded exponentially? What's holding us back?

It might be that it's easier than ever to draw an idea on the back of the napkin, it's still hard to quit your day job.

Napkin Entrepreneurs

One of the amazing consequences of the low cost of creating web and mobile apps is that you can get a lot of them up and running simultaneously and affordably. I call these app development projects: "science experiments."

These web science experiments are the logical extension of the Customer Discovery step in the Customer Development process. They're a great way to brainstorm outside the building, getting real customer feedback as you think through your ideas about value proposition/ customer/ demand creation/ revenue model.

They're the 21st century version of a product sketch on a back of napkin. But instead of just a piece of paper, you end up with a site that users can visit, use, and even pay for.

Ten of thousands of people who could never afford to start a company can now start several over their lunch break. And, with any glimmer of customer interest, they can decide whether they want to:

- run it as a part-time business
- commit full-time to build a "buyable startup" (~$5-$25 million exit)
- commit full-time and try to build a scalable startup

But it's important to note what these napkin projects/test are not. They are not a company, nor are they are a startup. Running them doesn't make you a founder. And while they are entrepreneurial experiments, until you actually commit to them by choosing one idea, quitting your day job, and committing yourself 24/7 it's not clear that the word "founder or entrepreneur" even applies.

Lessons Learned

- The web now allows you to turn your "back of the napkin" ideas into live experiments.

- Running lots of app experiments is a great idea.

- But these experiments are not a company, and you're not a "founder." You're just a "napkin entrepreneur."

- Founding a company is an act of complete commitment

Mentors, Coaches and Teachers

April 19, 2011 (Steve Blank)

> "When the student is ready, the master appears."
> — Buddhist Proverb

Lots of entrepreneurs believe they want a mentor. In fact, they're actually asking for a teacher or a coach. A mentor relationship is a two-way street. To make it work, you have to bring something to the party.

A Question from the Audience

Recently when I was at a conference taking questions from the audience, I got a question that I had never heard before. Someone asked, "How do I get you, or someone like you to become my mentor?" It made me pause (actually, cringe). As I gathered my thoughts, I realized that I've never thought much about the mentors I had, how I got them, and the difference between mentors, coaches, and teachers.

Teachers

What I do today is teach. At Stanford and Berkeley, I have students, with classes and office hours. For the brief time in the quarter I have students in my class, at worst I impart knowledge to them. At best, I try to help my students to discover and acquire the knowledge themselves. I try to engage them to see the startup world as part of a larger pattern; the lifecycle of how companies are born, grow, and die. I attempt to offer them both theory, as well as a methodology, about building early stage ventures. And finally, I have them experience all of this firsthand by teaching them theory side-by-side with immersive hands-on experience using Customer Development to find a business model.

At times, the coffees, lunches, and phone calls I have with current and past students are also a form of teaching. Most of the time students come with, "Here's the problem I have. Can you help me?" Usually, I'll give a direct answer, but sometimes my answer is a question.

In both cases, inside or outside the classroom, I consider those activities as teaching. At least for me, mentorship is something quite different.

Mentors

As an entrepreneur in my 20s and 30s, I was lucky to have four extraordinary mentors, each brilliant in his own field and each a decade or two older than me. Ben Wegbreit taught me how to think, Gordon Bell taught me what to think about, Rob Van Naarden taught me how to think about customers, and Allen Michels showed me how to turn thinking into direct, immediate, and outrageous action.

At this time in my life, I was the world's biggest pain in the rear. Lessons needed to be communicated by baseball bat, yet each one of these people not only put up with me, but also engaged me in a dialog of continual learning. Unlike coaching, there was no specific agenda or goal, but they saw I was competent and open to learning and they cared about me and my long-term development. I'm not sure it was a conscious effort on their part (I know it wasn't on mine), but it continued for years, and in some cases (with my partner Ben Wegbreit) for decades. What is interesting in hindsight is that although the relationship continued for a long time, neither of us explicitly acknowledged it.

Now I realize that what made these relationships a mentorship is this: I was giving as good as I was getting. While I was learning from them—and their years of experience and expertise—what I was giving back to them was equally important. I was bringing fresh insights to their data. It wasn't that I was just more up-to-date on the current technology, markets or trends, it was that I was able to recognize patterns and bring new perspectives to what these very smart people already knew. In hindsight, mentorship is a synergistic relationship.

Like every good student/teacher and mentor/mentee relationship, over time the student became the teacher, and this phase of relationship ends.

How Do I Find a Mentor?

All this was running through my head as I tried to think of how to answer the question from the audience.

Finally I replied, "At least for me, becoming someone's mentor means a two-way relationship. A mentorship is a back and forth dialog—it's as much about giving as it is about getting. It's a much higher-level conversation than just teaching. Think about what can we learn together? How much are you going to bring to the relationship?"

If it's not much, then what you really want/need is a teacher, not a mentor. If it's a specific goal or skill you want to achieve, hire a coach, but if you're prepared to give as good as you get, then look for a mentor. But never ask. Offer to give.

Lessons Learned

Teachers, coaches and mentors are each something different.

If you want to learn a specific subject find a teacher.

If you want to hone specific skills or reach an exact goal hire a coach.

If you want to get smarter and better over your career, find someone who cares about you enough to be a mentor.

The Apprentice—Entrepreneur Version

April 26, 2011 (Steve Blank)

"We are all apprentices in a craft where no one ever becomes a master."
—Ernest Hemingway

Silicon Valley is built on simple myths—one of the most pervasive is that all winning startups are founded straight out of school by 20 year olds from Stanford or Harvard. The reality is these are the exceptions not the rule.

Too Old at 30?

I was having coffee with an ex-student at the ranch, watching our bobcat hunt in the front lawn. This student had called and said he had to meet. "I'm having a career crisis," was how he described it. I invited him to make the drive down.

As the story unfolded, it turned out that he just turned 30 and realized that he hadn't founded a company yet. "Everyone now starts a company out of school. All my classmates who were interested in entrepreneurship have started their own companies. I've just been working my way up the ladder." He explained that he had a progressively set of better jobs at companies that were in the "build" phase. These ex-startups had found a repeatable business model and were putting the processes in place to grow into a large company. They had hired operating executives and were starting to scale.

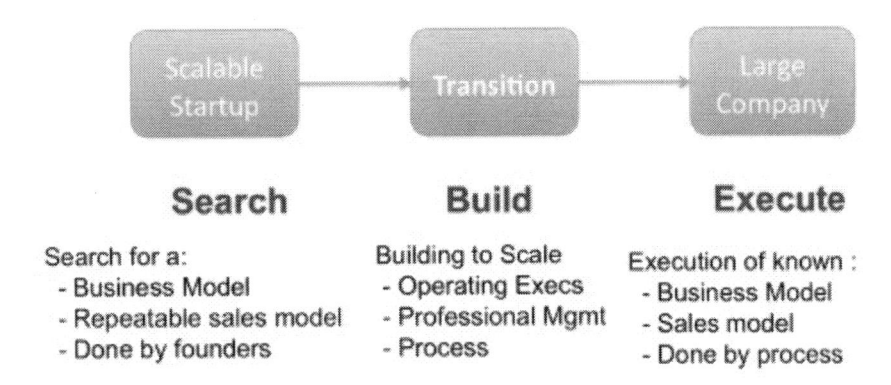

Search — Scalable Startup
Search for a:
- Business Model
- Repeatable sales model
- Done by founders

Build — Transition
Building to Scale
- Operating Execs
- Professional Mgmt
- Process

Execute — Large Company
Execution of known:
- Business Model
- Sales model
- Done by process

"Well what's wrong with what you've been doing?" I asked. "Oh, I've learned a ton," he replied. "If I had started a company out of school, I would have made all kind of stupid mistakes."

Okay, I wondered, the problem is what? "So how have your friends done?" We watched as the bobcat patiently stalked a gopher. "Hmm," he said. "A few did okay, but most of them cratered their startups. For the amount of money they made, most of them would have been better off working at Walmart."

Slow Learner

I told him he wasn't alone. Early in my career I apprenticed at companies that had recently been startups, hadn't yet gone public, and were still innovative. My career was a slow 20-year progression from training instructor to product marketing manager to VP of Marketing. It wasn't until my seventh startup that I was a CEO in a startup I co-founded (and its failure left a crater so deep it had its own Iridium layer).

Perhaps the most important part of this non-meteoric career trajectory was the mentoring I received. I managed to work for, with, and around people who were truly skilled at what they did. Some of them consciously taught and shared their skills. For others I tried my best to suck out every bit of what they knew and emulate the best of their skills. (At times the learning was painful, but it was never forgotten.)

While the Silicon Valley myth is that all winning startups are founded straight out of school, it's just not true.

No Longer a Startup

In raw numbers, most engineers and MBAs aren't founding companies, they're going to work for others who have; Facebook, Google, Zynga, FourSquare, Twitter, etc. While the jobs at these companies are still incredibly challenging, and passion and innovation may still pervade their company cultures, the startup risk ("will we run out of money before we find our customers?") is gone. As great as these companies may be, they are no longer startups. (A startup is a temporary organization searching for a repeatable and scalable business model.)

But employees in these ex-startups are getting the best hands-on education for entrepreneurship there is—as apprentices.

Apprentice

As we watched the bobcat make a meal out of the gopher I offered that his career was proceeding just fine. Someday, he'll hear a calling, pull his head out of his computer, look around, and say, "I can do this myself."

And the cycle of creative destruction will begin anew.

Lessons Learned

- Not all startups are founded by 20-somethings straight out of college.

- Working for companies that were recently startups is a great way to apprentice.

- These companies can you give a lifetime of mentorship hard to achieve in other ways.

- When you're ready, you'll hear a calling, and it won't be a job.

Killing Your Startup By Listening to Customers

February 27, 2012 (Steve Blank)

The art of entrepreneurship and the science of Customer Development is not just getting out of the building and listening to prospective customers. It's understanding who to listen to and why.

Five Cups of Coffee

I got a call from Satish, one of my ex-students, last week. He got my attention when he said, "following your customer development stuff is making my company fail." The rest of the conversation sounded too confusing for me to figure out over the phone, so I invited him out to the ranch to chat.

When he arrived, Satish sounded like he had five cups of coffee. Normally when I have students over, we'd sit in the house and we'd look at the fields trying to catch a glimpse of a bobcat hunting.

But in this case, I suggested we take a hike out to Potato Patch pond.

Potato Patch Pond

We took the trail behind the house down the hill, through the forest, and emerged into the bright sun in the lower valley. (Like many parts of the ranch, this valley has its own micro-climate and today was one of those days when it was ten degrees warmer than up at the house.)

As we walked up the valley Satish kept up a running dialog catching me up on six years of family, classmates, and how he started his consumer web company. It had recently rained and about every 50 feet we'd see another 3-inch salamander ambling across the trail. When the valley dead-ended in the canyon, we climbed 30-foot up a set of stairs and emerged looking at the water. A "hanging pond" is always a surprise to visitors. All of a sudden Satish's stream of words slowed to a trickle and just stopped. He stood at the end of the small dock for a while taking it all in. I dragged him away and we followed the trail through the woods, around the pond, through the shadows of the trees.

As we circled the pond I tried to both keep my eyes on the dirt trail while glancing sideways for pond turtles and red-legged frogs. When I'm out here alone it's quiet enough to hear the wind through the trees, and after a while the sound of your own heartbeat. We sat on the bench staring across the water, with the only noise coming from ducks tracing patterns on the flat water. Sitting there, Satish described his experience.

We Did Everything Customers Asked For

"We did everything you said: we got out of the building and talked to potential customers. We surveyed a ton of them online, ran A/B tests, brought a segment of those who used the product in-house for face-to-face meetings. " Yep, sounds good.

"Next, we built a minimum viable product." Okay, still sounds good.

"And then we built everything our prospective customers asked for." That took me aback. Everything? I asked? "Yes, we added all their feature requests, and we priced the product just like they requested. We had a ton of people come to our website and a healthy number actually activated." That's great I said, "but what's your pricing model?" "Freemium," came the reply.

Oh, oh. I bet I knew the answer to the next question, but I asked it anyway. "So, what's the problem?"

"Well everyone uses the product for a while, but no one is upgrading to our paid product. We spent all this time building what customers asked for. And now most of the early users have stopped coming back."

I looked at hard at Satish trying to remember where he had sat in my class. Then I asked, "Satish, what's your business model?

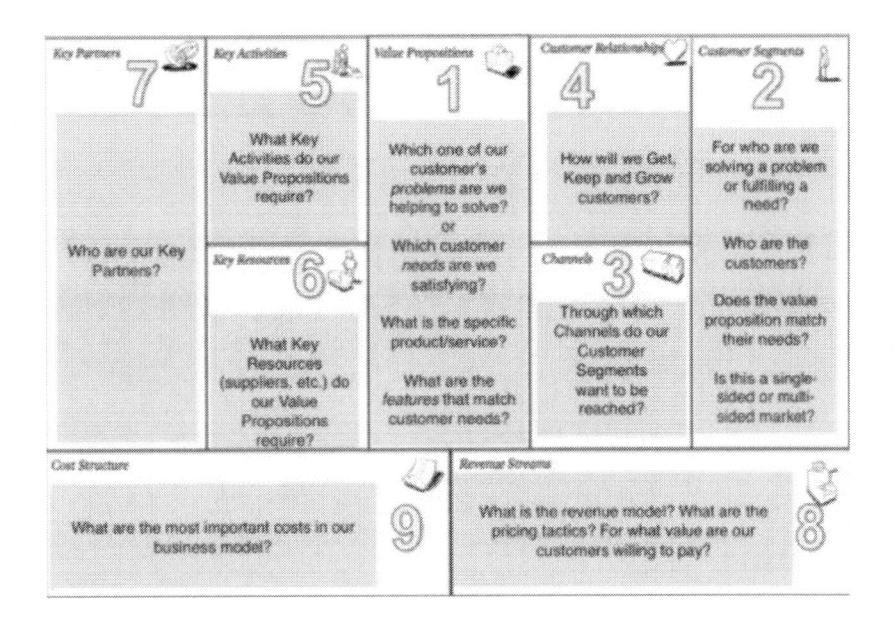

Key Partners 7	Key Activities 5	Value Propositions 1	Customer Relationships 4	Customer Segments 2
Who are our Key Partners?	What Key Activities do our Value Propositions require?	Which one of our customer's problems are we helping to solve? or Which customer needs are we satisfying?	How will we Get, Keep and Grow customers?	For who are we solving a problem or fulfilling a need? Who are the customers?
	Key Resources 6		Channels 3	Does the value proposition match their needs?
	What Key Resources (suppliers, etc.) do our Value Propositions require?	What is the specific product/service? What are the features that match customer needs?	Through which Channels do our Customer Segments want to be reached?	Is this a single-sided or multi-sided market?
Cost Structure 9			Revenue Streams 8	
What are the most important costs in our business model?			What is the revenue model? What are the pricing tactics? For what value are our customers willing to pay?	

What's Your Business Model?

"Business model? I guess I was just trying to get as many people to my site as I could and make them happy. Then I thought I could charge them for something later and sell advertising based on the users I had."

I pushed a bit harder.

"Your strategy counted on a freemium-to-paid upgrade path. What experiments did you run that convinced you that this was the right pricing tactic? Your attrition numbers mean users weren't engaged with the product. What did you do about it?"

"Did you think you were trying to get large networks of engaged users that can disrupt big markets?" Large is usually measured in millions of users. "What experiments did you run that convinced you could get to that scale?"

I realized by the look in his eyes that none of this was making sense. "Well I got out of the building and listened to customers."

The wind was picking up over the pond so I suggested we start walking.

We stopped at the overlook a top of the waterfall, after the recent rain I had to shout over the noise of the rushing water. I offered that it sounded like he had done a great job listening to customers. And better, he had translated what he had heard into experiments and tests to acquire more users and get a higher percentage of those to activate.

But he was missing the bigger picture. The idea of the tests he ran wasn't just to get data —it was to get insight. All of those activities—talking to customers, A/B testing, etc. needed to fit into his business model—how his company will find a repeatable and scalable business model and ultimately make money. And this is the step he had missed.

Customer Development = The Pursuit of Customer Understanding

Part of Customer Development is understanding which customers make sense for your business. The goal of listening to customers is not to please every one of them. It's to figure out which customer segment served his needs—both short and long term. And giving your product away, as he was discovering, is often a going out of business strategy.

The work he had done acquiring and activating customers were just one part of the entire business model.

As we started the long climb up the driveway, I suggested his fix might be simpler than he thought. He needed to start thinking about what a repeatable and scalable business model looked like.

I offered that acquiring users and then making money by finding payers assumed a multi-sided market (users/payers). But a freemium model assumed a single-sided market—one where the users became the payers.

He really needed to think through his Revenue Model (the strategy his company uses to generate cash from each customer segment). And how was he going to use Pricing, (the tactics of what he charged in each customer segment) to achieve that Revenue Model. Freemium was just one of many tactics. Single or multi-sided market? And which customers did he want to help him get there?

My guess was that he was going to end up firing a bunch of his customers—and that was okay.

As we sat back in the living room, I gave him a copy of The Startup Owner's Manual and we watched a bobcat catch a gopher.

Lessons Learned

- Getting out of the building is a great first step.

- Listening to potential customers is even better.

- Getting users to visit your site and try your product feels great.

- Your job is not to make every possible customer happy.

- Pick the customer segments and pricing tactics that drive your business model.

Blinded by the Light— The Epiphany

April 3, 2012 (Steve Blank)

Epiphany
e·piph·a·ny
/iˈpifənē/

Noun. A moment of sudden revelation or insight

We now know how to teach entrepreneurs how to think about business models and use customer development to turn hypotheses into facts. But there is no process to teach how to get an epiphany. We can only try to create the conditions where this might occur.

It All Just Came to Me in a Flash

Luis, one of the CEOs from our first National Science Foundation class, came in to speak to our next class. We had a couple of minutes to catch up between sessions and the conversation got strangely awkward when I asked him how their startup was going.

"I'm kind of embarrassed to tell you, but we dumped the entire business idea and are doing something else," he said, avoiding eye contact. "Oh, you pivoted when your team analyzed customer feedback?" I said as I grabbed some coffee. He looked uncomfortable. "No, I was standing in the shower when it just hit me that our nano-materials technology should be used for something completely different. I didn't change a few business model components, I changed all of them."

I guess my jaw dropped a bit because Luis just continued. "I'm feeling guilty because I was using Customer Development and The Startup Owner's Manual until I had that insight. But there was nothing in your book that prepared me for what just clicked in my head. I just saw our entire new business model in a flash, all of it at once. I'm now having the company execute on what came to me in the shower. A small part of me is confused whether I'm doing the right thing, but mostly I'm just convinced it's as right as anything I've ever done. But there's no chapter in your book or anyone else's on this."

Realizing what I was hearing, I pulled Luis outside the conference room into the quiet of the hall.

"Luis, did this ever happen to you before?" I asked. "Well no, not in a startup. This stuff is new to me."

"No," I replied. "I mean in your lab. Did you ever have this feeling where it all just came to you?

He thought for a bit as he stared in the distance and then responded, "Yeah, I never thought about that until now, but in fact I did. It felt a lot like when I was writing my thesis five years ago. I had struggled with the data for two years. Then one weekend I went for a walk by the ocean to clear my head—and I had an insight that won me the fellowship. I had to spend six more months checking the data and working my tail off, but my thesis was awarded best paper of the year."

I tried to stay calm as I realized what I was hearing. "Luis, you need to pay attention to me very carefully. You just had an epiphany. If you're lucky you may have a few more in your career. But while epiphanies are extremely rare, they are immensely important and need to be listened to. What you had was no accident. You were collecting enormous amounts of data on one side of your brain, but it was the other side that recognized the pattern. No one knows if epiphanies are always right, but people who follow them tend to get rich, famous, or both."

Epiphany Equals Insight

For thousands of years, every culture has had words to describe what happened to Luis: a flash of insight, an epiphany, strategic intuition, a revelation, etc. An epiphany is a different way of solving problems than the problem solving we do every day. In an epiphany, you see the entire answer to a complex problem without realizing you were even consciously thinking about it (very different from a snap answer or a quick response). We hear stories in almost every field, in art, science and business, about how "the idea just came to me."

The Customer Development process was a result of an Epiphany I had when writing my memoirs. After 80 pages, I realized in one instant that the stories I had been recounting weren't of interest (at least to anyone besides me), but the pattern behind the stories had much deeper meaning. Years later, the key ideas in The Startup Owner's Manual came to me in the same way—realizing that startups are a search for a Business Model, and that the Business Model Canvas was the organizing principle for Customer Development. All of these insights came fully formed.

Getting Ready for the Epiphany

While we can describe an epiphany, we don't know how to teach it or make it happen. But we do know how to set up the conditions for it to occur.

First interact with lots of people—the more they are different from you, with different ideas and different perspectives, the better. (Getting out of the building in the Customer Development process guarantees you'll do just that.) Next, attack whatever problem you're working on head-on. In Customer

Development that means building a set of business model hypotheses, and running customer discovery to test those hypotheses. Most of the time you'll be slogging through a ton of data operating in chaos trying to figure out what direction to take your company.

Here's the part that's counterintuitive—on a regular basis make time to take an hour, or even a day, to do something completely different. Go for a hike or a drive. Walk around the city. Don't distract yourself with something that makes you focus (the movies, TV, email or the net). Instead, shut it all down and do something that's relaxing and gives the problem solving part of your brain a rest—let the pattern recognition side take over.

It can be challenging for an entrepreneur to slow down, disengage from the relentless pace, and smell the roses. But making this kind of time for your right brain to process what your left-brain has learned can bring you insights you'd never uncover otherwise. You can't force an epiphany but when it comes, you'll know it.

You'll be blinded by the light.

Lesson Learned

An Epiphany is a moment of sudden revelation or insight.

Epiphanies cannot be planned or scheduled.

They require a constant stream of data from multiple sources.

An Epiphany is a pattern recognition moment.

Often they match a pattern from a different industry or field.

They happen when you disengage from execution.

II.

Startups Are Not Small Versions of Large Companies

A Startup Is Not a Smaller Version of a Large Company

January 14, 2010 (Steve Blank)

"A journey of a thousand miles begins with a single step."
– Lao-tzu

If you read the academic literature or business press, you might believe that large companies and their business models are brought by the stork.

This series of posts are going to offer a new three-stage model of how startups grow into large companies. And I'll end with some thoughts about a new approach to entrepreneurial education using this model.

Children, Adolescents, and Adults

In the Middle Ages, children were considered to be smaller versions of adults. We now know that the human life cycle is more complex; children aren't just small adults, and adolescents are not simply large children. Instead each is a unique stage of development with distinctive behavior, modes of thinking, physiology and more.

The same is true for startups and companies.

In the past, most business literature has treated the life cycle of corporation as if the practices that make sense for a large corporation were equally appropriate for a startup. They only differed by timing or scale.

I argue that as a scalable startup grows from a garage into a Google, it progresses through three distinct stages—each presenting a unique set of challenges and decisions— and each requiring vastly different resources, skills and strategy.

Let's take a closer look at the first two of these stages.

Stage 1: The Scalable Startup

A scalable startup is designed by intent from day one to become a large company. The founders believe they have a big idea—one that can grow to $100 million or more in annual revenue – by either disrupting an existing market and taking customers from existing companies or creating a new market. Scalable startups aim to provide an obscene return to their founders and investors using all available outside resources.

Entrepreneurs who have run a startup know that startups are not small versions of big companies. Rather they are different in every possible way—from goals, to measurements, from employees to culture. Very few skills, process, people or strategies that work in a startup are successful in a large established company and vice versa because a startup is a different organizational entity than a large established company.

Therefore, it follows that:

a) Startups need different management principles, people and strategies than large established companies

b) Any advice that's targeted to large established companies is irrelevant, distracting and potentially damaging in growing and managing a startup

Getting from Here to There

If you would ask a startup CEO to create a diagram showing how their startup will become a large company, you'd probably get a simple line extending from "here's where we are" to "here's where we're going."

- Total Available Market > $500m
- Company can grow to $100m/year
- Known business model
- Focused on execution and process

All the activities of a scalable startup such as Customer Development, Agile Development, and Pivots search for a repeatability, scale, business model, team building etc. would be inside the box to the left. In this simplistic model, on the day a startup achieves product/market fit, they would stop doing all the startup activities and magically become a "large company"—somehow acquiring a completely new set of skills, executing a known business model, generating profits and achieving liquidity for its founders and investors.

Since we know the world doesn't work like this, the question is, "what is the process that transforms a startup into a large company?"

Stage 2: Metamorphosis—The Transition

Any entrepreneur who has been successful (lucky) enough to grow their startup into a large company knows that this process is not a simple linear transition—it's a metamorphosis. Startups traverse a clearly defined and chaotic stage before they become a large enterprise.

And once again, very few skills, processes, people or strategies that work in a scalable startup or in a large established company are successful in this transitional stage.

Scalable Startup → Transition → Large Company >$100M/year

The transitional period between a startup and a company is a different organizational entity than either a startup or a large enterprise. While it is no longer an early stage scalable startup, it is not yet a large company.

This is the "they fired the founders and took away the free sodas" stage.

Summary

The new taxonomy for understanding how startups differ and grow into large company's looks like this:

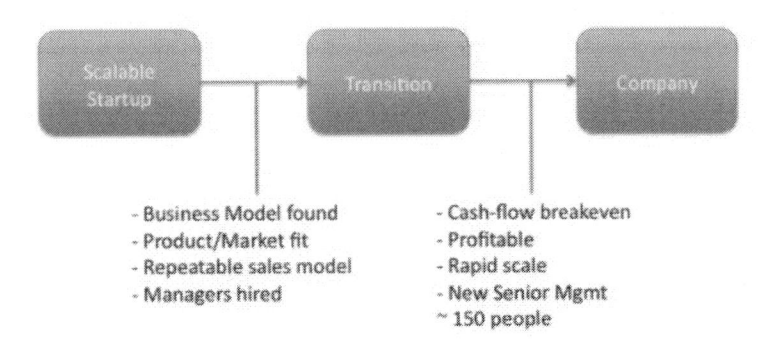

```
[Scalable Startup] → [Transition] → [Company]
```

- Business Model found
- Product/Market fit
- Repeatable sales model
- Managers hired

- Cash-flow breakeven
- Profitable
- Rapid scale
- New Senior Mgmt
- ~ 150 people

Each stage is an entirely different business entity with different management needs and requirements.

This three-step model calls for a new approach to entrepreneurial education — Durant School of Entrepreneurship™.

What's A Startup? First Principles

January 25, 2010 (Steve Blank)

"Success consists of going from failure to failure without loss of enthusiasm."
—— Winston Churchill

Everyone knows what a startup is for—don't they?

In this post we're going to offer a new definition of why startups exist: a startup is an organization formed to search for a repeatable and scalable business model.

A Business Model

Okay, but what is a business model?

A business model describes how your company creates, delivers and captures value. Or in English: A business model describes how your company makes money. (Or depending on your metrics for success, get users, grow traffic, etc.).

Think of a business model as a drawing that shows all the flows between the different parts of your company. A business model diagram also shows how the product gets distributed to your customers and how money flows back into your company. And it shows your company's cost structures, how each department interacts with the others and where your company fits with other companies or partners to implement your business.

While this is a mouthful, it's a lot easier to draw.

Drawing a Business Model

Lots of people have been working on how to diagram and draw a business. I had my students drawing theirs for years, but Alexander Osterwalder's work on business models is the clearest description I've read in the last decade. The diagram below is his Business Model template. In your startup's business model, the boxes will have specific details of your company's strategy.

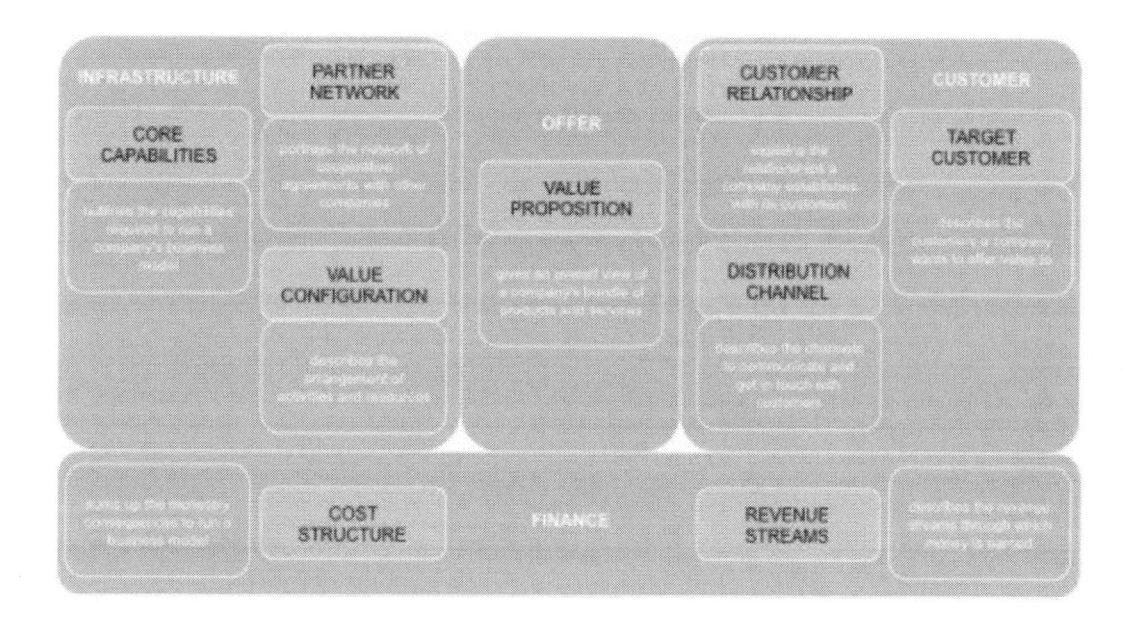

Alexander Osterwalder's Business Model Template

(At Stanford, Ann Miura-Ko and I have been working on a simplified Silicon Valley version of this model.)

But What Does a Business Model Have to Do With My Startup?

Your startup is essentially an organization built to search for a repeatable and scalable business model. As a founder you start out with:

1) a vision of a product with a set of features,

2) a series of hypotheses about all the pieces of the business model: Who are the customers/users? What's the distribution channel? How do we price and position the product? How do we create end user demand? Who are our partners? Where/how do we build the product? How do we finance the company, etc.?

Your job as a founder is to quickly validate whether the model is correct by seeing if customers behave as your model predicts. Most of the time the darn customers don't behave as you predicted.

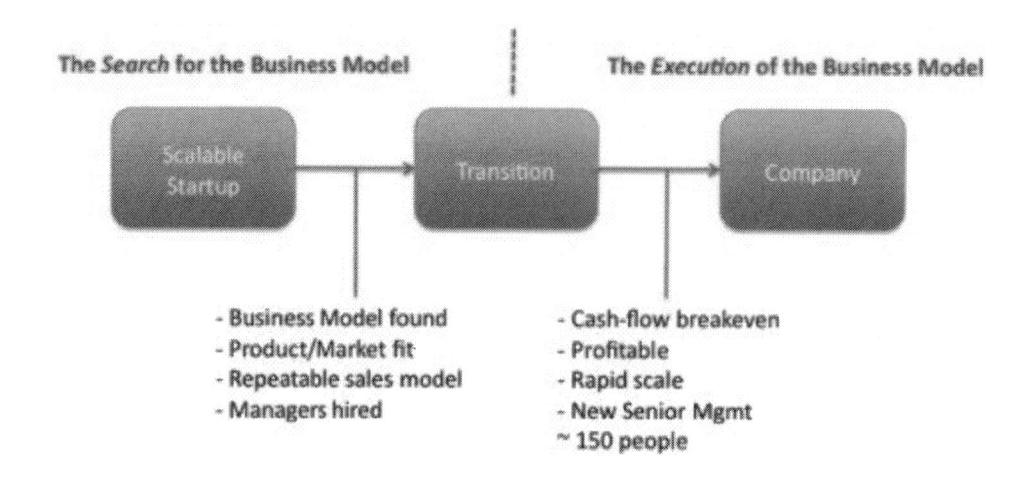

The Search for the Business Model | *The Execution of the Business Model*

Scalable Startup → Transition → Company

- Business Model found
- Product/Market fit
- Repeatable sales model
- Managers hired

- Cash-flow breakeven
- Profitable
- Rapid scale
- New Senior Mgmt
- ~150 people

How Do Customer Development, Agile Development, and Lean Startups Fit?

The Customer Development process is the way startups quickly iterate and test each element of their business model. Agile Development is the way startups quickly iterate their product as they learn. A Lean Startup is Eric Ries' description of the intersection of Customer Development, Agile Development and if available, open platforms and open source. (This methodology does for startups what the Toyota Lean Production System did for cars.)

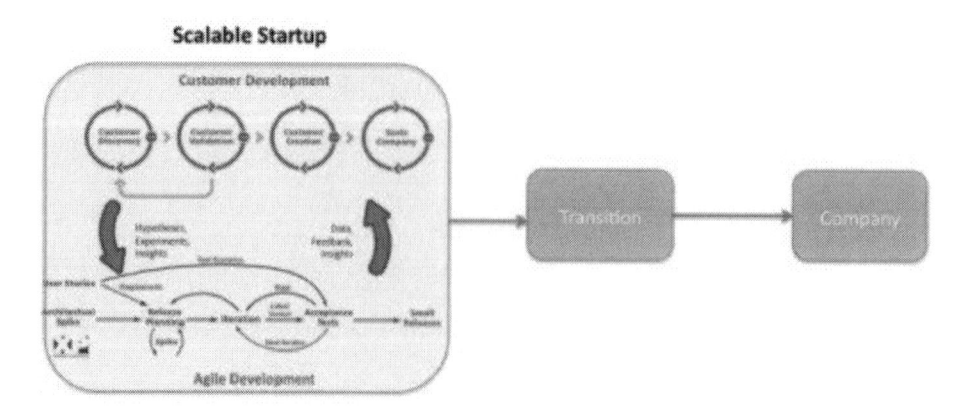

Business Plan Versus Business Model

Wait a minute, isn't the Business Model the same thing as my Business Plan? Sort of… but better. A business plan is useful place for you to collect your hypotheses about your business, sales, marketing, customers, market size, etc. (Your investors make you write one, but they never read it.) A Business Model is how all the pieces in your business plan interconnect.

The Pivot

How do you know your business model is the right one? When revenue, users, traffic, etc., start increasing in a repeatable way you predicted and make your investors happy. The irony is the first time this happens, you may not have found your company's optimal model. Most startups change their business model at least once if not several times. How do you know when reached the one to scale?

Lessons Learned

- A startup is an organization formed to search for a repeatable and scalable business model.

- The goal of your early business model can be revenue, or profits, or users, or click-throughs—whatever you and your investors have agreed upon.

- Customer and Agile Development is the way for startups to quickly iterate and test their hypotheses about their business model.

- Most startups change their business model multiple times.

Touching the Hot Stove— Experiential Versus Theoretical Learning

August 13, 2009 (Steve Blank)

I'm a slow learner. It took me eight startups and 21 years to get it right (and one can argue success was due to the Internet bubble rather than any brilliance).

In 1978 when I joined my first company, information about how to start companies simply didn't exist. No Internet, no blogs, no books on startups, no entrepreneurship departments in universities, etc. It took lots of trial and error, learning by experience and resilience through multiple failures.

The first few months of my startups were centered around building the founding team, prototyping the product and raising money. Since I wasn't an engineer, my contribution was around the team-building and fund raising.

I was an idiot.

Customer Development/Lean Startups

In hindsight startups and the venture capital community left out the most important first step any startup ought to be doing—hypothesis testing in front of customers— from day one.

I'm convinced that starting a company without talking to customers is like throwing your time and money in the street (unless you're already a domain expert).

This mantra of talking to customers and iterating the product is the basis of the Lean Startup Methodology that Eric Ries as been evangelizing and I've been teaching at U.C. Berkeley and at Stanford. It's what my textbook on Customer Development describes.

Experiential Versus Theoretical Learning

After teaching this for a few years, I've discovered that subjects like Lean Startups and Customer Development are best learned experientially rather than solely theoretically.

Remember your parents saying, "Don't touch the hot stove!" What did you do? I bet you weren't confused about what "hot" meant after that. That's why I make my students spend a lot of time "touching the hot stove" by talking to customers "outside the building" to test their hypotheses.

However, as hard as I emphasize this point to aspiring entrepreneurs every year I usually get a call or email from a past student asking me to introduce them to my favorite VCs. The first questions I ask are: "So what did you learn from testing your hypothesis?" and "What did customers think of your prototype?" These questions I know will be on top of the list that VCs will ask.

At least a third of the time the response I get is: "Oh that class stuff was real interesting, but we're too busy building the prototype. I'm going to go do that Customer Development stuff after we raise money."

Interestingly this response almost always comes from first-time entrepreneurs. Entrepreneurs who have a startup or two under their belt tend to rattle off preliminary customer findings and data that blow me away (not because I think their data is going to be right, but because it means they have built a process for learning and discovery from day one).

Sigh. Fundraising isn't the product. It's not a substitute for customer input and understanding.

Sometimes you need a few more lessons touching the hot stove.

Search Versus Execute

March 5, 2012 (Steve Blank)

One of the confusing things to entrepreneurs, investors, and educators is the relationship between customer development and business model design and business planning and execution.

When does a new venture focus on customer development and business models? And when do business planning and execution come into play?

Here's an attempt to put this all in context.

Don't Throw the Tomatoes

I was in Washington D.C. to present at the ARPA-E conference. I spent the next day working with the National Science Foundation on the Innovation Corps, and talking to congressional staffs about how entrepreneurial educational programs can reshape our economy. (And I even found time to go to the Spy Museum.)

One of the issues that came up is whether the new lexicon of entrepreneurial ideas— Customer Development, Business Model Design, Lean, Lean LaunchPad class, etc.— replace all the tools and classes that are currently being taught in entrepreneurship curriculums and business schools. I was a bit surprised since most of what I've been advocating is complementary to existing courses. However, I realize I've primarily written about business model design and customer development. Given that I'm speaking this month in front of entrepreneurship educators at the NCIIA conference, I thought I should put it in context before they throw tomatoes at me.

Search Versus Execution

One of the things startups have lacked is a definition of who they were. For years we've treated startups like they are just smaller versions of a large company. However, we now know that a startup is a temporary organization designed to search for a repeatable and scalable business model. Within this definition, a startup can be a new venture or it can be a new division or business unit in an existing company.

If your business model is unknown—that is just a set of untested hypotheses—you are a startup searching for a repeatable business model. Once your business model (market, customers, features, channels, pricing, Get/Keep/Grow strategy, etc.) is known, you will be executing it. Search versus execution is what differentiates a new venture from an existing business unit.

Strategy

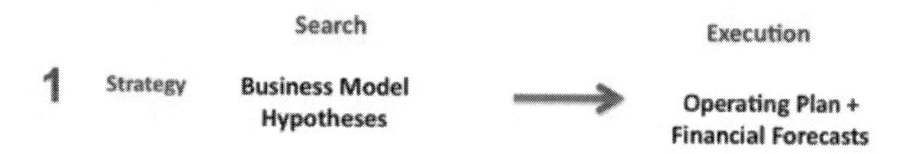

1 Strategy — Search: **Business Model Hypotheses** → Execution: **Operating Plan + Financial Forecasts**

The primary objective of a startup is to validate its business model hypotheses (and iterate and pivot until it does). Then it moves into execution mode. It's at this point the business needs an operating plan, financial forecasts and other well-understood management tools.

Process

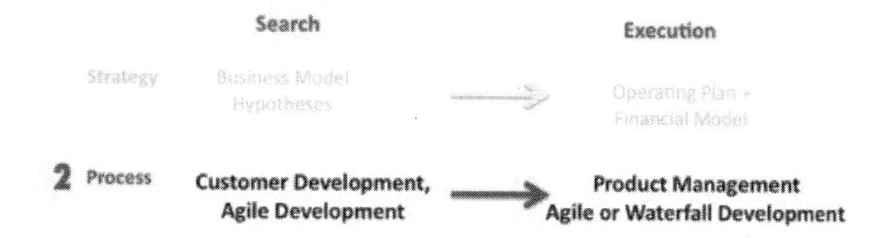

2 Process — Search: **Customer Development, Agile Development** → Execution: **Product Management, Agile or Waterfall Development**

The processes used to organize and implement the search for the business model are Customer Development and Agile Development. A search for a business model can be in any new business—in a brand new startup new or in a new division of an existing company.

In search, you want a process designed to be dynamic, so you work with a rough business model description knowing it will change. The model changes because startups use customer development to run experiments to test the hypotheses that make up the model. And most of the time these experiments fail. Search embraces failure as a natural part of the startup process. Unlike existing companies that fire executives when they fail to match a plan, we keep the founders and change the model.

Once a company has found a business model (it knows its market, customers, product/service, channel, pricing, etc.), the organization moves from search to execution.

The product execution process—managing the lifecycle of existing products and the launch of follow-on products—is the job of the product management and engineering organizations. It results in a linear process where you make a plan and refine it into detail. The more granularity you add to a plan, the better people can execute it: a Business Requirement Document (BRD) leads to a Market Requirements Document (MRD) and then gets handed off to engineering as a Functional Specifications Document (FSD) implemented via Agile or Waterfall development.

Organization

	Search	Execution
Strategy	Business Model Hypotheses	Operating Plan + Financial Model
Process	Customer Development, Agile Development	Product Management Agile or Waterfall Development
3 Organization	**Customer Development Team, Founder-driven**	**Functional Organization by Department**

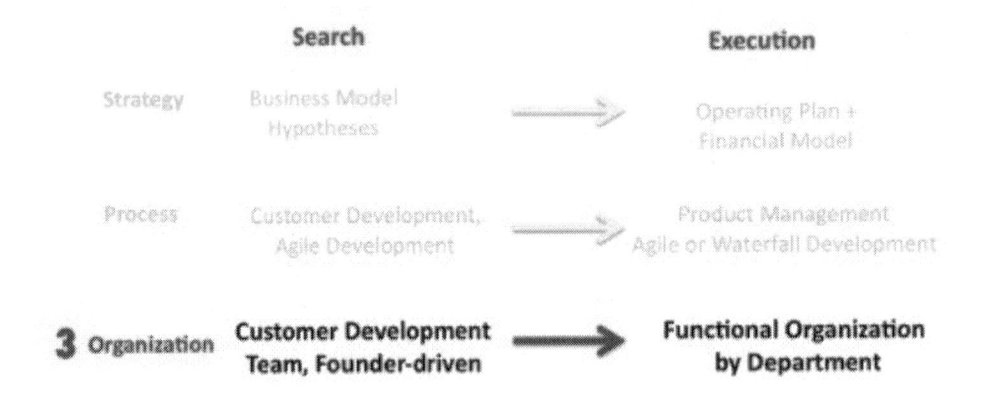

Searching for a business model requires a different organization than the one used to execute a plan. Searching requires the company to be organized around a customer development team led by the founders. In contrast, execution, (which follows search) requires the company to be organized by function (product management, sales, marketing, business development, etc.).

Companies in execution suffer from a "fear of failure culture" (quite understandable since they were hired to execute a known job spec). Startups with Customer Development Teams have a "learning and discovery" culture for search. The fear of making a move before the last detail is nailed down is one of the biggest problems existing companies have when they need to learn how to search.

The idea of not having a functional organization until the organization has found a proven business model is one of the hardest things for new startups to grasp. There are no sales, marketing or business development departments when you are searching for a business model. If you've organized your startup with those departments, you are not really doing customer development. (It's like trying to implement a startup using Waterfall engineering.)

Education

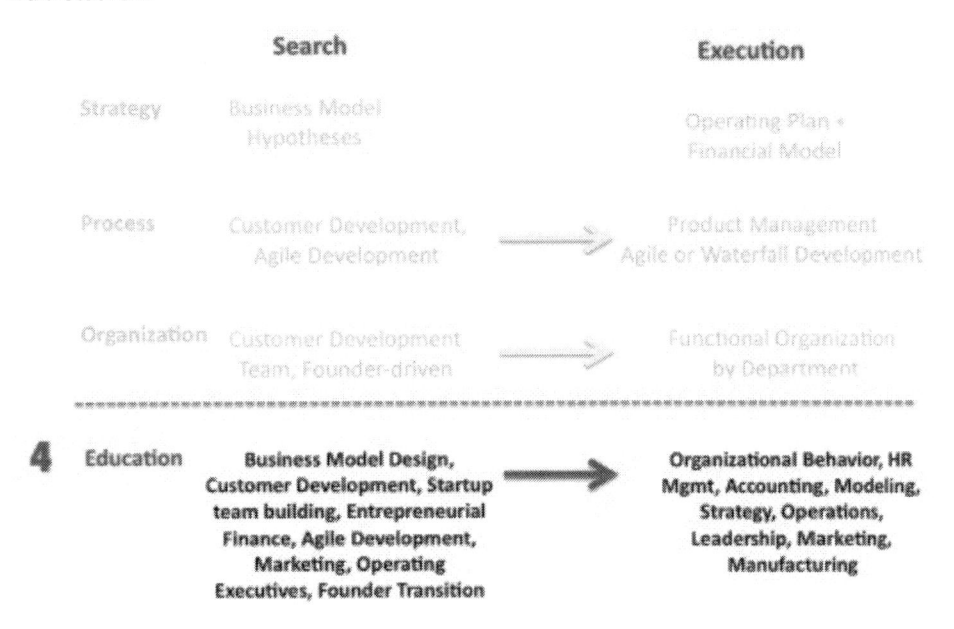

	Search	Execution
Strategy	Business Model Hypotheses	Operating Plan + Financial Model
Process	Customer Development, Agile Development	Product Management, Agile or Waterfall Development
Organization	Customer Development Team, Founder-driven	Functional Organization by Department
Education	Business Model Design, Customer Development, Startup team building, Entrepreneurial Finance, Agile Development, Marketing, Operating Executives, Founder Transition	Organizational Behavior, HR Mgmt, Accounting, Modeling, Strategy, Operations, Leadership, Marketing, Manufacturing

Entrepreneurship curriculums are only a few decades old. First taught as electives and now part of core business school curriculums, the field is still struggling to escape from the bounds of the business plan-centric view that startups are "smaller versions of a large company." VCs who've watched as no startup business plan survived first contact with customers continue to insist that startups write business plans as the price of entry to venture funding. Even as many of the best VCs understand that the business "planning" and not the "plan" itself, are what is important.

The trouble is that, over time, this key message has gotten lost. As business school professors, many of whom lack venture experience, studied how VCs made decisions, they observed the apparently central role of the business plan and proceeded to make the plan [not the planning] the central framework for teaching entrepreneurship. As new generations of VCs with MBAs came into the business, they compounded the problem ("that's how we always done it" or "that's what I learned (or the senior partners learned) in business school.")

Entrepreneurship educators have realized that plan-centric curriculum may get by for teaching incremental innovation but they're not turning out students prepared for the realities of building new ventures. Educators are now beginning to build their own E- School curriculum with a new class of management tools built around "search and discovery." Business Model Design, Product/Service Development, CustomerDevelopment, Startup Team-Building, Entrepreneurial Finance, Marketing, Founder Transition, etc. all provide the startup equivalent of the management tools MBAs learn for execution.

Instructional Strategy

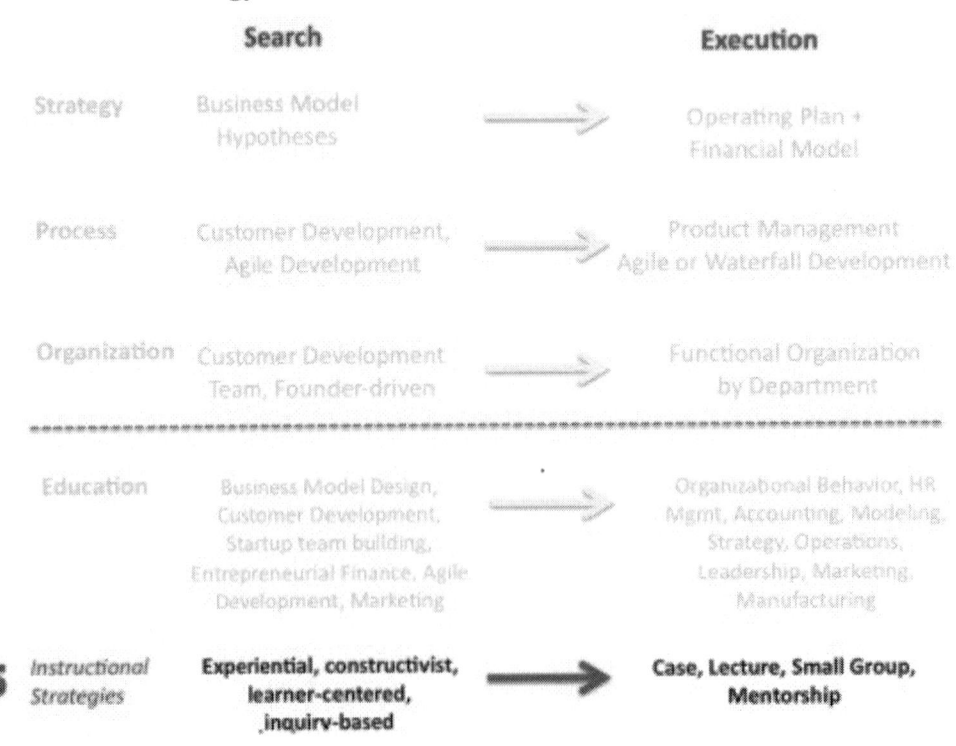

	Search	Execution
Strategy	Business Model Hypotheses	Operating Plan + Financial Model
Process	Customer Development, Agile Development	Product Management Agile or Waterfall Development
Organization	Customer Development Team, Founder-driven	Functional Organization by Department
Education	Business Model Design, Customer Development, Startup team building, Entrepreneurial Finance, Agile Development, Marketing	Organizational Behavior, HR Mgmt, Accounting, Modeling, Strategy, Operations, Leadership, Marketing, Manufacturing
5 Instructional Strategies	Experiential, constructivist, learner-centered, inquiry-based	Case, Lecture, Small Group, Mentorship

Entrepreneurial education is also changing the focus of the class experience from case method to hands-on experience. Invented at Harvard, the case method approach assumes that knowledge is gained when students actively participate in a discussion of a situation that may be faced by decision makers.

The search for a repeatable business model for a new product or service is not a predictable pattern. An entrepreneur must start with the belief that all her assumptions are simply hypotheses that will undoubtedly be challenged by what she learns from customers. Analyzing a case in the classroom removed from the realities of chaos and conflicting customer responses adds little to an entrepreneur's knowledge. Cases can't be replicated because the world of a startup is too chaotic and complicated. The case method is the antithesis of how entrepreneurs build startups—it teaches pattern recognition tools for the wrong patterns—and therefore has limited value as an entrepreneurship teaching tool.

The replacement for cases are not better cases written for startups. Instead, it would be business model design—using the business model canvas as a way to 1) capture and visualize the evolution of business learning in a company, and 2) see what patterns match real world iterations and pivots. It is a tool that better matches the real-world search for the business model.

An entrepreneurial curriculum obviously will have some core classes based on theory, lecture and mentorship. There's embarrassing little research on entrepreneurship education and outcomes, but we do know that students learn best when they can connect with the material in a hands-on way—personally making the mistakes and learning from them directly.

As much as possible the emphasis ought to be on experiential, learner-centric and inquiry-based classes that help to develop the mindset, reflexes, agility and resilience an entrepreneur needs to search for certainty in a chaotic world.

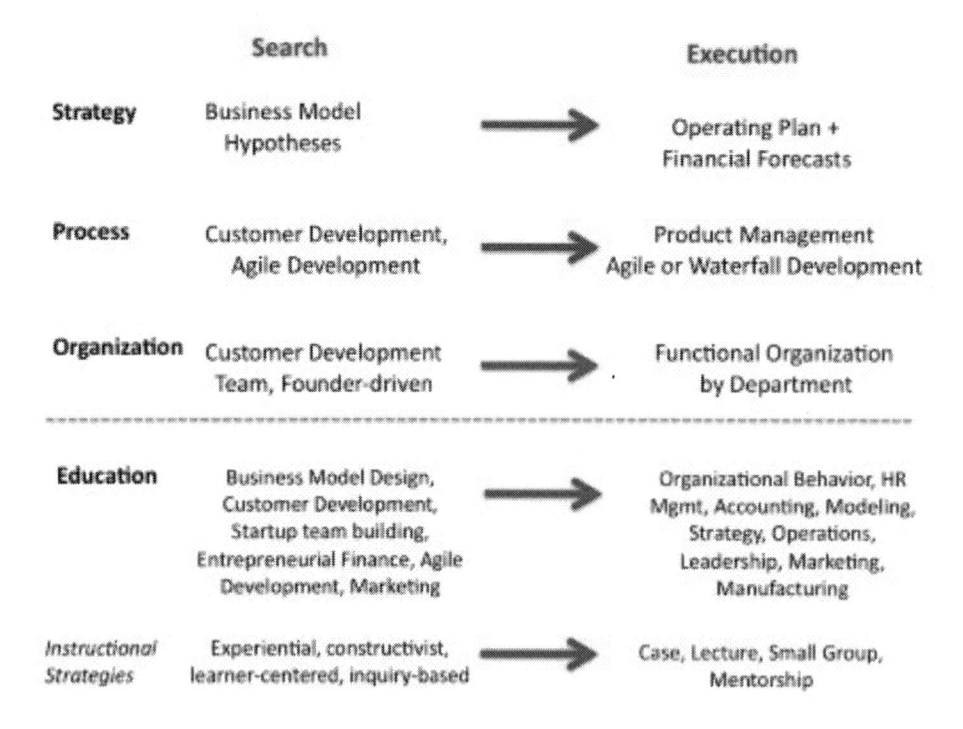

	Search		Execution
Strategy	Business Model Hypotheses	→	Operating Plan + Financial Forecasts
Process	Customer Development, Agile Development	→	Product Management Agile or Waterfall Development
Organization	Customer Development Team, Founder-driven	→	Functional Organization by Department
Education	Business Model Design, Customer Development, Startup team building, Entrepreneurial Finance, Agile Development, Marketing	→	Organizational Behavior, HR Mgmt, Accounting, Modeling, Strategy, Operations, Leadership, Marketing, Manufacturing
Instructional Strategies	Experiential, constructivist, learner-centered, inquiry-based	→	Case, Lecture, Small Group, Mentorship

Lessons Learned

- The search for the business model is the front end of the startup process.

- This is true in the smallest startup or largest company.

- The goal is to find a repeatable/scalable model, and then execute.

- Execution requires operating plans and financial forecasts.

- Customer and Agile Development are the processes to search and build the model.

- Product management is the process for executing the model.

- Entrepreneurial education needs to develop its own management stack

- Starting with how to design and search for a business model

- Adding all the other skills startups needs

- The case-method is the antithesis of an entrepreneurial teaching method

Make No Little Plans—Defining the Scalable Startup

January 4, 2010 (Steve Blank)

"Make no little plans. They have no magic to stir men's blood …"
—Daniel Burnham

A lot of entrepreneurs think that their startup is the next big thing when, in reality, they're just building a small business. How can you tell if your startup has the potential to be the next Google, Intel, or Facebook? A first order filter is whether the founders are aiming for a scalable startup.

Go for Broke

A few years ago I sat on the board of IMVU when the young company faced a choice my mother used to describe as "you should be so lucky to have this problem." For its first year IMVU had funded itself with money from friends and family. Now with customers and early revenue, it was out raising its first round of venture money. (Not only did their sales curve look like a textbook case of a VC-friendly hockey stick, but their Lessons Learned funding presentation was an eye-opener.)

Staring at us in the board meeting were three term-sheets from brand name VCs and an unexpected buy-out offer from Google. In fact, Google's offer for $15 million was equal to the highest valuation from the venture firms. The question was: what did the founders want to do?

Will Harvey, Eric Ries and the other founders were unequivocal—"Screw the buy-out, we're here to build a company. Lets take venture capital and grow this thing into a real business."

The Scalable Startup

Will and Eric implicitly had already made six decisions that defined a scalable startup.

1. Their vision for IMVU was broad and deep and very big—3D avatars and virtual goods would eventually be everywhere in the online world. They wanted to build an industry not just a product or a company.

2. Their personal goal wasn't to have a company that stayed small and paid them well. Nor did they think flipping the company to make a few million dollars would be a win. They believed their vision and work was going to be worth a lot more—or zero.

3. They envisioned that their tiny startup was to going to be a $100 million per year company by creating an entirely new market—selling virtual goods.

4. They used Customer and Agile development to search for a scalable and repeatable business model to become a large company. It reduced risk while allowing them to aim high.

5. They hired a world-class team with co-founders and early employees who shared their vision.

6. They fervently believed that only they were the ones who could and would make this happen.

These decisions guaranteed that the outcome of the board meeting was preordained. Selling out to Google would mean that someone else would define their vision. They were too driven and focused to let that happen. A few million dollars wasn't their goal. Taking venture money was just a means to an end. Their goal was to get profitable and big. And risk capital allowed them to do that sooner than later. Venture money also meant that the VC's goals of obscene returns were aligned with the founders. For the entire team, turning down the Google deal was equivalent to burning the boats on the shore. (One founder quit and joined Google.) After that, there was no doubt to existing employees and new hires what the company was aiming for.

Take No Prisoners

A "scalable startup" takes an innovative idea and searches for a scalable and repeatable business model that will turn it into a high growth, profitable company. Not just big but huge. It does that by entering a large market and taking share away from incumbents or by creating a new market and growing it rapidly.

A scalable startup typically requires external "risk" capital to create market demand and scale. And the founders must have a reality distortion field to convince investors their vision is not a hallucination and to hire employees and acquire early customers. A scalable startup requires incredibly talented people taking unreasonable risks with an unreasonable effort from the founders and employees.

Not All Startups Are Scalable

The word "entrepreneur" covers a lot of ground. It means someone who organizes, manages, and assumes the risks of a business. Entrepreneurship often describes a small business whose owner starts up a company i.e. a plumbing supply store, a restaurant, a consulting firm. In the U.S., 5.7 million companies with fewer than 100 employees make up 99.5-percent of all businesses. These small businesses are the backbone of American capitalism. But small business startups have very different objectives than scalable startups.

First, their goal is not scale on an industry level. They may want to grower larger, but they aren't focused on replacing an incumbent in an existing market or creating a new market. Typically the size of their opportunity and company doesn't lend itself to attracting venture capital. They grow their business via profits or traditional bank financing. Their primary goal is a predictable revenue stream for the owner, with reasonable risk and reasonable effort and without the need to bring in world-class engineers and managers.

The Web and Startups

The Internet has created a series of new and innovative business models. Herein lies the confusion; not every business on the web can scale big. While the Internet has enabled scalable Internet startups like Google and

Facebook it has also created a much, much larger class of web-based small businesses that can't or won't scale to a large company. Some are in small markets, some are run by founders who don't want to scale or can't raise the capital, or acquire the team. (The good news is that there is an emerging class of investors who are more than happy to fund and flip Web small businesses.)

Scalable Startup or Small Business—Which One Is Right?

There's nothing wrong with starting a small business. In fact, it is scalable startups that are the abnormal condition. You have to be crazy to make the bet the IMVU founders did. Unfortunately the popular culture and press have made scalable startups like Google and Facebook the models that every entrepreneur should aspire to and disparages technology small businesses with pejoratives like "lifestyle business." That's just plain wrong. It's simply a choice.

Just make it a conscious choice.

Lessons Learned

- Not all startups are scalable startups.

- Six initial conditions differentiate a scalable startup from a small business:

    1. Breadth of an entrepreneur's vision
    2. Founders' personal goals
    3. Size of the target market
    4. Customer and Agile development to find the business model
    5. World-class founding team and initial employees
    6. Passionate belief and a reality distortion field

- Understand your personal risk profile, and don't try to be someone you're not.

- Which one is "right" is up to you, not the crowd.

Lean Startups Aren't Cheap Startups

November 2, 2009 (Steve Blank)

At an entrepreneurs panel last week questions from the audience made me realize that the phrase "Lean Startup" was being confused with "Cheap Startup."

For those of you who have been following the discussion, a Lean Startup is Eric Ries' description of the intersection of Customer Development, Agile Development and, if available, open platforms and open source.

Lean Startups Aren't Cheap Startups

A Lean Startup is not about the total amount of money you may spend over the life of your startup. It is about when in the life of your company you do the spending.

Over its lifetime a Lean Startup may spend less money than a traditional startup. It may end up spending the same amount of money as a traditional startup. And I can even imagine cases where it might burn more cash than a traditional startup.

Let's see why.

The Price of Mistakes Are Inversely Proportional to Available Capital

In times of abundant venture capital if you miss your revenue plan, additional funding from your investors is usually available to cover your mistakes—i.e., you get "do-overs" or iterations without onerous penalties (assuming your investors still believe in the technology and vision). In times when venture capital is hard to get, investors extract high costs for failure (down-rounds, cramdowns, new management teams, shut down the company).

The key contributors to an out-of-control burn rate is 1) hiring a sales force too early, 2) turning on the demand creation activities too early, 3) developing something other than the minimum feature set for first customer ship. Salespeople cost money, and when they're not bringing in revenue, their wandering in the woods is time consuming, cash-draining and demoralizing. Marketing demand creation programs (Search Engine Marketing, Public Relations, Advertising, Lead Generation, Trade Shows, etc.) are all expensive and potentially fatal distractions if done before you have found product/market fit and a repeatable sales model. And most startup features and code end up on the floor as customers never really wanted them.

Therefore when money is hard to come by, entrepreneurs (and their investors) look for ways to reduce cash burn rate and increase the chance of finding product/market fit before waste you bunch of money. The Customer Development process (and the Lean Startup) is one way to do that.

Repeatable and Scalable Sales Model

In Customer Development your goal is not to avoid spending money but to preserve your cash as you search for a repeatable and scalable sales model and then spend like there is no tomorrow when you find one.

This is the most important sentence in this post and worth deconstructing.

- Preserve your cash: When you have unlimited cash (internet bubbles, frothy venture climate), you can iterate on your mistakes by burning more dollars. When money is tight, when there aren't dollars to redo mistakes, you look for processes that allow you to minimize waste. The Customer Development process says preserve your cash by not hiring anyone in sales and marketing until the founders turn hypotheses into facts and you have found product/market fit.

- As you search: Customer Development observes that when you start your company, all you and your business plan have are hypotheses, not facts—and that the founders are the ones who need to get out of the building to turn these hypotheses into customer data. This "get out of the building" activity is the Customer Discovery step of the Customer Development Model.

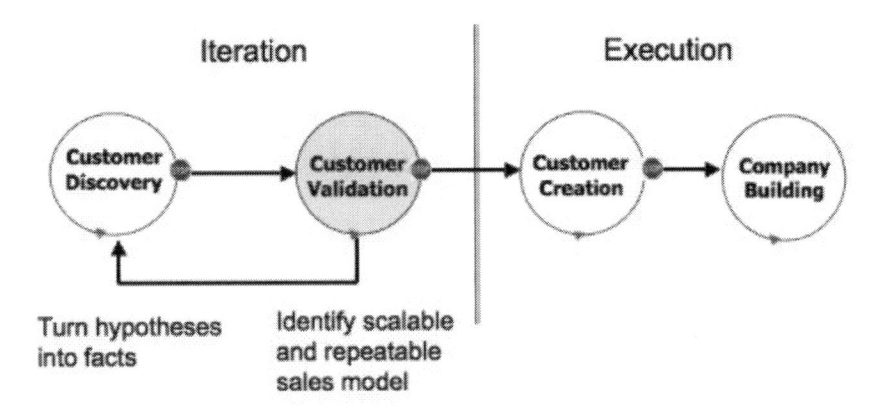

Customer Development Model

- Repeatable: Startups may get orders that come from board members' customer relationships or heroic, single-shot efforts of the CEO. These are great, but they are not repeatable by a sales organization. What you are searching for is not the one-off revenue hits but rather a repeatable pattern that can be replicated by a sales organization selling off a price list or by customers coming to your web site.

- Scalable: The goal is not to get one customer but many—and to get those customers so each additional customer adds incremental revenue and profit. The test is: If you add one more salesperson or spend more marketing dollars, does your sales revenue go up by more than your expenses?

- Sales model: A sales model answers the basic questions involved in selling your product: "Is this a revenue play or a freemium model going for users? Something else? Who's the customer? Who influences a sale? Who recommends a sale? Who is the decision maker? Who is the economic buyer? Where is the budget for purchasing the type of product you're selling? What's the customer acquisition cost? What's the lead and/or traffic generation strategy? How long does an average sale take from beginning to end? Etc."

- Finding out whether you have a repeatable, scalable sales model is the Customer Validation step of Customer Development. This is the most important phase in customer development. Have you learned how to sell your product to a target customer? Can you do this without running out of money?

Scale like there is no tomorrow The goal of an investor-backed startup is not to build a lifestyle business. The goal is to reach venture-scale (around 10-times return on investment). When you and your board agree you've found a repeatable and scalable sales model (i.e. have product/market fit,) then you invest the dollars to create end user demand and drive those customers into your sales channel.

If you confuse Lean with Cheap when you do find a repeatable and scalable sales model, you will starve your company for resources needed to scale. Customer Development (and Lean) is about continuous customer contact/iteration to find the right time for execution.

How to Build a Billion Dollar Startup

April 19, 2012 (Steve Blank)

The quickest way to create a billion dollar company is to take basic human social needs and figure out how to mediate them online.

(Look at the first wave of the web/mobile/cloud startups that have done just that: Facebook, Twitter, Instagram, Match.com, Pandora, Zynga, WordPress, LinkedIn.)

It's your turn.

Hard-Wired

This week I'm in New York teaching a 5-day version of my Lean LaunchPad class at Columbia University. While the class teaches a process to search and validate a business model, it does not offer any hints on how to create a killer startup idea. So after teaching several hundred teams in the last few years, one of my students finally asked this question—"So how do we come up with an idea for the next billion dollar company?"

Is It a Problem or a Need?

I've now come to believe that the value proposition in a business model (value proposition is the fancy name for your product or service) fits into either one of two categories:

- It solves a problem and gets a job done for a consumer or a company (accounting software, elevators, air-conditioning, electricity, tablet computers, electric toothbrushes, airplanes, email software, etc.)

- Or it fulfills a fundamental human social need (friendship, dating, sex, entertainment, art, communication, blogs, confession, networking, gambling, religion, etc.)

Moving Needs to Bits = A Billion Dollars

Friendship, dating, sex, art, entertainment, communication, confession, networking, gambling, religion—would our hearts still beat and would our lungs still breathe without them? Of course. But these are things that make us human. They are hard-wired into our psyche. We've been doing them for tens of thousands of years.

Ironically, the emergence of the digital world has made us more efficient yet has left us with less time for face-to-face interaction. Yet it's these interactions that define our humanity.

Facebook takes our need for friendship and attempts to recreate that connection on-line. Twitter allows us to share and communicate in real time. Zynga allows us to mindlessly entertain ourselves on-line. Match.com allows us to find a spouse.

At the same time these social applications are moving on-line, digital platforms (tablets and smartphones) are becoming available to hundreds of millions. It's not hard to imagine that in a decade, the majority of people on our planet will have 24/7 access to these applications. For better or worse social applications are the ones that will reach billions of users.

Yet they are all only less than 5 years old.

It cannot be that today we have optimally recreated and moved our all social interactions on-line.

It cannot be that Facebook, Twitter, Instagram, Pandora, Zynga, LinkedIn are the pinnacle of social software.

Others will do better.

Others will discover the other unmet and unfilled social needs that can move online. It could be you.

Lessons Learned

- Value propositions come in two forms: they solve a problem or they fulfill a human social need.

- Social Needs are friendship, dating, sex, entertainment, art, communication, blogs, confession, networking, gambling, religion, etc.

- They have always been fulfilled face-to-face.

- They are now moving on-line.

- The market size for these applications equals the entire human race.

- These are the ultimate applications.

9 Deadliest Startup Sins

May 14, 2012 (Bob Dorf)

Inc. magazine is publishing a 12-part series of excerpts from The Startup Owner's Manual, the new step-by-step "how to" guide for startups. The excerpts, which appeared first at Inc.com, highlight the Customer Development process, best practices, tips and instructions contained in our book. Feedback from my readers suggested you'd appreciate seeing the series posted here, as well.

Whether your venture is a new pizza parlor or the hottest new software product, beware: These nine flawed assumptions are toxic.

1. Assuming You Know What the Customer Wants

First and deadliest of all is a founder's unwavering belief that he or she understands who the customers will be, what they need, and how to sell it to them. Any dispassionate observer would recognize that on Day One, a startup has no customers, and unless the founder is a true domain expert, he or she can only guess about the customer, problem, and business model. On Day One, a startup is a faith-based initiative built on guesses.

To succeed, founders need to turn these guesses into facts as soon as possible by getting out of the building, asking customers if the hypotheses are correct, and quickly changing those that are wrong.

2. The "I Know What Features to Build" Flaw

The second flawed assumption is implicitly driven by the first. Founders, presuming they know their customers, assume they know all the features customers need.

These founders specify, design, and build a fully featured product using classic product development methods without ever leaving their building. Yet without direct and continuous customer contact, it's unknown whether the features will hold any appeal to customers.

3. Focusing on the Launch Date

Traditionally, engineering, sales, and marketing have all focused on the immovable launch date. Marketing tries to pick an "event" (trade show, conference, blog, etc.) where they can "launch" the product. Executives look at that date and the calendar, working backwards to ignite fireworks on the day the product is launched. Neither management nor investors tolerate "wrong turns" that result in delays.

The product launch and first customer ship dates are merely the dates when a product development team thinks the product's first release is "finished." It doesn't mean the company understands its customers or how to market or sell to them, yet in almost every startup, ready or not, departmental clocks are set irrevocably to "first customer ship." Even worse, a startup's investors are managing their financial expectations by this date as well.

4. Emphasizing Execution Instead of Testing, Learning, and Iteration

Established companies execute business models where customers, problems, and necessary product features are all knowns; startups, on the other hand, need to operate in a "search" mode as they test and prove every one of their initial hypotheses.

They learn from the results of each test, refine the hypothesis, and test again—all in search of a repeatable, scalable, and profitable business model. In practice, startups begin with a set of initial guesses, most of which will end up being wrong. Therefore, focusing on execution and delivering a product or service based on those initial, untested hypotheses is a going-out-of-business strategy.

5. Writing a Business Plan That Doesn't Allow for Trial and Error

Traditional business plans and product development models have one great advantage: They provide boards and founders an unambiguous path with clearly defined milestones the board presumes will be achieved. Financial progress is tracked using metrics like income statement, balance sheet, and cash flow. The problem is, none of these metrics are very useful because they don't track progress against your startup's only goal: to find a repeatable and scalable business model.

6. Confusing Traditional Job Titles With a Startup's Needs

Most startups simply borrow job titles from established companies. But remember, these are jobs in an organization that's executing a known business model. The term "sales" at an existing company refers to a team that repeatedly sells a known product to a well-understood group of customers with standard presentations, prices, terms, and conditions. Startups by definition have few, if any, of these. In fact, they're out searching for them!

The demands of customer discovery require people who are comfortable with change, chaos, and learning from failure and are at ease working in risky, unstable situations without a roadmap.

7. Executing on a Sales and Marketing Plan

Hiring VPs and execs with the right titles but the wrong skills leads to further trouble as high-powered sales and marketing people arrive on the payroll to execute the "plan." Executives and board members accustomed to measurable signs of progress will focus on these execution activities because this is what they know how to do (and what they believe they were hired to do). Of course, in established companies with known customers and markets, this focus makes sense.

And even in some startups in "existing markets," where customers and markets are known, it might work. But in a majority of startups, measuring progress against a product launch or revenue plan is simply false progress, since it transpires in a vacuum absent real customer feedback and rife with assumptions that might be wrong.

8. Prematurely Scaling Your Company Based on a Presumption of Success

The business plan, its revenue forecast, and the product introduction model assume that every step a startup takes proceeds flawlessly and smoothly to the next. The model leaves little room for error, learning, iteration, or customer feedback.

Even the most experienced executives are pressured to hire and staff per the plan regardless of progress. This leads to the next startup disaster: premature scaling.

9. Management by Crisis, Which Leads to a Death Spiral

The consequences of most startup mistakes begin to show by the time of first customer ship, when sales aren't happening according to "the plan." Shortly thereafter, the sales VP is probably terminated as part of the "solution."

A new sales VP is hired and quickly concludes that the company just didn't understand its customers or how to sell them. Since the new sales VP was hired to "fix" sales, the marketing department must now respond to a sales manager who believes that whatever was created earlier in the company was wrong. (After all, it got the old VP fired, right?)

Here's the real problem: No business plan survives first contact with customers. The assumptions in a business plan are simply a series of untested hypotheses. When real results come in, the smart startups pivot or change their business model based on the results. It's not a crisis, it's part of the road to success.

Why Too Many Startups (er) Suck

September 21, 2012 (Bob Dorf)

While statistics are weak on startup success rates, the worst one I've seen suggests that 2 in 1000 venture backed startups will ever achieve $100 million or more in valuation. Another stat puts that number at 2-percent rather than 0.2-percent. Either way, the "hurdle" for successful, scalable startups is high, and it gets higher every day as customer acquisition challenges continue to increase.

I've spent more than four decades founding, coaching, teaching and investing in startups, and nothing breaks my heart more than meeting a starry-eyed founder who says "we're almost ready to show it to people." The "it" is a physical or web product they've often been locked-down, pounding away at, for many weeks.

In my view, this is the nastiest of all startup sins: failing to involve customers and their feedback from literally the first day of a startup's life, keeping the most vital opinions silent—those of the eventual customers—for far longer than necessary.

When I hear this comment, as I do far too often, I switch to pleading mode: "Please. Take a week. Get some feedback. Does anybody really care, or are they giving you polite nods and little more. This generally leads to the second biggest reason too many startups suck: they're solving a non-problem.

Does Anybody Care? Many Startup Owner's Manual readers ask why Steve Blank and I are adamant that Customer Discovery happen in two separate, distinct phases: "problem" discovery and, later, "solution" discovery. There's just no other way but, as Steve Blank has said for a decade, to "get out of the building" and talk to the only folks who matter—your customers.

Building a solution to a problem of moderate or lukewarm interest to users is a long-term death sentence for startups, where founders will almost certainly commit to 20,000 hours of their lives (or 5 years of 80-hour workweeks) in order to "beat the odds" and deliver a breakout success: a sustainable, scalable, profitable business.

Why, then, are so many founders so reluctant to invest even 500 or 1,000 hours upfront to be sure that, when they're done, the business they're building will face genuine, substantial demand or enthusiasm. Without passionate customers, even the most passionate entrepreneur will flounder at best. Dropbox is a great example. It scaled like lightning by solving an urgent, painful problem for millions of consumers. The product is so good, helpful, and easy to use that it literally almost does its own marketing organically through the product's viral nature, just as Hotmail and Gmail have done since inception.

What's the Honest Trajectory? There can only be one Mark Zuckerberg, and at least he's young and healthy. Can every startup skyrocket like Facebook or Square or Google? It's downright impossible. The solution: understand your startup's "honest trajectory" and align objectives of the founding team and—importantly—its investors to define and agree about what "success" looks like. Thousands of entrepreneurs would be a lot happier if their focus was a solid, growable, defensible niche business that might never go public or be worth $100 million. There's a ton of money to be made "in the middle," a broad swath between struggling or gasping for cash and ringing the bell at the NASDAQ.

Find the right trajectory for your business and focus not only on reaching it, but on ensuring that the result is a sustainable, repeatable profit engine that can perform and grow healthily over time. Use Customer Development to identify and refine the potential profitable niche and stay in close contact with customers as you build, to be sure you're building something they'll want to have… and keep.

Stand Out in the Crowd: If you're solving an important problem, make sure your solution stands out in the crowd. Hundreds of entrepreneurs I've met never spent an entire day Googling their industry, other ways to solve "their" problem, and few have spent time "playing consumer," trying to find "their" own product, or one like it, and creating a "market map" that assesses all the competitive solutions, their strengths/weaknesses, and where the new product fits clearly and distinctly in its competitive environment. If you can't figure this out on your own, and relate it to customers succinctly, it's a certainty that your customers never will.

Going Forward Is NOT About Standing Still: Another of my high-frequency "sad" moments happens when visiting with a team that is consistently "flatlining," or delivering minimal or trivial user growth week after week or worse. Clearly, something's terribly wrong, and everyone just keeps showing up, doing their jobs, without attacking the core problem that's almost always a lack of palpable customer enthusiasm. What's the point? What are they waiting for? It's time to bring the leadership team into a room, dissect each key element of the business model, and identify pivots that are worth exploring smartly—where else—with customers.

Going Forward Is Often About Going Backward First: Entrepreneurs pride themselves in their problem-solving abilities, tenacity, and willingness to run through brick walls to make things "go." More often than not, the DNA strand that makes entrepreneurs great is the one that's their undoing when confronted with "flatlining" user adoption, growth, referrals, or frequency. These entrepreneurs need to switch smartly out of "do" mode and return to the earliest "discovery" steps to find a distinctive, exciting solution to a seriously painful customer need or problem.

It's the only way to make a startup not suck.

Startup Suicide— Rewriting the Code

January 25, 2011 (Steve Blank)

The benefits of customer and agile development and minimum features set are continuous customer feedback, rapid iteration and little wasted code. But over time if developers aren't careful, code written to find early customers can become unwieldy, difficult to maintain and incapable of scaling. Ironically it becomes the antithesis of agile. And the magnitude of the problem increases exponentially with the success of the company. The logical solution? "Re-architect and re-write" the product.

For a company in a rapidly changing market, that's usually the beginning of the end.

It Seems Logical

I just had lunch (at my favorite Greek restaurant in Palo Alto forgetting it looked like a VC meetup) with a friend who was technical founder of his company and is now its chairman. He hired an operating exec as the CEO a few years ago. We caught up on how the company was doing ("very well, thank you, after five years, the company is now at a $50 million run rate,") but he wanted to talk about a problem that was on his mind. "As we've grown we've become less and less responsive to changing market and customer needs. While our revenue is looking good, we can be out of business in two years if we can't keep up with our customer's rapid shifts in platforms. Our CEO doesn't have a technology background, but he's frustrated he can't get the new features and platforms he wants (Facebook, iPhone and Android, etc.). At the last board meeting, our VP of Engineering explained that the root of our problems was "our code has accumulated a ton of 'technical debt,' it's really ugly code, and it's not the way we would have done it today." He told the board that the only way to deliver these changes is to "re-write our product." My friend added, "It sounds logical to the CEO so he's about to approve the project."

Shooting Yourself in the Head

"Well didn't the board read him the riot act when they heard this?" I asked. "No," my friend replied, sadly shaking his head. "The rest of the board said it sounded like a good idea."

With a few more questions I learned that the code base, which had now grown large, still had vestiges of the original exploratory code written back in the early days when the company was in the discovery phase of Customer Development. Engineering designs made back then with the aim of figuring out the product were not the right designs for the company's current task of expanding to new platforms.

I reminded my friend that I've never been an engineering manager so any advice I could give him was just from someone who had seen the movie before.

The Siren Song to CEOs Who Aren't Technical

CEOs face the "rewrite" problem at least once in their tenure. If they're an operating exec brought in to replace a founding technical CEO, then it looks like an easy decision— just listen to your engineering VP compare the schedule for a rewrite (short) against the schedule of adapting the old code to the new purpose (long). In reality, this is a fool's choice. The engineering team may know the difficulty and problems adapting the old code, but has no idea what difficulties and problems it will face writing a new code base.

A CEO who had lived through a debacle of a rewrite or understood the complexity of the code would know that with the original engineering team no longer there, the odds of making the old mistakes over again are high. Add to that introducing new mistakes that weren't there the first time, Murphy's Law says that unbridled optimism will likely turn the one-year rewrite into a multi-year project.

My observation was that the CEO and VP of Engineering were confusing cause and effect. The customers aren't asking for new code. They are asking for new features and platforms—now. Customers couldn't care less whether it was delivered via spaghetti code, alien spacecraft, or a completely new product. While the code rewrite is going on, competitors who aren't enamored with architectural purity will be adding features, platforms, customers, and market share. The difference between being able to add them now versus a year or more in the future might be the difference between growing revenue and going out of business.

Who Wants to Work on The Old Product
Perhaps the most dangerous side-effect of embarking on a code rewrite is that the decision condemns the old code before a viable alternative exists. Who is going to want to work on the old code with all its problems when the VP Engineering and CEO have declared the new code to be the future of the company? The old code is as good as dead the moment management introduces the word "rewrite." As a consequence, the CEO has no fallback. If the VP Engineering's schedule ends up taking four years instead of one year, there is no way to make incremental progress on the new features during that time.

What We Have Is a Failure of Imagination

I suggested that this looked like a failure of imagination in the VP of Engineering—made worse by a CEO who's never lived through a code rewrite—and compounded by a board that also doesn't get it and hasn't challenged either of them for a creative solution.

My suggestion to my friend? Given how dynamic and competitive the market is, this move is a company-killer. The heuristic should be "don't rewrite the code base in businesses where time to market is critical and customer needs shift rapidly." Rewrites may make sense in markets where the competitive cycle time is long.

I suggested that he lay down on the tracks in front of this train at the board meeting. Force the CEO to articulate what features and platforms he needs by when, and what measures he has in place to manage schedule risk. Figure out whether a completely different engineering approach was possible. (Refactor only the modules for the features that were needed now? Rewrite the new platforms on a different code-base? Start a separate skunk works team for the new platforms? etc.)

Lessons Learned

- Not all code rewrites are the same. When the market is stable and changes are infrequent, you may have time to rewrite.

- When markets/customers/competitors are shifting rapidly, you don't get to declare a "time-out" because your code is ugly.

- This is when you need to understand 1) what problem are you solving (hint it's not the code) and 2) how to creatively fix what's needed.

- Making the wrong choice can crater your company.

- This is worth a brawl at the board meeting.

Open Source Entrepreneurship

November 27, 2012 (Steve Blank)

One of the great things about being a retired entrepreneur is that I get to give back to the community that helped me. I assembled this collection of free and almost-free tools, class syllabi, presentations, books, lectures, and videos in hopes that it can make your path as an entrepreneur or educator easier.

Free:

Startup Tools

If you're building a startup, the Startup Tools tab has curated links to hundreds of startup resources. Specific links are:

- A list of startup tools

- Market research tools to help you figure out the size of the opportunity your startup is pursuing

- Some of the best advice on founding and running a startup from other smart voices

The Lean LaunchPad Course Online

I teach potential founders a hands-on, experiential class called "The Lean LaunchPad" at Berkeley, Stanford, Columbia and Caltech. The class teaches the three basic skills all entrepreneurs need to know:

- business model design

- customer development

- agile engineering

For my Innovation Corps class for the National Science Foundation, it made sense to record the lectures and put them online. In my regular classes, I now "flip" the classroom and have my students watch these online lectures as homework and we use the class time for discussion.

The free online class is hosted at Udacity.com

Class Syllabi, My Lecture Slides, and Student Presentations
You'll also find

- Syllabi for all my classes

- Educators Training Guide (it's part of the Educators Course where we teach how to design a Lean Entrepreneurship Curriculum and how to teach the Lean LaunchPad class—described in the Educators section below.)

- Secret Notes for Instructors

- Latest presentations posted

- Stanford presentations, lectures and syllabus

- Berkeley presentations, lectures and syllabus

- Columbia five-day presentations, lectures and syllabus

- Caltech five-day presentations, lectures and syllabus

- Some general customer development slides click

The Entrepreneur's Checklist

The good folks at Udemy have taken a few of my lectures at Stanford and put them together in a free series online.

Online Guide to How to Build a Startup: The Lean LaunchPad

Startupplays.com, publisher of online entrepreneurs processes guides, drew from my Udacity course and The Startup Owner's Manual to create a free step-by-step guide to understanding your customers and creating your value proposition. Called "How to Build a Startup: The Lean LaunchPad" it walks you through the Business Model Canvas and an overview of the customer development process.

Videos
This section has a number of my talks on entrepreneurship, customer development and startup, some short, some long, and a few interesting.

Recommended Reading
These books have influenced my thinking. There's a short synopsis of why I like each book.

Updates and suggestions for books that I've missed are welcomed on the books comment page.

Visitors Guide to Silicon Valley
I got tired watching dignitaries fly into Silicon Valley, visit Google, Facebook, Apple, and Stanford and then say they understand startups and entrepreneurship. So for the rest of us, I put together a Visitors Guide to Silicon Valley.

Secret History of Silicon Valley
What began as a hobby of mine—research in the intersection of my military, intelligence, and Silicon Valley careers combined with my interest in the history of Silicon Valley and technology entrepreneurship—ended up in a video and Power Point presentation. I first gave the Secret History of Silicon Valley presentation as an invited talk at Google, then at the Computer History Museum.

When I gave the talk to audience of CIA staffers they asked how I came up with the talk, so I wrote series of posts as the back-story.

I still love giving this talk to people who lived it and people curious about it.

Almost Free:

Startup Weekend Next

Startup Weekend NEXT is a three-week version of the Lean LaunchPad class with hands- on instructors and mentors—offered in hundreds of cities around the world.

- The class is organized, led and delivered by Startup Weekend, the global non-profit

  that teaches entrepreneurs how to launch a startup in 54 hours.

- TechStars and Startup America are partnering to provide mentors in the U.S.

They don't ask for equity and charge just enough to cover the costs of pizza and the room rental.

The Lean LaunchPad Educators Course

Hosted by NCIIA, Stanford University and U.C. Berkeley, Jerry Engel and I teach a course for educators interested in learning how to update and revise their entrepreneurship curriculum for the 21st century as well as learning how to teach the Lean LaunchPad class.

The Lean LaunchPad Educators Training Guide is part of this course.

The Startup Owner's Manual

The Startup Owner's Manual with Bob Dorf, has become the step-by-step reference manual for anyone even thinking about a startup. Each section offers detailed guidance and how-tos, helping you make your way through the Customer Development process using MVPs and Pivots as you search for a Business Model.

We added a Kindle version, incorporating hundreds of links to websites, blog posts, and presentations.

The Founder's Workbook

Zoomstra, the publisher of online workbooks offers The Founders Workbook to help you track and monitor your progress through every step of the Customer Development process. It takes the static 57 checklists from The Startup Owner's Manual and makes them dynamic and accessible by putting them online as an interactive checklist. Use it to keep your team on track and ensure you have completed each critical task as you search for a scalable business model.

The Four Steps to the Epiphany

The Four Steps to the Epiphany as been described as the book that launched the Lean

Startup movement. The book is still relevant today as when it was written. The last two chapters deal with scale and management of growing startups.

Now get out of the building and make something happen!

Holding a Cat by the Tail

III.

The Customer Development Manifesto—A Startup's Guiding Light

The Product Development Model

February 23, 2009 (Steve Blank)

I realized that traditional ways to think about startups—have an idea, raise some money, do product development, go through an alpha test, beta test and first customer ship was the canonical model of how entrepreneurs thought about early stage ventures.

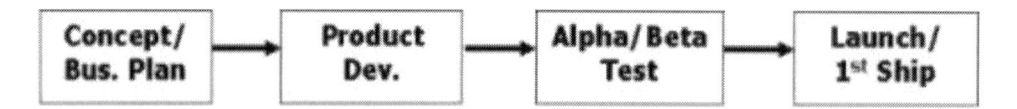

Concept/Bus. Plan → Product Dev. → Alpha/Beta Test → Launch/1st Ship

This product development diagram had become part of the DNA of Silicon Valley. So much so that after I started teaching I'd ask, "Can anybody recognize this model of startups?" And when everyone raised their hands I used to joke, "Even the waiters in San Francisco could draw this model." But in 2002, a student with a pained look on his face raised his hand and said, "Well, we're now waiters in San Francisco because we used to be CEOs of dot-com companies." So I no longer make that joke.

When I looked at the diagram while sitting in a ski cabin after my eighth and likely final startup, E.piphany, I realized there was a fundamental question I couldn't answer: if all startups follow that model, why is it that some companies are opening bottles of champagne at their IPO and others who almost followed the same rules are selling off their furniture? What was the difference here? Were all startups the same? Were startups failing because of product failures or was there some other failure mode? Is there any way to predict success or failure? And even more importantly, was there any way to reduce risk in early stage ventures?

That day, alone in the cabin I knew I had to find the answer.

The Customer Development Manifesto: Reasons for the Revolution (part 1)

August 31, 2009 (Steve Blank)

After 20 years of working in startups, I decided to take a step back and look at the product development model I had been following and see why it usually failed to provide useful guidance in activities outside the building—sales, marketing and business development.

Every startup has some methodology for product development, launch and life-cycle management. At their best, these processes provide detailed plans, checkpoints and milestones for every step in getting a product out the door: sizing markets, estimating sales, developing marketing requirements documents, prioritizing product features. Yet at the end of the day, even with all these processes, 9 out of 10 new products are failures.

So what's wrong the product development model? The first hint lies in its name; this is a product development model, not a marketing model, not a sales hiring model, not a customer acquisition model, not even a financing model (and we'll also find that in most cases, it's even a poor model to use to develop a product). Yet startup companies have traditionally used this model to manage and pace not only engineering but also non-engineering activities.

In this post I'm going to describe the flaws of the product development model. In the next few posts that follow, I'll describe more specifically how this model distorts startup sales, marketing and business development. And how thinking of a solution to this commonly used model's failures led to a new model—the Customer Development Model—that offers a new way to approach startup activities outside the building. Finally, I'll write about how Eric Ries and the

Lean Startup concept provided the equivalent model for product development activities inside the building and neatly integrates customer and agile development.

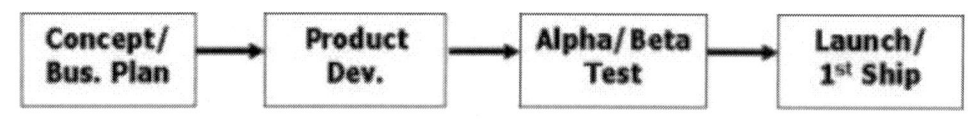

Concept/Bus. Plan → Product Dev. → Alpha/Beta Test → Launch/1st Ship

Product Development Diagram

1. Where Are the Customers?

To begin with, the product development model completely ignores a fundamental truth about startups and new products. The greatest risk in startups —and hence the greatest cause of failure—is not the technology risk of developing a product but in the risk of developing customers and markets. Startups don't fail because they lack a product; they fail because they lack customers and a profitable business model. This alone should be a pretty good clue about what's wrong with using the product development diagram as the sole guide to what a startup needs to be doing. Look at the Product Development model and you might wonder, "Where are the customers?"

The reality for most startups today is that the product development model focuses all their attention on activities that go on inside a company's own building. While customer input may be a checkpoint or "gate" in the process, it doesn't drive it.

2. The Focus on a First Customer Ship Date

Using the Product Development model also forces sales and marketing to focus on the end point of the process—the first customer ship date. Most sales and marketing executives hired into a startup look at the "first customer ship date," look at the calendar on the wall, and then work backwards figuring out how to do their job in time so that the fireworks start the day the product is launched.

The flaw in this thinking is that "first customer ship" is simply the date when engineering thinks they "finished" the 1.0 release of the product. The first customer ship date does not mean that the company understands its customers, how to market or sell to them or how to build a profitable business. (Read the preceding sentence again. It's a big idea.)

Even worse, a startup's investors are managing their financial milestones by the first customer ship date as well.

The product development model is so focused on building and shipping the product that it ignores the entire process of testing your basic hypothesis about your business model (customers, channel, pricing, etc.) before you ship. Not testing these hypotheses upfront is a fundamental and, in many cases, fatal error most startups make.

Why? Because it isn't until after first customer ship that a startup discovers that their initial hypotheses were simply wrong (i.e. customers aren't buying it, the cost of distribution is too high, etc.) As a result the young company is now saddled with an expensive, scaled-up sales organization frustrated trying to execute a losing sales strategy and a marketing organization desperately trying to create demand without a true understanding of customers' needs.

As Marketing and Sales flail around in search of a sustainable market, the company is burning through its most precious asset: cash.

3. The Focus on Execution Versus Learning and Discovery

The product development model assumes that customers' needs are known, the product features are known, and your business model is known. Given this certainty, it's logical that a startup will hire a sales and marketing team to simply execute your business plan. You interview sales and marketing execs for prior relevant experience and their rolodexes, and hope they execute the playbook that worked for them in prior companies.

All of this is usually a bad idea. No one asks, "Why are we executing like we know what we are doing? Where exactly did the assumptions in our startup business plan come from?" Was the sales revenue model based on actually testing the hypotheses outside the building? Or were they a set of spreadsheets put together over late night beers to convince an investor that this is going to be a great deal?

No newly hired sales and marketing exec is going to tell a founder, "Hey, my prior experience and assumptions may not actually be relevant to this new startup." Great sales and marketing people are great at execution—that's what you hired for. But past experience may not be relevant for your new company. A new company needs to test a series of hypothesis before it can successfully find a repeatable and scalable sales model. For startups in a new or re-segmented market, these are not merely execution activities, they are learning and discovery activities that are critical to the company's success or failure.

4. The Focus on Execution Versus Agility

The product development diagram has a linear flow from left to right. Each step happens in a logical progression that can be PERT charted with milestones and resources assigned to completing each step.

Anyone who has ever taken a new product out to a set of potential customers can tell you that the real world works nothing like that. A good day in front of customers is two steps forward and one step back. In fact, the best way to represent what happens outside the building is more like a series of recursive circles—recursive to represent the iterative nature of what actually happens in a learning and discovery environment. Information and data are gathered about customers and markets incrementally, one step at a time. Yet sometimes those steps take you in the wrong direction or down a blind alley. You find yourself calling on the wrong customers, not understanding why people will buy, not understanding what product features are important. Other times potential customers will suggest a new use for the product, new positioning or even a much better idea.

The ability to learn from those missteps, to recognize new opportunities, and to rapidly change direction is what distinguishes a successful startup from those whose names are forgotten among the vanished.

5. The Outsourcing of Founders' Responsibility

The Product Development model separates founders from deeply understanding their customers and market. The responsibility for validating the founders' original hypotheses is delegated to employees—the sales and marketing team.

This means the founders are isolated from directly hearing customer input—good, bad, and ugly. Worse, founders really won't understand whether customers will buy and what features are saleable until after first customer ship.

When an adroit and agile founder gets outside the building and hears for the nth time that the product is unsellable they will recognize, regroup and change direction. A process to give the founders continuous customer interaction—from day one—is essential.

6. Focus on a Finished Product Rather Than a Minimum Feature Set

The passion of an entrepreneur coupled with the product development diagram drives you to believe that all you need to do is build the product (in all its full-featured glory) and customers will come. A waterfall development process reinforces that insanity. The reality is quite different. Unless you are in an Existing Market (making a better version of what customers are already buying), you'll find that your hypothesis about what features customers want had no relationship to what they really wanted. Most startup code ends up on the floor.

7. Investor Focus on a Broken Model

Ask VCs why they use the Product Development model to manage a startup and you get answers like: "It's the way my firm has always done it. Why change something that has worked so well over the last three decades?" Or: "Look at our returns, it's always worked for us." Or at times an even more honest answer: "My senior partners say this is the only way to do it."

Some firms correctly point out that, "It's fine if 8 out of 10 of our companies fail if the remaining two return 20-times our money. That's a better return than having 10 out of 10 companies succeed and each return 2-times our money. Therefore we don't want startups doing anything but swinging for the fences."

The fallacy is that the product development model is the most efficient model for new ventures swinging for the fences—this year, last year, last decade, or since the first startup met their first investor.

Venture portfolio companies don't succeed because they used the Product Development model they succeeded in spite of using it. The fact is most successful startups abandon the product development model as soon as they encounter customers.

Today, startups using the product development model iterate and learn and discover by burning investor cash. When cash is tight, they go out of business—or they adopt a more efficient model.

The Customer Development Manifesto: Reasons for the Revolution (part 2)

September 3, 2009 (Steve Blank)

This post describes how the traditional product development model distorts startup sales, marketing and business development. In the next few posts that follow, I'll describe how thinking of a solution to this model's failures led to the Customer Development Model— that offers a new way to approach startup sales and marketing activities. Finally, I'll write about how Eric Ries and the Lean Startup concept provided the equivalent model for product development activities inside the building and neatly integrates customer and agile development.

8. The Lack of Meaningful Milestones for Sales, Marketing, and Business Development

The one great thing about the product development methodology is that it provides an unambiguous structure with clearly defined milestones. The meaning of alpha test, beta test, and first customer ship are pretty obvious to most engineers. In contrast, sales and marketing activities before first customer ship are ad hoc, fuzzy, and don't have measurable, concrete objectives. They lack any way to stop and fix what's broken (or even to know if it is broken.)

What kind of objectives would a startup want or need for sales and marketing? Most sales executives and marketers tend to focus on execution activities because at least these are measurable. For example, some startup sales execs believe hiring the core sales team is a key objective. Others focus on acquiring early "lighthouse" customers (prominent customers who will attract others). Once the product begins to ship, startup sales execs use orders and revenue as its marker of progress in understanding customers. (Freemium models have their own scorekeeping.) Marketers believe creating a killer web presence, corporate presentation, are objectives. Some think that hiring a PR agency, starting the buzz and getting coverage in hot blogs or on the cover of magazines at launch are objectives.

While these objectives provide an illusion of progress, in reality they do little to validate the business plan hypotheses about customers and what they will buy. They don't help a startup move toward a deep understanding of customers and their problems, discovering a repeatable road map of how they buy, and building a financial model that results in profitability.

9. The Use of a Product Development Model to Measure Sales

Using the product development diagram for startup sales activities is like using a clock to tell the temperature. They both measure something, but not the thing you wanted.

Here's what the product development diagram looks like from a sales perspective:

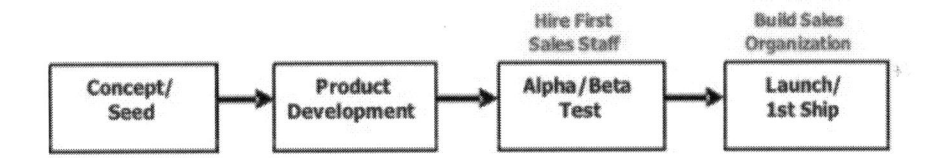

Concept/Seed → Product Development → Alpha/Beta Test (Hire First Sales Staff) → Launch/1st Ship (Build Sales Organization)

A VP of Sales looks at the diagram and says, "Hmm, if beta test is on this date, I'd better get a small sales team in place before that date to acquire my first 'early customers.' And if first customer ship is on this date over here, then I need to hire and staff a sales organization by then." Why? "Well, because the revenue plan we promised the investors shows us generating customer revenue from the day of first customer ship."

I hope this thinking already sounds insane to you. The plan calls for selling in volume the day engineering is finished building the product. What plan says that? Why, the business plan, crafted with a set of hypotheses now using the product development model as a timeline for execution. This approach is not predicated on discovering the right market or learning whether any customers will actually shell out cash for your product. Instead you use product development to time your readiness to sell. This "ready or not, here we come" attitude means that you won't know if the sales strategy and plan actually work until after first customer ship. What's the consequence if your stab at a sales strategy is wrong? You've built a sales organization and company that's burning cash before you know if you have demand for your product or a repeatable and scalable sales model. No wonder the half-life of a startup VP of Sales is about nine months post-first customership.

"Build and they will come" is not a strategy, it's a prayer.

10. The Use of a Product Development Model to Measure Marketing
The head of Marketing looks at the same product development diagram and sees something quite different.

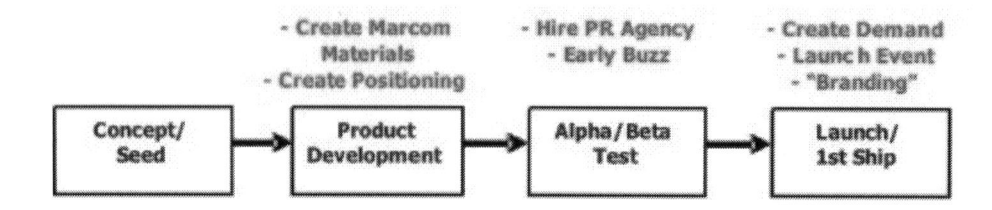

Concept/Seed → Product Development → Alpha/Beta Test → Launch/1st Ship

- Create Marcom Materials
- Create Positioning
- Hire PR Agency
- Early Buzz
- Create Demand
- Launch Event
- "Branding"

For Marketing, first customer ship means feeding the sales pipeline with a constant stream of customer prospects. To create this demand at first customer ship, marketing activities start early in the product development process. While the product is being engineered, Marketing begins to create web sites, corporate presentations and sales materials. Implicit in these materials is the corporate and product "positioning." Looking ahead to the product launch, the marketing group hires a public relations agency to refine the positioning and to begin generating early "buzz" about the company. The PR agency helps the company understand and influence key bloggers, social networks, industry analysts, luminaries, and references. All this leads up to a flurry of press events and interviews, all geared to the product/web site launch date. (During the Internet bubble, one more function of the marketing department was to "buy" customer loyalty with enormous advertising and promotion spending to create a brand.)

At first glance this process may look quite reasonable, until you realize all this marketing activity occurs before customers start buying—that is, before the company has had a chance to actually test the positioning, marketing strategy, or demand-creation activities in front of real customers. In fact, all the marketing plans are made in a virtual vacuum of real customer feedback and information. Of course, smart marketers have some early interaction with customers before the product ships, but if they do, it's on their own initiative, not as part of a well-defined process. Most first-time marketers spend more of their time behind their desks inside the building then outside talking to potential customers.

This is somewhat amazing since in a startup no facts exist inside the building—only opinions.

Yet even if we get the marketing people out from behind their desks into the field, the deck is still stacked against their success. Look at the product development diagram. When does Marketing find out whether the positioning, buzz, and demand creation activities actually work? After first customer ship. The inexorable march to this date has no iterative loop that says: "If our assumptions are wrong, maybe we need to try something different."

11. Premature Scaling

The Product Development model leads Sales and Marketing to believe that by first customer ship, come hell or high water, they need fully staffed organizations leads to another disaster: premature scaling.

Startup executives have three documents to guide their hiring and staffing; a business plan, a product development model and a revenue forecast. All of these are execution documents—they direct the timing and hiring of spending as if all assumptions in the business plan are 10-percent correct. As mentioned earlier there are no milestones that alert a startup to stop or slow down hiring until you have proven until you understand you customers. Even the most experienced executives succumb to the inexorable pressure to hire and staff to "plan" regardless of the limited customer feedback they've collected to this point in Alpha and Beta test.

Premature scaling is the immediate cause of the startup Death Spiral. More on this in the next post.

The Customer Development Manifesto: The Startup Death Spiral (part 3)

September 7, 2009 (Steve Blank)

This post describes how following the traditional product development can lead to a "startup death spiral." In the next posts that follow, I'll describe how this model's failures led to the Customer Development Model—offering a new way to approach startup sales and marketing activities. Finally, I'll write about how Eric Ries and the Lean Startup concept provided the equivalent model for product development activities inside the building and neatly integrates customer and agile development.

12. The Startup Death Spiral: The Cost of Getting Product Launch Wrong

By the time of first customer ship, if a startup does not understand its market and customers, failure unfolds in a stylized ritual, almost like a Japanese Noh play.

Three to six months after first customer ship, if Sales starts missing its numbers, the board gets concerned. The VP of Sales comes to a board meeting, still optimistic, and provides a set of reasonable explanations—"our pipeline looks great, but orders will close next quarter" or "we've got lots of traffic to our site, we just need to work on conversion." The board raises a collective eyebrow. The VP of Sales goes back and exhorts the troops to work harder.

To support sales, Marketing tries to "make up a better story," and the website and/or product presentation slides start changing (sometimes weekly or even daily). Morale in Sales and Marketing starts to plummet.

Meanwhile, if you have a direct sales force, smart salespeople realize that the sales strategy and marketing materials the company headquarters provided don't work. Each starts inventing and testing their own alternatives about how to sell and position the product. They try different customers, different customer contacts, different versions of the presentations, etc. Instead of a Sales team and organized to sell with a consistent and successful sales road map generating revenue, it is a disorganized and unhappy organization burning lots of cash.

You're Just Not Selling It Right

By the next board meeting, the VP of Sales looks down at his shoes and shuffles his feet as he reports that the revenue numbers still aren't meeting plan. Now the board collectively raises both eyebrows and looks quizzically at the CEO. The VP of Sales, forehead bathed in sweat, leaves the board meeting and has a few heated motivational sessions with the sales team.

Fire the First VP of Sales

By the next board meeting, if the sales numbers are still poor, the stench of death is in the air. No one wants to sit next to the VP of Sales. Other company execs are moving their chairs to the other side of the room. Having failed to deliver the numbers, he's history. Whether it takes three board meetings or a year is irrelevant; the VP of Sales in a startup who does not make the numbers is called an ex-VP of Sales.

Now the company is in crisis mode. Not only hasn't the sales team delivered the sales numbers, but now the CEO is sweating because the company is continuing to burn cash at what now seems like an alarming rate. Why is it only alarming now? Because the company based its headcount and expenses on the expectation that the Sales organization will bring in revenue according to plan. The rest of the organization (product development, marketing, support) has been burning cash, all according to plan, expecting Sales to make its numbers. Without the revenue to match its expenses, the company is in now danger of running out of money.

Blame It on Marketing

In the next three to six months, a new VP of Sales is hired. She quickly comes to the conclusion that the company's positioning and marketing strategy were incorrect. There isn't a sales problem, the problem is that marketing just did not understand its customers and how to create demand or position the product.

Now the VP of Marketing starts sweating. Since the new VP of Sales was brought on board to "fix" sales, the marketing department has to react and interact with someone who believes that whatever was created earlier in the company was wrong. The new VP of Sales reviews the sales strategy and tactics that did not work and comes up with a new sales plan. She gets a brief honeymoon of a few months from the CEO and the board.

In the meantime, the original VP of Marketing tries to come up with a new positioning strategy to support the new Sales VP. Typically this results in conflict, if not outright internecine warfare. If the sales aren't fixed in a short time, the next executive to be looking for a job will not be the new VP of Sales (she hasn't been around long enough to get fired), it's the VP of Marketing—the rationale being, "We changed the VP of Sales, so that can't be the problem. It must be Marketing's fault."

Time for an Experienced CEO

Sometimes all it takes is one or two iterations to find the right sales roadmap and marketing positioning that connects a startup with exuberant customers ready to buy. Unfortunately, more often than not, this is just the beginning of an executive death spiral. If changing the sales and marketing execs doesn't put the company on the right sales trajectory, the investors start talking the "we need the right CEO for this phase" talk. This means the CEO is walking around with an unspoken corporate death sentence. Moreover, since the first CEO was likely to have been one of the founders, the trauma of CEO removal begins. Typically, founding CEOs hold on to the doorframe of their offices as the investors try to pry their fingers off the company. It's painful to watch and occurs in a majority of startups with first-time CEOs after First Customer Ship.

In flush economic times the company may get two or three iterations to fix a failed launch and bad sales numbers. In tougher times investors are tighter with their wallets and make the "tossing good money after bad" calculations with a more frugal eye. A startup might simply not get a next round of funding and have to shut down.

Customer Development Manifesto: Market Type (part 4)

September 10, 2009 (Steve Blank)

13. Not All Startups Are Alike

There's an urban legend that Eskimos-Aleuts have more words to describe snow than other cultures. While that's not true, it is a fact that entrepreneurs only have one word for "startup." This post points out that the lack of adequate words to describe very different "types" of startups can lead not only to confusion in execution but also at times to disaster.

The product development model treats all startups like they are in an Existing Market—an established market with known customers. With that implicit assumption, startups hire a VP of Sales with a great Rolodex and call on established mainstream companies while marketing creates a brand and buzz to create demand and drive it into the sales channel (web, direct salesforce, etc.)

Most startups following the Product Development Model never achieve their revenue plan and burn through a ton of cash not knowing what hit them.

They never understood Market Type.

Why Does Market Type Matter?

Depending on the type of market it enters, a startup can have very different rates of customer adoption and acceptance and their sales and marketing strategies would be dramatically different. Even more serious, startups can have radically different cash needs. A startup in a New Market (enabling customers to do something they never could before) might be unprofitable for five or more years, (hopefully with the traditional hockey stick revenue curve) while one in an Existing Market might be generating cash in 12 to 18 months.

Handspring in an Existing Market

As an example, imagine it's October 1999 and you are Donna Dubinsky the CEO of a feisty new startup, Handspring, entering the billion dollar Personal Digital Assistant (PDA) market. Other companies in the 1999 PDA market were Palm, the original innovator, as well Microsoft and Hewlett Packard. In October 1999 Donna told her VP of Sales, "In the next 12 months I want Handspring to win 10-percent of the Personal Digital Assistant market." The VP of Sales swallowed hard and turned to the VP of Marketing and said, "I need you to take end user demand away from our competitors and drive it into our sales channel." The VP of Marketing looked at all the other PDAs on the market and differentiated Handspring's product by emphasizing its superior expandability and performance. End result? After twelve months Handspring's revenue was $170 million. This was possible because in 2000, Donna and Handspring were in an Existing Market. Handspring's customers understood what a Personal Digital Assistant was. Handspring did not have to educate them about the market. They just need to persuade customers why their new product was better than the competition—and they did it brilliantly.

Palm in a New Market

What makes this example really interesting is this: rewind the story four years earlier to 1996. Before Handspring, Donna and her team had founded Palm Computing, the pioneer in Personal Digital Assistants. Before Palm arrived on the scene, the Personal Digital Assistant market did not exist. (A few failed science experiments like Apple's Newton had come and gone.) But imagine if Donna had turned to her VP of Sales at Palm in 1996 and said, "I want to get 10-percent of the Personal Digital Assistant market by the end of our first year." Her VP of Sales might had turned to the VP of Marketing and said, "I want you to drive end user demand from our competitors into our sales channel." The VP of Marketing might have said, "Let's tell everyone about how fast the Palm Personal Digital Assistant is and how much memory it has." If they had done this, there would have been zero dollars in sales. In 1996 no potential customer had even heard of a Personal Digital Assistant. Since no one knew what a PDA could do, there was no latent demand from end users, and emphasizing its technical features would have been irrelevant. What Palm needed to do first was to educate potential customers about what a PDA could do for them. In 1996 Palm was selling a product that allowed users to do something they couldn't do before. In essence, Palm created a New Market. In contrast, in 2000 Handspring entered an Existing Market. ("Disruptive" and "sustaining" innovations, eloquently described by Clayton Christensen, are another way to describe new and existing Market Types.)

The lesson is that even with essentially identical products and team, Handspring would have failed if it had used the same sales and marketing strategy that Palm had used so successfully. And the converse is true; Palm would have failed, burning through all their cash, using Handspring's strategy. Market Type changes everything.

Market Type Changes Everything

Here's the point. Market Type changes how you evaluate customer needs, customer adoption rate, how the customer understands his needs, and how you should position the product to the customer. Market Type also affects the market size as well as how you launch the product into the market. As a result different market types require dramatically different sales and marketing strategies.

As a result, the standard product development model is not only useless, it is dangerous. It tells the finance, marketing and sales teams nothing about how to uniquely market and sell in each type of startup, nor how to predict the resources needed for success.

Customer Development Manifesto: The Path of Warriors and Winners (part 5)

September 17, 2009 (Steve Blank)

Most startups lack a process for discovering their markets, locating their first customers, validating their assumptions, and growing their business. A few successful ones do all these things. The difference is that the ones that succeed invent a Customer Development model. This post describes such a model.

The Customer Development Model

Customer Development is designed to solve the problems of the Product Development model I described in the four previous posts. Its strength is its rigor and flexibility. The Customer Development model delineates all the customer-related activities in the early stage of a company into their own processes and groups them into four easy-to-understand steps: Customer Discovery, Customer Validation, Customer Creation, and Company Building. These steps mesh seamlessly and support a startup's ongoing product development activities. Each step results in specific deliverables.

The Customer Development model is not a replacement for the Product Development model, but rather a companion to it. As its name should communicate, the Customer Development model focuses on developing customers for the product or service your startup is building.

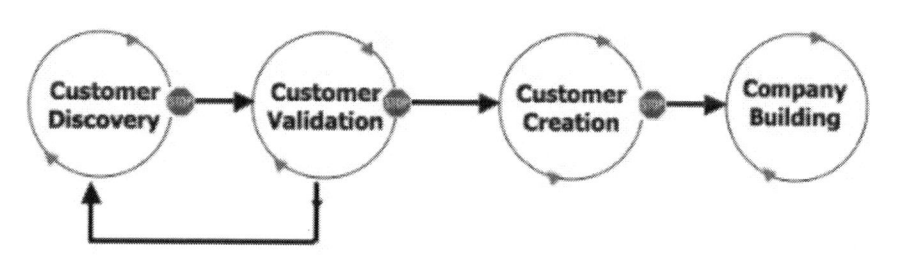

The Customer Development Model

Four Steps

While startups are inherently chaotic (and will never be run from a spreadsheet or checklist inside your building), the Four Steps of Customer Development are designed to help entrepreneurs leverage the chaos and turn it into actionable data:

- Customer Discovery focuses on testing hypotheses and understanding customer problems and needs—in front of customers—by the founders.

- Customer Validation is where you develop a sales model that can be replicated and scaled.

- Customer Creation is creating and driving end user demand to scale sales.

- Company Building transitions the organization from one designed for learning and discovery to a well-oiled machine engineered for execution.

Market Type

Integral to the Customer Development model is the notion that Market Type choices affect the way the company will deploy its sales, marketing, and financial resources. Market Type changes how you evaluate customer needs, customer adoption rate, how the customer understands his needs, and how you should position the product to the customer, etc. As a result, different market types modify what you do in each step of Customer Development.

Customer Development Is Iterative

Learning and discovery versus linear execution is a major difference between this model and the traditional product development model. While the product development model is linear in one direction, the customer development model is a circular track with recursive arrows. The circles and arrows highlight the fact that each step in Customer Development is iterative. That's a polite way of saying, "Unlike product development, finding the right customers and market is unpredictable, and we will screw it up several times before we get it right." (Only in business school case studies does progress with customers happen in a nice linear fashion.) The nature of finding a market and customers guarantees that you will get it wrong several times.

The Customer Development model assumes that it will take several iterations of each of the four steps until you get it right. It's worth pondering this point for a moment because this philosophy of "It's okay to screw it up if you plan to learn from it" is the heart of the methodology.

The Facts Reside Outside Your Building

Customer Development starts by testing your hypotheses outside the building. Not in planning meetings, not in writing multiple pages of nicely formatted Marketing Requirements Documents, but by getting laughed at, ignored, thrown out, and educated by potential customers as you listen to their needs and test the fundamental hypotheses of your business.

Failure Is an Option

Notice that the circle labeled Customer Validation in the diagram has an additional iterative loop going back to Customer Discovery. As you'll see later, Customer Validation is a key checkpoint in understanding whether you have a product that customers want to buy and a roadmap of how to sell it. If you can't find enough paying customers in the Customer Validation step, the model returns you to Customer Discovery to rediscover what you failed to hear or understand the first time through the loop.

Customer Development Is Low Burn by Design

The Customer Development process keeps a startup at a low cash burn rate until the company has validated its business model by finding paying customers. In the first two steps of Customer Development, even an infinite amount of cash is useless because it can only obscure whether you have found a market. (Having raised lots of money tempts you to give products away, steeply discount to buy early business, etc., all while saying "we'll make it up later." It rarely happens that way.) Since the Customer Development model assumes that most startups cycle through these first two steps at least twice, it allows a well-managed company to carefully estimate and frugally husband its cash. The company doesn't build its non-product development teams (sales, marketing, business development) until it has proof in hand (a tested sales road map and valid purchase orders) that it has a business worth building. Once that proof is obtained, the company can go through the last two steps of Customer Creation and Company Building to capitalize on the opportunity it has found and validated.

Customer Development Is for Winners and Warriors

The interesting thing about the Customer Development model is that the process represents the best practices of winning startups. Describe this model to entrepreneurs who have taken their companies all the way to a large profitable business, and you'll get heads nodding in recognition. It's just that until now, no one has ever explicitly mapped their journey to success.

Even more surprising, while the Customer Development model may sound like a new idea for entrepreneurs, it shares many features with a U.S. war fighting strategy known as the "OODA Loop," articulated by John Boyd and adopted by the U.S. Armed Forces in both Gulf Wars —and by others.

Building a Company with Customer Data—Why Metrics Are Not Enough

December 17, 2009 (Steve Blank)

Gathering real-world feedback from customers is a core concept of Customer Development as well as the Lean Startup. But what information to collect?

Only 57 Questions

Yesterday I got an email from an ex-student lamenting that only 2-percent of their selected early testers responded to their online survey. The survey said in part:

"The survey has 57 questions, the last three of which are open ended, and should take about 20 minutes to complete. Please note that you must complete the entire survey once you begin. You cannot stop along the way and have your responses to that point saved."

If it wasn't so sad, it would be funny. I called the founder and noted that there are SAT tests that are shorter than the survey. When I asked him if he actually had personally left the building and talked to these potential customers, or even had gotten them on the phone, he sounded confused. "We're a web startup, all our customers are on the web. Why can't I just get them to give me the answers I need this way?"

Continual Data Flow

Customer Development suggests that founders have continual and timely customer, channel and market information.

Founders need three views of information to truly understand what is going on:

- First-hand knowledge
- A "bird's-eye view"
- The view from the eyes of customers and competitors

First-Hand Knowledge

First-hand knowledge is "getting outside the building" and talking to potential or actual customers. Customer Development proposes that the best way to get customer data is through personal observation and experience—getting out from behind your desk and getting up close and personal with customers, competitors, and the market.

Web startups are at real disadvantage here as founders may confuse web metrics, A/B testing and online surveys as the entirety of first-hand knowledge—for most web business models they are not. In fact, this mistake can be a "going out of business" strategy. Metrics tell you that something is happening. A/B testing can tell you that one something is better than another. But neither can tell you why. And getting answers back from customers only with online surveys when you can't watch their pupils dilate or hear the intonation of their voice is not something I'd build a business on.

Of course you need to collect metrics, do A/B testing and run online surveys. It's just that without having founders "get outside the building," you are missing a key point of Customer Development—the numeric data you collect may be blinding you to the fact that you're more than likely working to optimize the wrong business model. Customer needs are non-deterministic.

"Birds-Eye View"

The second picture founders need is a synthesized "birds-eye view" of the customer, market, and competitive environment. You assemble this view by gathering information from a variety of sources: web sites, social media (Facebook, Twitter, blogs, et al) sales data, win/loss information, market research data (i.e. compete.com, Alexa, etc.,) competitive analyses, and so on.

From this big-picture view, founders try to make sense of the shape of the market and the overall patterns in the unfolding competitive and customer situation. At the same time, they can gauge how well industry data and the actual sales match the company's revenue and market-share expectations.

(Just remember that most market research firms are excellent at predicting the past. If they could predict the future, they'd be entrepreneurs.)

My test for how well you understand this "order of battle" is to hand the founder a marker, have them go up to the whiteboard and diagram the players in the market and where they fit. (Try it.)

See Through the Eyes of Customers and Competitors

The third view is of the action as seen through the eyes of customers and competitors. Put yourself in your customers' and competitors' shoes in order to deduce possible competitors' moves and anticipate customer needs. In an existing market this is where you ask yourself, "If I were my own competitor and had its resources, what would my next move be?" In looking through the eyes of a customer, the question might be, "Why should I buy from this company versus the incumbent." In a new or re-segmented market, the questions might be "Why would more than a few early adopters use this app, web site or buy this product? How would I get my 90-year grandmother to understand and buy this product?"

Think of this technique as playing chess. You need to be looking at all the likely moves from both sides of the chessboard. What would we do if we were our competitors? How would we react? What would we be planning? After a while this type of role playing will become an integral part of everyone's thinking and planning.

Putting It All Together

First-hand knowledge is clearly the most detailed and essential, but offers a narrow field of view. Founders who focus only on this information risk losing sight of the big picture.

The "birds-eye view" provides a view of the market but lacks the critical detail. Founders who focus only on this image risk missing the "ground truth."

Seeing through the eyes of customers and competitors is a theoretical exercise limited by the fact that you can never be sure what your customers and competitors are up to.

The combination of all three views helps founders form an accurate picture of what is going on in their business and help them hone in on product/market fit.

Even with information from all three views, founders need to remember there will never be enough information to make a perfect decision.

Building an Information Culture

The most important element of data gathering is what to do with the information once you collect it. Customer information dissemination is a cornerstone of Lean and agile companies. This information, whether good or bad, must not be guarded like some precious commodity. Large company cultures reward executives who hoard knowledge or suppress bad news. In any of my companies, that is a firing offense.

All news, but especially bad news, needs to be shared, dissected, understood, and acted upon.

This means that understanding poor click-through rates, retention numbers and sales losses are more important than understanding sales wins; understanding why a competitor's products are better is more important than rationalizing ways in which yours is still superior. Winning startups build a startup culture that reward not punish messengers of bad news.

Lessons Learned

- Three views of information: First-hand knowledge, "birds-eye" view, view from the eyes of customers and competitors.

- Web startups can fall into the trap of confusing metrics, testing and surveys with Customer Interaction.

- Goal is to build an information culture to help you get to product/market fit.

Why Startups are Agile and Opportunistic—Pivoting the Business Model

April 12, 2010 (Steve Blank)

> "Startups are the search to find order in chaos."
> — Steve Blank

At a board meeting last week I watched as the young startup CEO delivered bad news. "Our current plan isn't working. We can't scale the company. Each sale requires us to handhold the customer and takes way too long to close. But I think I know how to fix it." He took a deep breath, looked around the boardroom table and then proceeded to outline a radical reconfiguration of the product line (repackaging the products rather than reengineering them) and a change in sales strategy, focusing on a different customer segment. Some of the junior investors blew a gasket. "We invested in the plan you sold us on." A few investors suggested he add new product features, others suggested firing the VP of Sales. I noticed that through all of this, the lead VC just sat back and listened.

Finally, when everyone else had their turn, the grey-haired VC turned to the founder and said, "If you do what we tell you to do and fail, we'll fire you. And if you do what you think is right and you fail, we may also fire you. But at least you'd be executing your plan not ours. Go with your gut and do what you think the market is telling you. That's why we invested in you." He turned to the other VCs and added, "That's why we write the checks and entrepreneurs run the company."

The Search for the Business Model

A startup is an organization formed to search for a repeatable and scalable business model.

Investors bet on a startup CEO to find the repeatable and scalable business model.

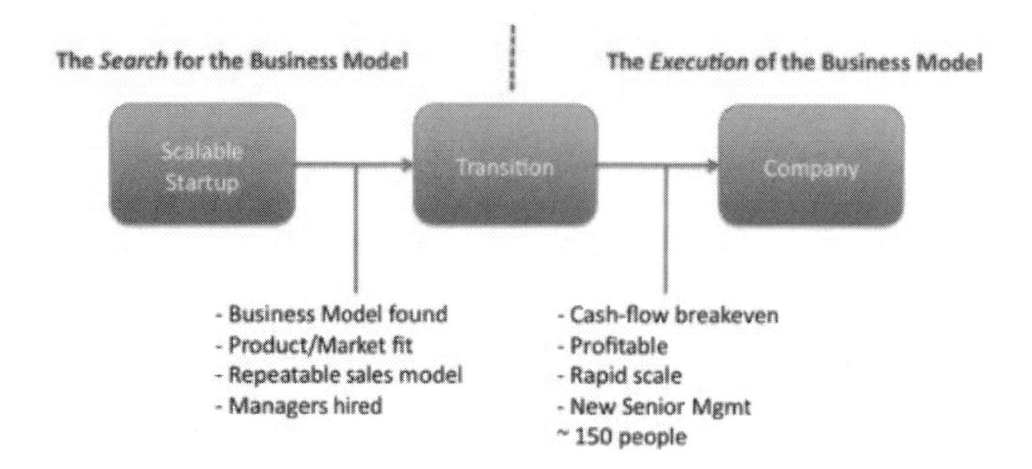

The *Search* for the Business Model | **The *Execution* of the Business Model**

Scalable Startup → Transition → Company

- Business Model found
- Product/Market fit
- Repeatable sales model
- Managers hired

- Cash-flow breakeven
- Profitable
- Rapid scale
- New Senior Mgmt
~ 150 people

Unlike the stories in the popular press, entrepreneurs who build successful companies don't get it right the first time. (That only happens after the fact when they tell the story.) The real world is much, much messier. And a lot more interesting. Here's what really happens.

Observe, Orient, Decide, and Act

Whether they're using a formal process to search for a business model like Customer Development or just trial and error, startup founders are intuitively goal-seeking to optimize their business model. They may draw their business model formally or they may keep the pieces in their head. In either case founders who succeed observe that something isn't working in their current business model, orient themselves to the new facts, decide what part of their business model needs to change and then act decisively.

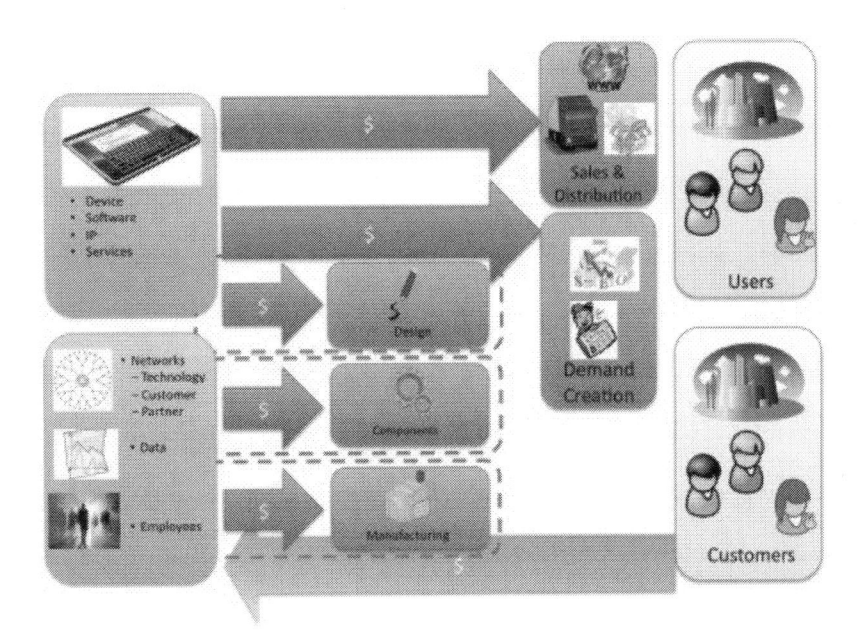

(A U.S. Air Force strategist, Colonel John Boyd, first described this iterative Observe, Orient, Decide and Act (OODA) loop. The Customer Development model that I write and teach about is the entrepreneur's version of Boyd's OODA loop.)

Pivoting the Business Model

What happens when the startup's leader recognizes that the original business model is not working as planned? In traditional startups this is when the VP of Sales or Marketing gets fired and the finger-pointing starts. In contrast, in a startup following the Customer Development process, this is when the founders realize that something is wrong with the business model (because revenue is not scaling). They decide what to change and then take action to reconfigure some part(s) of their model.

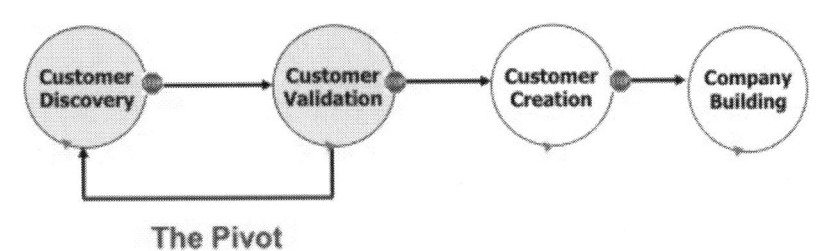

The Customer Development process assumed that many of the initial assumptions about your business model would probably be wrong, so it built in a iteration loop to fix them. Eric Ries coined this business model iteration loop— the Pivot.

(One of the Pivot's positive consequences for the startup team is realizing that a lack of scalable revenue is not the fault of the Sales or Marketing or Engineering departments—and the solution is not to fire executives—it's recognizing that there's a problem with the assumptions in the initial business model.)

Types of Pivots

"Pivoting" is when you change a fundamental part of the business model. It can be as simple as recognizing that your product was priced incorrectly. It can be more complex if you find the your target customer or users need to change, or the feature set is wrong, or you need to "repackage" a monolithic product into a family of products or you chose the wrong sales channel or your customer acquisition programs were ineffective.

If you draw your business model, figuring out how to Pivot is simpler as you can diagram the options of what to change. There are lots of books to help you figure out how to get to "Plan B," but great entrepreneurs (and their boards) recognize that this process needs to occur rapidly and continuously.

Operating in Chaos + Speed + Pivots = Success

Unlike a large profitable company, startups are constrained by their available cash. If a startup does not find a profitable and scalable business model, it will go out of business (or worse end up in the "land of the living dead" eking out breakeven revenue.) This means CEOs of startups are continually looking to see if they need to make a Pivot to find a better model. If they believe one is necessary, they do not hesitate to make the change. The search for a profitable and scalable business model might require a startup to make multiple pivots—some small adjustments and others major changes.

As a founder, you need to prepare yourself to think creatively and independently because more often than not, conditions on the ground will change so rapidly that your original well-thought-out business model will quickly become irrelevant.

Summary

Startups are inherently chaotic. The rapid shifts in the business model are what differentiates a startup from an established company. Pivots are the essence of entrepreneurship and the key to startup success. If you can't pivot or pivot quickly, chances are you will fail.

Pivot.

Lessons Learned

A startup is an organization formed to search for a repeatable and scalable business model.

Most startup business models are initially wrong.

The process of iteration in search of the successful business model is called the Pivot.

Pivots need to happen quickly, rapidly and often.

At the seed stage, microcap funds/ superangels understand that companies are still searching for a business model—they get Pivots.

Most of the time when startups go out for Series A or B round, the VC assumption is that a scalable business model has already been found.

Pivots are why startups must be agile and opportunistic and why their cultures are different from large companies.

The Phantom Sales Forecast—Failing at Customer Validation

July 22, 2010 (Steve Blank)

Startup CEOs can't delegate sales and expect it to happen. Customer Validation needs to have the CEO actively involved.

Here's an example in a direct sales channel.

Customer Development Diagnostics Over Lunch

A VC asked me to have lunch with the CEO of a startup building cloud-based enterprise software. (Boy, did I feel like Rip Van Winkle.) The board was getting nervous as the company was missing its revenue plan.

These lunches always start with the CEO looking like they had much better things to do. Before lunch even came the CEO ticked off the names of forty or so customers he talked to during the company's first nine months and gave me a great dissertation on the day-in-the-life of his target customers and what their problems were. He went through his product feature by feature and matched them to the customer problems. He talked about how his business model would make money and how the prospects he talked to seem to agree with his assumptions.

It certainly sounded like he had done a great job of Customer Discovery.

Sales Process

Next, he took me through his sales process. They had five salespeople supported by two in marketing. (They had beta customers, using but not paying for the product.)

Over lunch the CEO told me he had stopped talking to customers since he had been tied up helping get the product out the door and his VP of Sales (a successful sales executive from a large company) had managed the sales process for the last six months. In fact, the few times he had asked to go out in the field the VP of Sales said, "Not yet, I don't want to waste your time."

Too Good to Be True

For the first time I started squirming in my seat. He said, "I insist on getting weekly status reports with forecasted deal size and probability of close. We have a great sales pipeline." When I asked how close any of the deals on the forecast were to getting closed, he assured me the company's two beta customers—well-known companies that would be marquee accounts if they closed—were imminent orders.

"How do you know this?" I asked. "Have you heard it personally from the customers?"

Now it was his turn to squirm a bit. "No, not exactly," he replied, "but our VP of Sales assures me we will have a purchase order in the next few weeks or so."

I put my fork down. Very few large companies write big checks to unknown startups without at least meeting the CEO. When I asked if he could draw the sales road map for these two accounts that were about to close, he admitted he didn't know any of the details, given it was all in the VP of Sales' head. Since we were running out of time, I said, "Your sales pipeline sounds great. In fact, it sounds too good to be true. If you really do close any of these accounts, my hat is off to you and your sales team. If, as I suspect they don't close, do me a favor."

"What's that?" He asked, looking irritated.

"You need to pick up the phone and call the top five accounts on your sales pipeline. Ask them this question: if you gave them your product today for free, are they prepared to install and use it across their department and company? If the answer is no, you have absolutely no customers on your forecast who will be prepared to buy from you in the next six months."

He smiled and stuck me with the tab for lunch. I didn't expect to hear from him ever again.

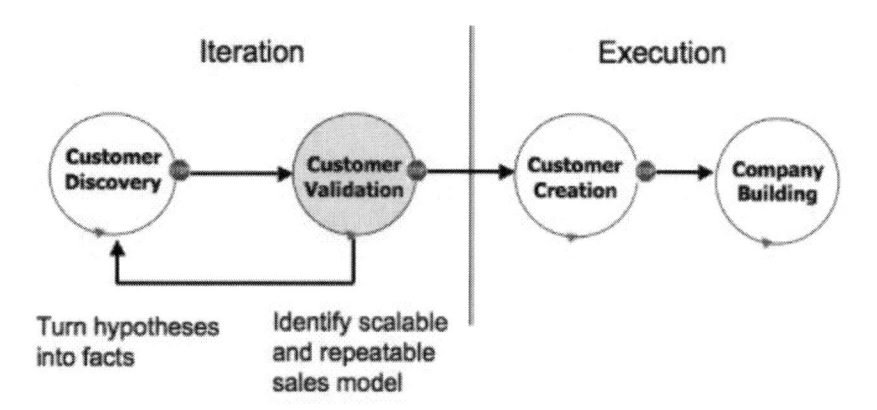

What If the Price Were Zero?

Less than two weeks later, I got a call and was surprised to hear the agitated voice of the CEO. "Steve, our brand-name account, the one we have been working on for the last eight months, told us they weren't going to buy the product this year. They just didn't see the urgency." Listening, I got the rest of the story.

"When my VP of Sales told me that," he said, "I got on the phone and spoke to the account personally. I asked them your question—would they deploy the product in their department or company if the price were zero? I'm still stunned by the answer. They said the product wasn't mission critical enough for their company to justify the disruption."

"Wow, that's not good," I said, trying to sound sympathetic.

"It only gets worse," he said. "Since I was hearing this from one of the accounts my VP of Sales thought was going to close, I insisted we jointly call our other 'imminent' account. It's the same story as the first. Then I called the next three down the list and got essentially the same story. They all think our product is 'interesting,' but no one is ready to put serious money down now. I'm beginning to suspect our entire forecast is not real. What am I going to tell my board?"

My not-so-difficult advice was that he was going to have to tell his board exactly what was going on. But before he did, he needed to understand the sales situation in its entirety, and then come up with a plan for fixing it. Then he was going to present both the problem and suggested fix to his board. (You never want a board to have to tell you how to run your company. When that happens, it's time to update your resume.)

The Phantom Sales Forecast

The implications of a phantom sales forecast meant something fundamental was broken. In talking to each of his salespeople, he discovered the sales team had no standardized sales process. Each was calling on different levels of an account and trying whatever seemed to work best. This was just a symptom of something deeper—while they thought they understood the target customer their initial hypotheses from Customer Discovery were wrong. But no one had told the CEO.

He realized the company was going to have to start from scratch, Pivot back to Customer Discovery and find out how to develop a sales road map. He presented his plan to the board, fired the VP of Sales and kept his best salesperson and the marketing VP. Then he went home, kissed his family goodbye, and went out to the field to discover what would make a customer buy. His board wished him luck and started the clock ticking on his remaining tenure. He had six months to get and close customers.

Customer Validation

The CEO had discovered what happens when you do a good job on Customer Discovery but get too "busy" for to personally get involved in Customer Validation. It wasn't that he didn't need a VP of Sales, but he had entirely outsourced the Validation step to him. Until a scalable and repeatable business model is found the CEO needs to be intimately involved in the sales process.

Lessons Learned

- Ownership of Customer Validation belongs to the CEO.
- A VP of Sales can assist but the CEO needs to answer:
- Do I understand the sales process in detail?
- Is the sales process repeatable?
- Can I prove it's repeatable? (Proof is multiple full-price orders in sufficient quantity.)
- Can we get these orders with the current product and release spec?
- Do we have a workable sales and distribution channel?
- Am I confident we can scale a profitable business?

Entrepreneurship as a Science— The Business Model/Customer Development Stack

October 25, 2010 (Steve Blank)

Over the last 50 years, engineers have moved from building computers out of individual transistors to building with prepackaged logic gates. Then they adopted standard microprocessors (e.g., x86, ARM.) At the same time every computer company was writing its own operating system. Soon standard operating systems (e.g., Windows, Linux) emerged. In the last decade, open source software (e.g., LAMP) emerged for building web servers.

Each time a standard solution emerged, innovation didn't stop. It just allowed new innovation to begin at a higher level.

In this post I want offer a solution stack for Entrepreneurship. It's the combination of Business Model Design and Customer Development.

Business Model Design

Today every business organization from startup to large company uses the words "business model." Some use it with certainty like they know what it means. Others use it with an implied question mark realizing they don't have a clue to its components.

Alexander Osterwalder and Yves Pigneur refined a business model as how an organization creates, delivers, and captures value. More importantly they showed how any company's business model could be defined in nine boxes. It's an amazing and powerful tool. It instantly creates a shared visual language while defining a business. Their book "Business Model Generation" is the definitive text on the subject. (And their forthcoming Business Model Toolbox is a killer iPad app for business strategy.)

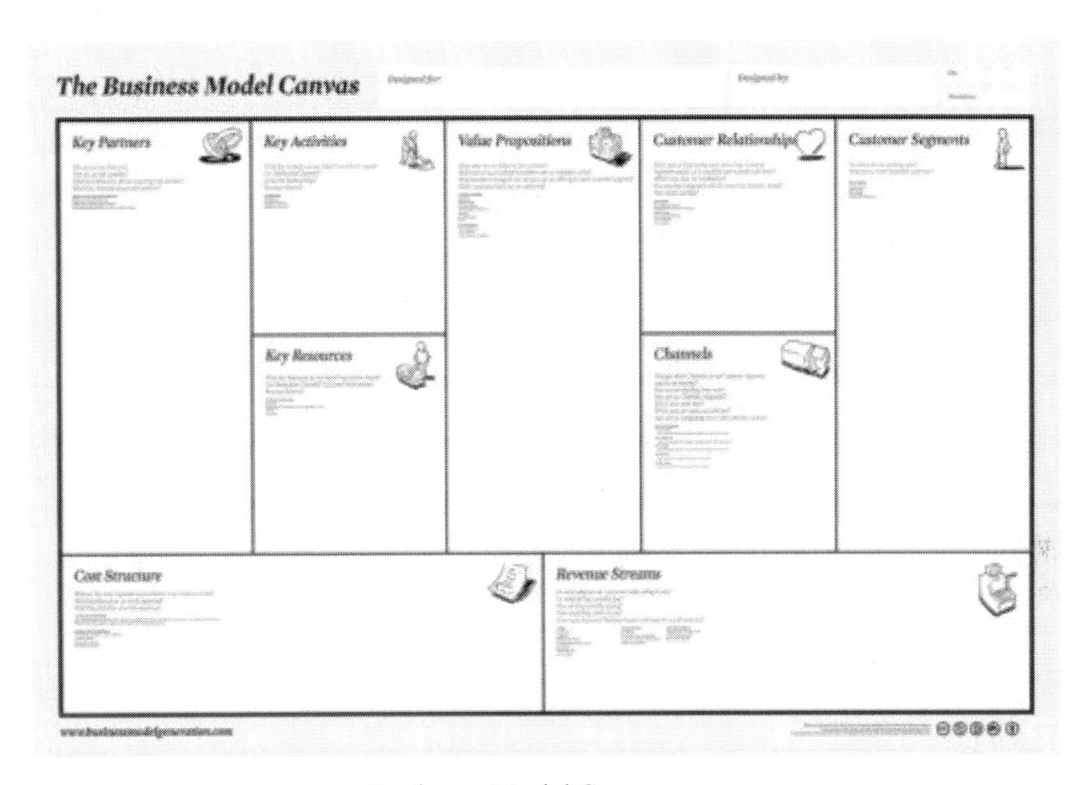

Business Model Canvas

Yet as powerful as the Business Model Canvas (a template with the nine blocks of a business model) is, at the end of the day it was a tool for brainstorming hypotheses without a formal way of testing them.

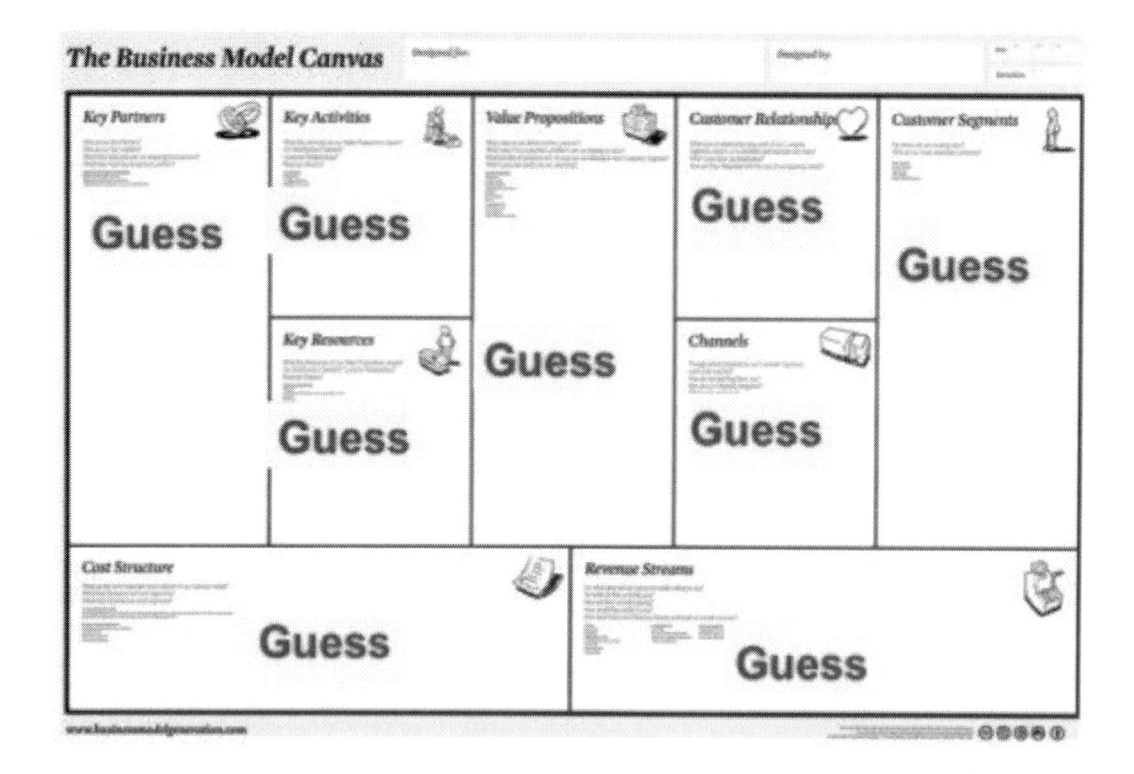

Business Model Design Gets Dynamic, Customer Development Gets Strategic

One of the key tenets of Customer Development is that your business model is nothing more than a set of untested hypotheses. Yet Customer Development has no structured and systematic way of describing a business model.

In the last year I found that the Osterwalder Business Model canvas could be used for something much more than a static planning tool. I realized that it was the launch-pad for setting up the hypotheses to test, and a scorecard for visually tracking iterations and Pivots during Customer Discovery and Validation.

Meanwhile on the other side of the world Alexander Osterwalder was coming to the same conclusion: tying the two processes together would create a "strategy stack for entrepreneurship." We got together this weekend (along with our partners Alan Smith and Bob Dorf and my student Max Marmer) to try to integrate the two.

Business Model Design Meets Customer Development

In its simplest form the way to think about the intersection of the two processes is that you start by designing your business model. Next, each one of the nine business model canvas boxes then directly translates into a set of Customer Discovery hypotheses that are described in Customer Development and The Four Steps to the Epiphany.

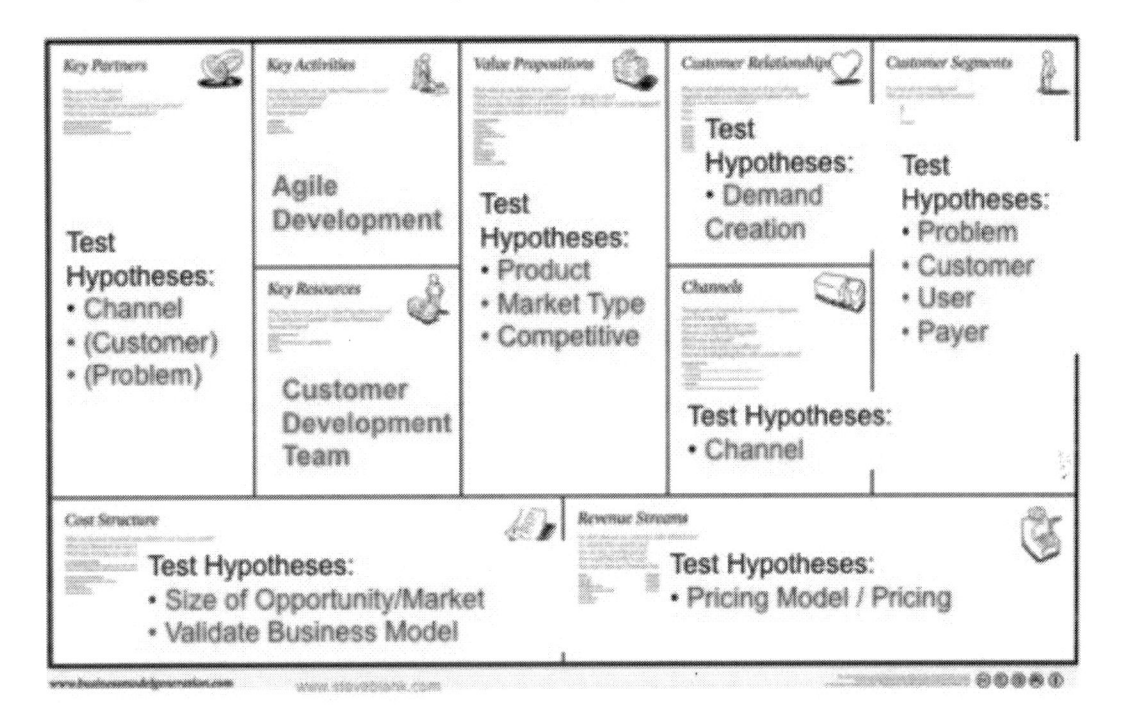

Business Model Design Meets Customer Development

Pivots and Iterations

Many entrepreneurs assume that the assumptions in their original business model (or business plan if they wrote one) will be correct. Confronting the reality that one of these hypotheses is wrong (finding out you have the wrong sales channel, revenue model, target market, or customer) creates a crisis.

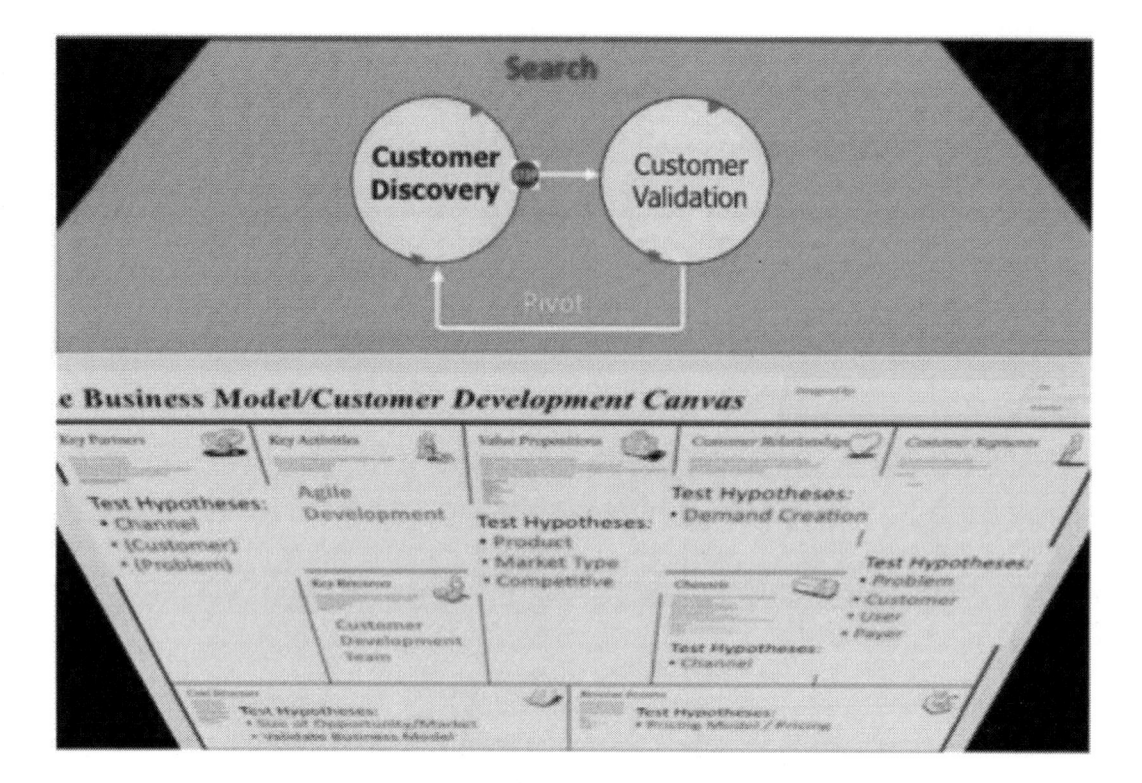

Pivots are Business Model Insights

Tying Osterwalder's Business Model Canvas with the Customer Development process turns these potential crises into learning opportunities called the Pivot. Customer Development forces you to get out of the building and discover and validate each one of the assumptions behind the business model. A Pivot is when reality leads you to change one or more business model hypotheses. The result is an updated business model not a fired VP of Sales.

The Pivot turns a failed business model hypotheses into insight.

Lessons Learned

- Business Model design is the standard for describing a business model.

- Customer Development is the standard for testing business model hypotheses.

- The two are the strategy stack for entrepreneurship.

Crisis Management by Firing Executives—There's A Better Way

November 18, 2010 (Steve Blank)

> "Insanity is doing the same thing over and over again and expecting different results."
> — Albert Einstein

For decades startups were managed by pretending the company would follow a predictable path (revenue plan, scale, etc.) and being continually surprised when it didn't.

That's the definition of insanity. Luckily most startups now realize there is a better way.

Startups Are Not Small Versions of Large Companies

As we described in previous posts, startups fail on the day they're founded if they are organized and managed like they are a small version of a large company. In an existing company with existing customers you 1) understand the customers problem and 2) since you do, you can specify the entire feature set on day one. But startups aren't large companies, but for decades VCs insisted that startups organize and plan like they were.

Traditional Product Introduction Model:
Two Implicit Assumptions

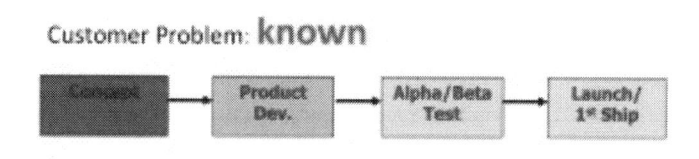

Customer Problem: **known**

Concept → Product Dev. → Alpha/Beta Test → Launch/1st Ship

Product Features: **known**

These false assumptions—that you know the customer problem and product features— led startups to organize their product introduction process like the diagram below— essentially identical to the product management process of a large company. In fact, for decades if you drew this diagram on day one of a startup VCs would nod sagely and everyone would get to work heading to first customer ship.

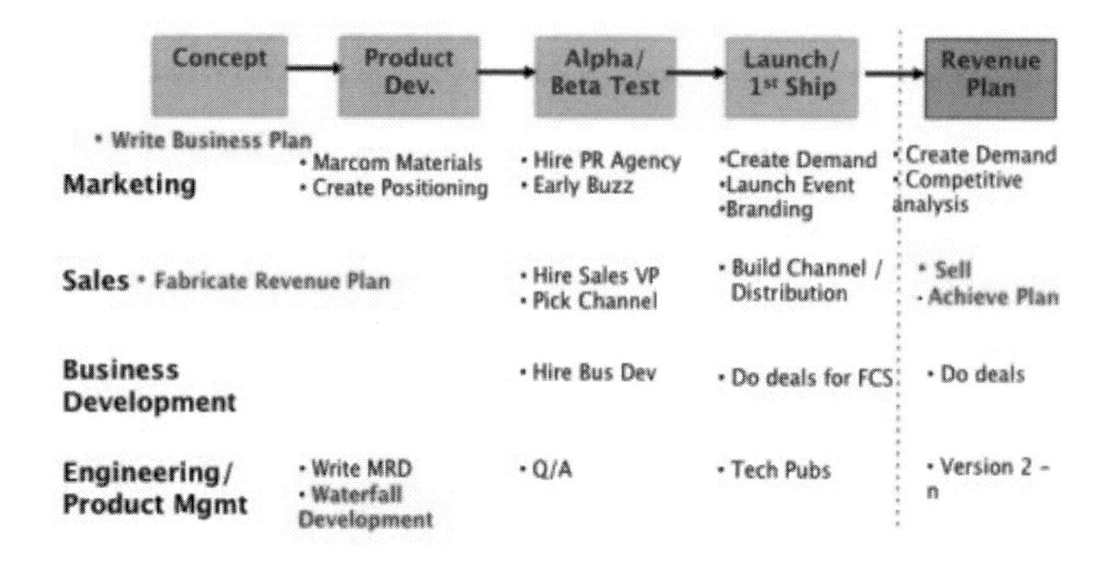

	Concept	Product Dev.	Alpha/Beta Test	Launch/1st Ship	Revenue Plan
Marketing	• Write Business Plan	• Marcom Materials • Create Positioning	• Hire PR Agency • Early Buzz	•Create Demand •Launch Event •Branding	•Create Demand •Competitive analysis
Sales	• Fabricate Revenue Plan		• Hire Sales VP • Pick Channel	• Build Channel / Distribution	• Sell • Achieve Plan
Business Development			• Hire Bus Dev	• Do deals for FCS	• Do deals
Engineering/Product Mgmt		• Write MRD • Waterfall Development	• Q/A	• Tech Pubs	• Version 2 – n

The Revenue Plan—The Third Fatal Assumption

Notice that the traditional product introduction model leads to a product launch and the execution of a revenue plan. The revenue numbers and revenue model came from a startup's original Business Plan. A business plan has a set of assumptions (who's the customer, what's the price, what's the channel, what are the product features that matter, etc.) that make up a business model. All of these initial assumptions must be right for the revenue plan to be correct. Yet by first customer ship most of the business model hasn't been validated or tested. Yet startups following the traditional product introduction model are organized to execute the business plan as if it were fact.

Unless you were incredibly lucky, most of your assumptions are wrong. What happens next is painful, predictable, avoidable, yet built into to every startup business plan.

Ritualized Crises

Trying to execute a startup revenue plan is why crises unfold in a stylized, predictable ritual after first customer ship.

You can almost set your watch to six months or so after first customer ship, when Sales starts missing its "numbers," the board gets concerned and Marketing tries to "make up a better story." The web site and/or product presentation slides start changing and Marketing and Sales try different customers, different channels, new pricing, etc. Having failed to deliver the promised revenue, the VP of Sales in a startup who does not make the "numbers" becomes an ex-VP of Sales. (The half-life of the first VP of sales of a startup is around 18 months.)

Now the company is in crisis mode because the rest of the organization (product development, marketing, etc.) has based its headcount and expenses on the business plan, expecting Sales to make its numbers. Without the revenue to match its expenses, the company is in now danger of running out of money.

Pivots by Firing Executives

A new VP of Sales (then VP of Marketing, then CEO) looks at their predecessors' strategy, and if they are smart, they do something different (they implement a different pricing model, pick a new sales channel, target different customers and/or partners, reformulate the product features, etc.)

Surprisingly we have never explicitly articulated or understood that what's really happening when we hire a new VP or CEO in a startup is that the newly hired executive is implicitly pivoting (radically changing) some portion of the business model. We were changing the business model when we changed executives.

Startups were pivoting by crisis and firing executives. Yikes.

Business Model Design and Customer Development Stack

The alternative to the traditional product introduction process is the Business Model Design and Customer Development Stack. It assumes the purpose of a startup is the search for a business model (not execution). This approach has a startup drawing its initial business model hypotheses on the Business Model Canvas.

... just a set of hypotheses

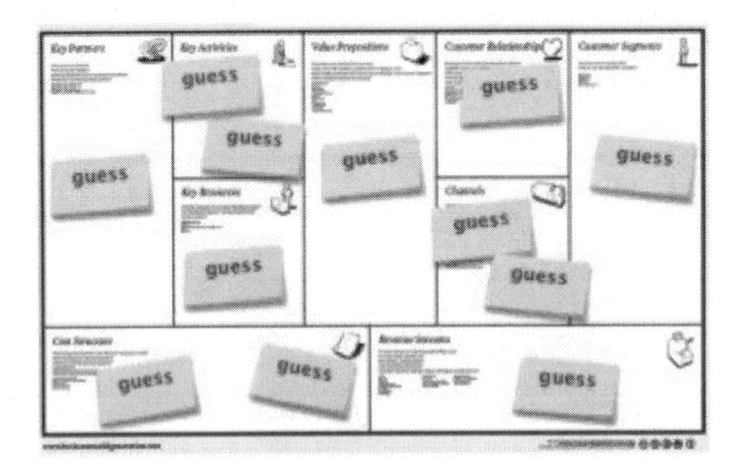

Each of the nine business model building blocks has a set of hypotheses that need to be tested. The Customer Development process is then used to test each of the nine building blocks of the business model. Each block in the business model canvas maps to hypotheses in the Customer Discovery and Validation steps of Customer Development.

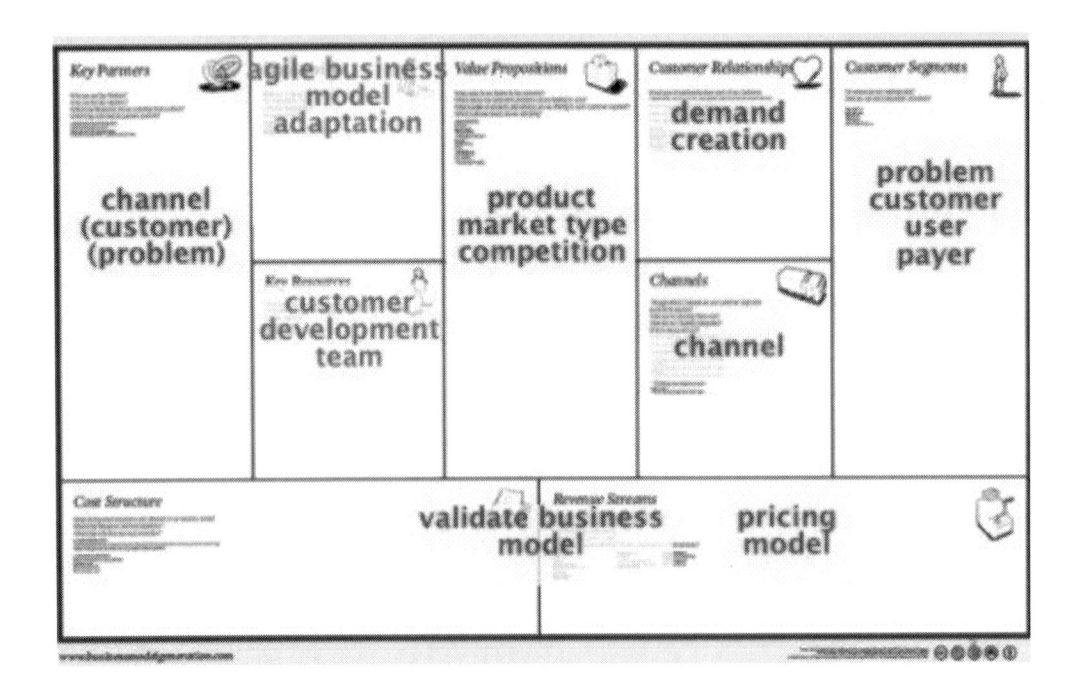

Simultaneously the engineering team is using an Agile Development methodology to iteratively and incrementally build the Minimum Feature Set to test the product or service that make up the Value Proposition.

Pivots Versus Crises

If we accept that startups are engaged in the search for a business model, we recognize that radical shifts in a startups business model are the norm, rather than the exception.

This means that instead of firing an executive every time we discover a faulty hypothesis, we expect it as a normal course of business.

Why it's not a crisis is that the Customer Development process says, "Do not staff and hire like you are executing. Instead keep the burn rate low during Customer Discovery and Validation while you are searching for a business model." This low burn rate allows you to take several swings at the bat (or shots on the goal, depending on your country.)

Each pivot gets you smarter but doesn't put you out of business. And when you finally find a scalable and repeatable model, you exit Customer Validation, pour on the cash, and scale the company.

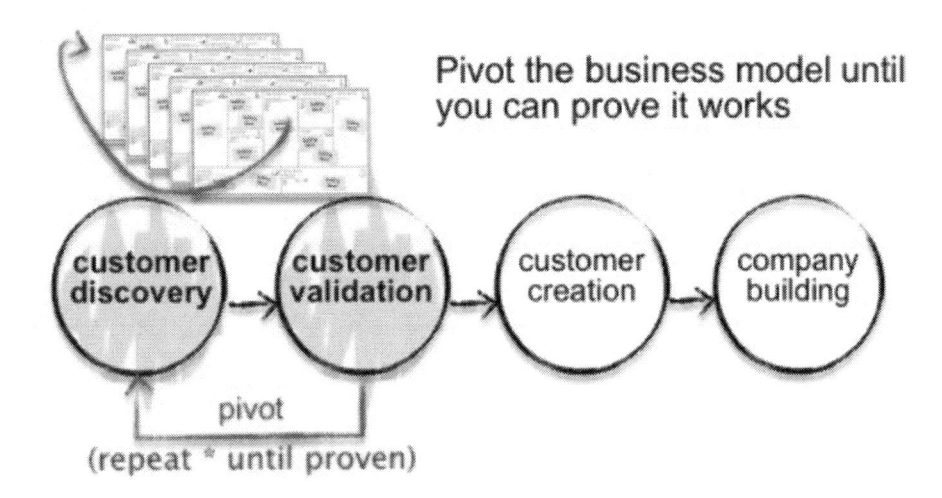

Lessons Learned

- "I know the Customer problem" and "I know the features to build" are rarely true on day-one in a startup.

- These hypotheses lead to a revenue plan that is untested, yet becomes the plan of record.

- Revenue shortfalls are the norm in a startup yet they create a crisis.

- The traditional solution to a startup crisis is to remove executives. Their replacements implicitly iterate the business model.

- The alternative to firing and crises is the Business Model/Customer Development process.

- It says faulty hypotheses are a normal part of a startup.

- We keep the burn rate low while we search and pivot allowing for multiple iterations of the business model.

- No one gets fired.

Consultants Don't Pivot, Founders Do

May 13, 2010 (Steve Blank)

Consultants can help startups leverage their limited resources. But startups can shoot themselves in the foot when founders use consultants at the wrong time or in the wrong way. Here's why.

Your Process Doesn't Work

A friend of mine asked me to chat with a startup he'd invested in. "They're deep into Customer Development," he said. I waited for the shoe to drop—and it did, as he continued carefully. "But they don't seem to be making much progress. I think your process doesn't work."

So I met the entrepreneur and asked him how his search for a business model was going. "Great, but we're having a bit of a problem getting traction." (Anytime I hear an entrepreneur talking in euphemisms, I get nervous.) After a bit more discussion, I discovered the "problem in getting traction" meant revenue was zero.

"We're in Customer Validation but we can't seem to close a deal." Hmm, I asked, "Can you go back to the beginning and tell me about your Customer Discovery process? What were your original hypotheses and what did you find?" I wanted to smack him when he said, "Well our consultants said…"

The rest of his story was mostly a blur. Honestly I didn't hear much detail other than a long litany of how other people who didn't work for the company got out of the building and talked to customers. I started paying attention to the words again when he concluded with, "I just don't know what we're doing wrong?"

You Can't Outsource Personal Experience

Here's what I told him:

A startup exists to search for a scalable and repeatable business model.

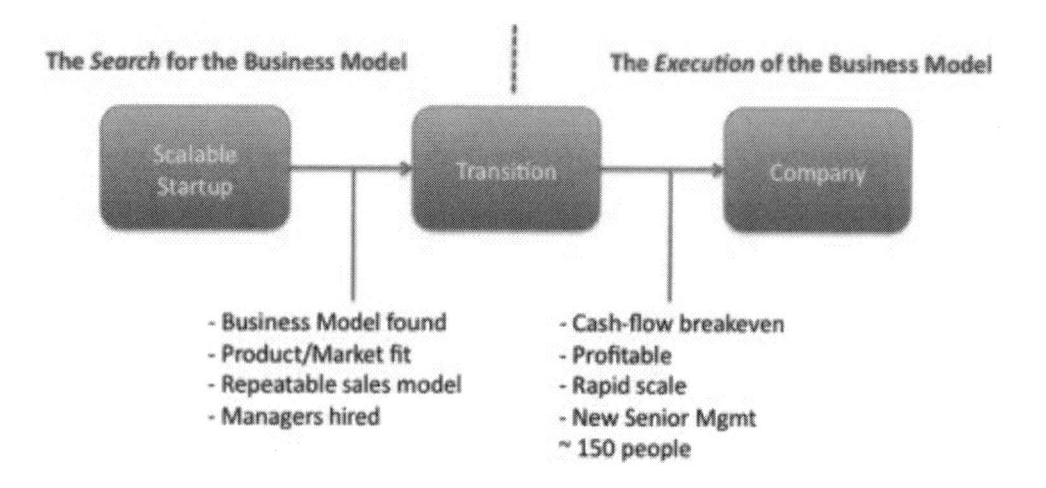

The *Search* for the Business Model — Scalable Startup → Transition

- Business Model found
- Product/Market fit
- Repeatable sales model
- Managers hired

The *Execution* of the Business Model — Transition → Company

- Cash-flow breakeven
- Profitable
- Rapid scale
- New Senior Mgmt
- ~150 people

Customer Development is the process of how you get out of the building and search for the model. Customer Development is designed so that you the founder(s) gather first hand experience about customer and market needs.

It can't be delegated.

Let me say it again: Getting customer feedback cannot be delegated.

Why? Founders get out of the building (physically or virtually) to test their hypotheses against reality. There are times when customers are going to tell you something that you don't want to hear. Or you're going to hear something completely unexpected or orthogonal to what you expected.

Consultants Don't Pivot, Founders Do

It's hearing this first-hand data that makes a founder decide to Pivot (the process of iteration in search of the successful business model).

The Pivot

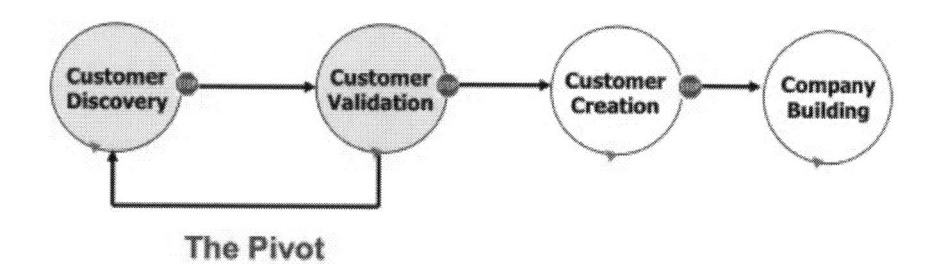

Pivots need to happen quickly, rapidly and often. Consultants cannot do that for you. In fact, startups that use consultants almost never pivot fast enough. Why? Because it's easy to ignore what consultants say and remain deluded by your own passion. Couple that with consultants that can't and don't understand the business deeply enough to know when to pivot. You have the vision, they don't.

The breakthroughs and aha moments can be random, unpredictable—but only the founders can find and make them.

Coming out of my daze, I asked: "Why weren't you the one talking to customers?" The answer, "Well I was too busy coding and building the product. But I knew getting customer input was important so I hired this great consultant who told me all about the features customers need." Ouch.

Using consultants as your proxy when you were supposed to be out there learning means you're not really doing Customer Development and don't understand the process.

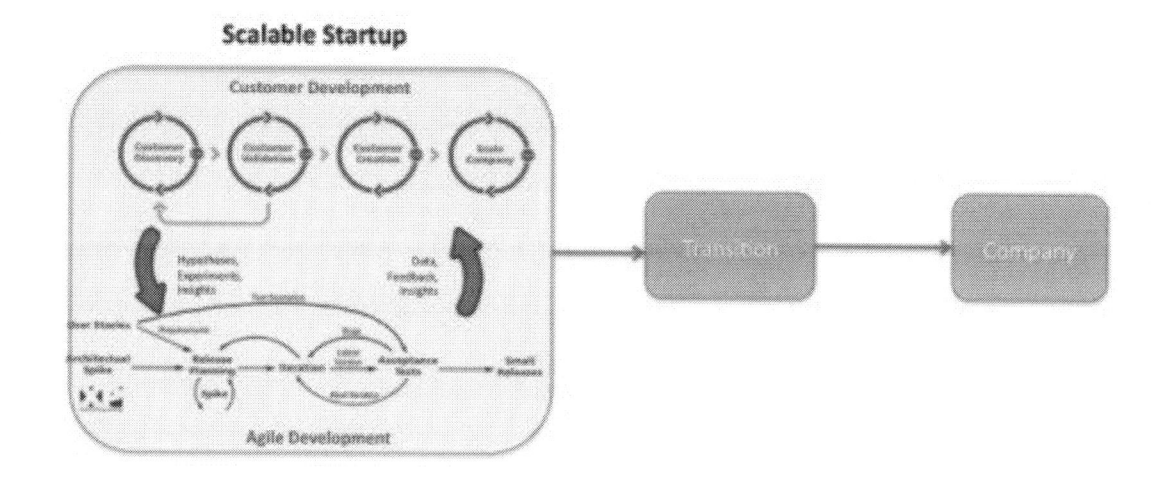

When Do I Use a Consultant?

So should your startup ever use a consultant? Of course.

Consultants can add tremendous value to your start up once you believe you have found a scalable business model—i.e. you think you have product/market fit.

Sean Ellis, a consultant who works with early stage companies, believes that "the cost of a consultant's time can never be justified working with startups pre product/market fit— the failure rate is just too high."

Sean believes that, "Consultants can improve the growth trajectory after your first business model is found. (In reality, once you think you found the right model, most startups will go through multiple iterations on optimizing revenue and their business model.) This help in finding the optimal model, (which can easily result in millions of dollars in incremental valuation) is where a consultant can help. At that point it is easy to find a win/win on the cost of the consultant's time."

I couldn't agree more.

Lessons Learned

- No consultants as you search for your business model.

- Get all the help you need after you find a repeatable model.

- If you're too busy coding to get out of the building yourself, find a co-founder.

Death By Revenue Plan

February 16, 2010 (Steve Blank)

I described what happened when a company prematurely scales sales and marketing before adequately testing its hypotheses in Customer Discovery. You would think that would be enough to get wrong, but entrepreneurs and investors compound this problem by assuming that all startups grow and scale by executing the Revenue Plan.

They don't.

The appendix of your business plan has one of the leading cause of death of startups: the financial spreadsheets you attached as your Income Statement, Balance Sheets, and Cash Flow Statements.

Reality Meets the Plan

I got to see this first hand as an observer at a board meeting I wish I could have skipped. We were at the board meeting of a company building a radically new type of communication hardware. The company was going through some tough times. It had taken the company almost twice as long as planned to get their product out the door. But that wasn't what the heat being generated at this board meeting was about. All discussion focused on "missing the revenue plan."

Spread out in front of everyone around the conference table were the latest Income Statement, Balance Sheets, and Cash Flow Statements. The VCs were very concerned that the revenue the financial plan called for wasn't being delivered by the sales team. They were also looking at the Cash Flow Statement and expressed their concern (i.e. raised their voices in a annoyed investor tone) that the headcount and its attendant burn rate combined with the lack of revenue meant the company would run out of money much sooner than anyone planned.

Let's Try to Make the World Match Our Spreadsheet

The VCs concluded that the company needed to change direction and act aggressively to increase revenue so the company could "make the plan." They told the CEO (who was the technical founder) that the sales team should focus on "other markets." Another VC added that engineering should redesign the product to meet the price and performance of current users in an adjacent market.

The founder was doing his best to try to explain that his vision today was the same as when he pitched the company to the VCs and when they funded the company. He said, "I told you it was going to take it least five years for the underlying industry infrastructure to mature, and that we had to convince OEMs to design in our product. All this takes time." But the VCs kept coming back to the lack of adoption of the product, the floundering sales force, the burn rate—and "the plan."

Given the tongue-lashing the VCs were giving the CEO and the VP of Sales, you would have thought that selling the product was something any high-school kid could have done.

What went wrong?

Revenue Plan Needs to Match Market Type

What went wrong was that the founder had built a product for a New Market and the VCs allowed him to execute, hire and burn cash like he was in an Existing Market.

The failure of this company's strategy happened almost the day the company was funded.

Make the VCs Happy—Tell Them It's a Big Market

There's a common refrain that VCs want to invest in large markets greater than $500 million and see companies that can generate $100 million per year in revenue by year five. Enough entrepreneurs have heard this mantra that they put together their revenue plan working backwards from this goal. This may actually work if you're in an existing market where customers understand what the product does and how to compare it with products that currently exist. The company I observed had in fact hired a VP of Sales from a competitor and staffed their sales and marketing team with people from an existing market.

Inconsistent Expectations

The VCs had assumed that the revenue plan for this new product would look like a straight linear growth line. They expected that sales should be growing incrementally each month and quarter.

Why did the VCs make this assumption? Because the company's initial revenue plan (the spreadsheet the founders attached to the business plan) said so.

What Market Type Are We?

Had the company been in an Existing Market, this would have been a reasonable expectation.

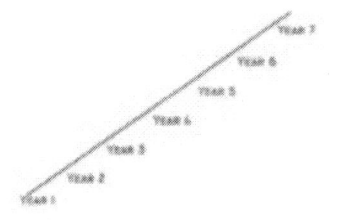

Existing Market Revenue Curve

But no one (founders, management, investors) bothered to really dig deep into whether that sales and marketing strategy matched the technical founder's vision or implementation. Because that's not what the founders had built. They had designed something much, much better—and much worse.

The New Market

The founders had actually built a new class of communication hardware, something the industry had never seen before. It was going to be the right product—someday—but right now it was not the mainstream.

This meant that their revenue plan had been a fantasy from day one. There was no chance their revenue was going to grow like the nice straight line of an existing market. More than likely the revenue projection would resemble the hockey stick like the graph on the right.

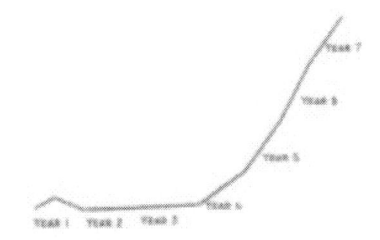

New Market Revenue Curve

(The small hump in year 1 is from the early adopters who buy one of anything. The flat part of the graph, years 1 to 4 is the Death Valley many companies never leave.)

Companies in New Markets that hire and execute like they're in an Existing Market burn through their cash and go out of business.

Inexperienced Founders and Investors

I realized I was watching the consequences of Catch22 of fundraising. Most experienced investors would have understood new markets take time, money and patience. This board had relatively young partners who hadn't quite grasped the consequences of what they had funded and had allowed the founder to execute a revenue plan that couldn't be met.

Six months later, the VCs were still at the board table but the founder was not.

Lessons Learned

   Customers don't read your revenue plan.

   Market Type matters. It affects timing of revenue, timing of spending to create demand, etc.

   Make sure your revenue and spending plan matches your Market Type.

   Make sure the founders and VCs agree on Market Type strategy.

It Must Be A Marketing Problem

February 11, 2010 (Steve Blank)

The Customer Development process is the way startups quickly iterate and test each element of their business model, reducing customer and market risk. The first step of Customer Development is called Customer Discovery. In Discovery, startups take all their hypotheses about the business model: product, market, customers, channel, etc. outside the building and test them in front of customers.

At least that's the theory. Helping out some friends I got to see firsthand the consequence of skipping Customer Discovery.

It's a Marketing Problem

After I retired, I would get calls from VCs to help with "marketing problems" in their portfolio companies. The phone call would sound something like: "We have a company with great technology and a hot product but at the last board meeting we determined that they have a marketing problem. Can you take a look and tell us what you think?"

A week later I was in the conference room of the company having a meeting with the CEO.

We Have a Marketing Problem

"So VC x says you guys have a marketing problem. How can I help?" CEO: "Well, we've missed our sales numbers for the last six months."

Me: "I'm confused. I thought you guys have a marketing problem. What does this have to do with missing your sales plan?"

CEO: "Well our VP of Sales isn't making the sales plan and he says it's a marketing problem, and he's a really senior guy."

Now, I'm intrigued. The CEO asks the VP of Sales to join us in the conference room. (Note that most VP of Sales' have world-class antenna for career danger. Being invited to chat with the CEO and an outside consultant that a board member brought in creates enough tension in a room to create static discharge.)

No One Is Buying Our Product

"Tell me about the marketing problem."

VP of Sales: "Marketing's positioning and strategy is all

wrong." Me: "How's that?"

VP of Sales: "No one is interested in buying our product."

If you've been in marketing long enough, you recognize the beginning of the sales versus marketing finger pointing. (It usually ends up bad for all concerned.) Sales is on the hook for making the numbers, and things aren't looking good.

Six Is a Proxy for Burn Rate

"How many salespeople do you have?" VP of Sales: "Six in the field, plus me."

Later I realized six salespeople without revenue to match was a proxy for an out-of- control burn rate that now had the board's serious attention.

There's Always One in Boston

"Is there a salesperson in Boston?" VP of Sales: "Sure."

Me: "What sales presentation is he using?

VP of Sales: "The corporate presentation. What else do you think he'd be using?"

Me: "Let's get him on the phone and ask."

Sure enough we'd get the sales person on the phone and find out that he stopped using the corporate presentation months ago. Why? The standard corporate presentation wasn't working, so the Boston sales rep made up his own. (I asked for the Boston sales rep because, in the U.S., they're farthest from the Silicon Valley corporate office and any oversight.)

We call the five other sales people and find that they are also "winging it."

Early Orders Were a Detriment

I learned that the founders received their initial product orders from their friends in the industry and through board members personal connections. These "friends and family orders" made the first nine months of their revenue plan. With that initial sales "success" they began to hire and staff the sales department per the "plan." That's how they ended up with seven people in sales (plus three more in marketing).

But now the bill had come due. It turned out that these "friends and family orders" meant the company really hadn't understood how and why customers would buy their product. There was no deep corporate understanding about customers or their needs. The company had designed and built their product and assumed it was going to sell well based on their initial early orders. Marketing was writing presentations and data sheets without having a clue what real problems customers had. And without that knowledge, sales essentially was selling blind.

Advice You Don't Want to Hear

My report back to the VC? Missing the sales numbers had nothing to do with marketing. The problem was much, much worse. The company had failed to do any Customer Discovery. Neither the CEO, VP of Sales, nor VP of Marketing had any idea what a repeatable sales model would look like before they scaled the sales force. Now they had a sales force in Brownian motion in the field, and a marketing department changing strategy, and the corporate slide deck weekly. Cash was flowing out of the company and the VP of Sales was still hiring.

I suggested they cut the burn rate back by firing all the salespeople in the field (keeping one in Silicon Valley) and get rid of all of marketing. The CEO needed to get back to basics and personally get out of the building in front of customers to learn and discover what problems customers had and why the company's product solved them.

The VC's response? "Nah, it can't be that bad, it's a marketing problem." I'll leave it to you to guess what the VCs did six months later.

Lessons Learned

- Premature Scaling of sales and marketing is the leading cause of hemorrhaging cash in a startup.

- Scale sales and marketing after the founders and a small team have found a repeatable sales model.

- Early sales from board members or friends are great for morale and cash but may not be indicative of learning and discovering a business model.

Nail the Customer Development Manifesto to the Wall

March 29, 2012 (Steve Blank)

When Bob Dorf and I wrote The Startup Owner's Manual we listed a series of Customer Development principles. I thought they might be worth enumerating here:

A Startup Is a Temporary Organization Designed to Search for A Repeatable and Scalable Business Model

1. There Are No Facts Inside Your Building, So Get Outside.

2. Pair Customer Development with Agile Development.

3. Failure is an Integral Part of the Search for the Business Model.

4. If You're Afraid to Fail, Then You're Destined to Do So.

5. Iterations and Pivots are Driven by Insight.

6. Validate Your Hypotheses with Experiments.

7. Success Begins with Buy-In from Investors and Co-Founders.

8. No Business Plan Survives First Contact with Customers.

9. Not All Startups Are Alike.

10. Startup Metrics are Different from Existing Companies.

11. Agree on Market Type—It Changes Everything.

12. Fast, Fearless Decision-Making, Cycle Time, Speed and Tempo.

13. If it's not About Passion, You're Dead the Day You Opened your Doors.

14. Startup Titles and Functions Are Very Different from a Company's.

15. Preserve Cash While Searching. After It's Found, Spend.

16. Communicate and Share Learning.

17. Startups Demand Comfort with Chaos and Uncertainty.

IV.

Corporate Innovation —Making Elephants Dance

The Future of Corporate Innovation and Entrepreneurship

December 3, 2012 (Steve Blank)

Almost every large company understands it needs to build an organization that deals with the ever-increasing external forces of continuous disruption, the need for continuous innovation, globalization and regulation.

But there is no standard strategy and structure for creating corporate innovation. We outline the strategy problem in this post.

—

I'm sitting at the ranch with Alexander Osterwalder, Henry Chesbrough, and Andre Marquis listening to them recount their lessons-learned consulting for some of the world's largest corporations. I offered what I just learned from spending a day at the ranch with the R&D group of a $100 billion corporation along with the insights my Startup Owner's Manual co-author, Bob Dorf, who has several Fortune 100 clients.

(Full disclosure: I'm recovering from a reading spree of Chandler's Strategy and Structure, Gary Hamel's The Future of Management and The Other Side of Innovation by Trimble and Govindarajan, Henry Chesbrough's Open Innovation, as well as The Innovator's DNA from Dyer, Gregersen, and Christensen. So some or most of this post **might be that I've** overdosed on business books for the month.)

Collectively we're beginning to see a pattern, and we want to offer some concrete suggestions about Corporate Management and Innovation strategy and the structural (i.e., organizational) changes corporations need to make.

If we're right, it will give 21st century companies a way to deal with innovation—both sustaining and disruptive—as a normal course of business rather than by exception or crisis. Companies will be organized around Continuous Innovation.

Strategy and Structure in the 21st Century

While companies have existed for the last 400 years, their modern form is less than 150 years old. In the U.S., the growth of railroads, telegraph, meat packers, steel and industrial equipment forced companies to deal with the strategies of how to organize a complex organization. In turn, these new strategies drove the need for companies to be structured around functions (manufacturing, purchasing, sales, etc.).

Ninety years ago, companies faced new strategic pressures as physical distances in the United States limited the reach of day-to-day hands-on management. In addition, firms found themselves now managing diverse product lines. In response, another structural shift in corporate organization occurred. In the 1920s, companies restructured from monolithic functional organizations (sales, marketing, manufacturing, purchasing, etc.) and reorganized into operating divisions (by product, territory, brand, etc.) each with its own profit and loss responsibility. This strategy-to-structure shift from functional organizations to operating divisions was led by DuPont and popularized by General Motors and quickly followed by Standard Oil and Sears.

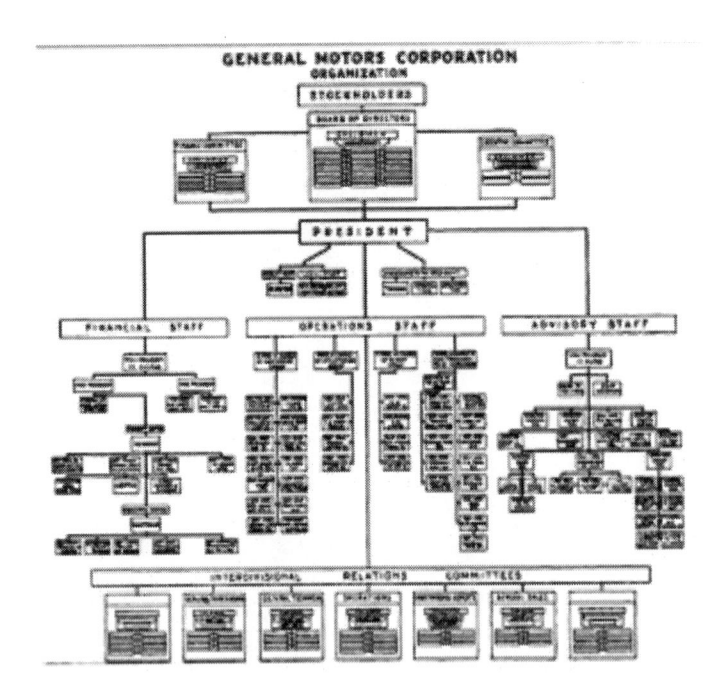

General Motors Organization Chart, 1925

In each case, whether it was organizing by functions or organizing by operating divisions, the diagram we drew for management was an organization chart. Invented in 1854 by Daniel McCallum, superintendent of the New York and Erie railroad, the org chart became the organizing tool for how to think about strategy and structure. It allowed companies to visually show command and control hierarchies—who's responsible, what they are responsible for and who they manage underneath them, and report to above them. (The irony is that while the org chart may have been new for companies, the hierarchies it described paralleled military organization and had been around since the Roman Legion.)

While org charts provided the "who" of a business, companies were missing a way to visualize the "how" of a business. In the 1990s, Strategy Maps provided the "How." Evolved from Balanced Scorecards by Kaplan and Norton, Strategy Maps are a visual representation of an organization's strategy. Strategy Maps are a tool to translate the strategy into specific actions and objectives to measure the progress of how the strategy gets implemented (but offer no help on how to create new strategies).

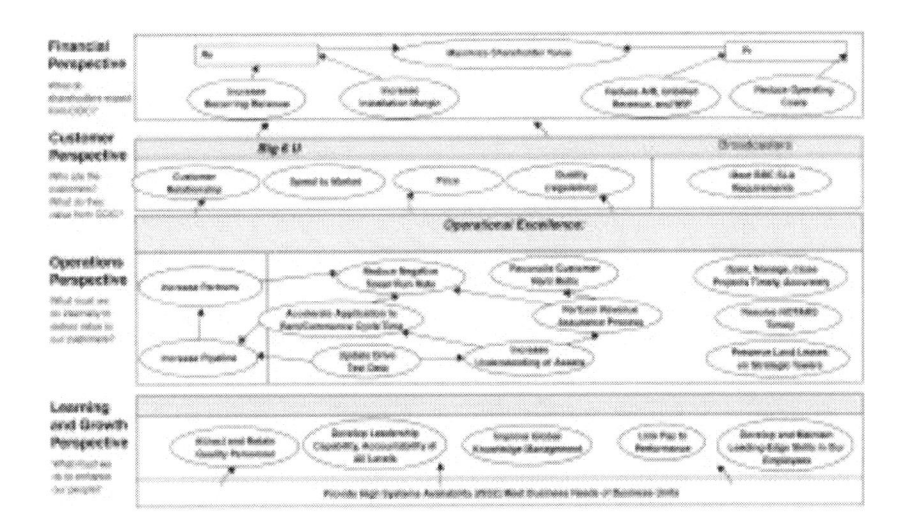

Strategy Maps from Robert Kaplan

By the 21st century, organizations still lacked a tool to create and formulate new strategies. Enter the Business Model Canvas. The canvas describes the rationale of how an organization **creates**, delivers, and captures **value** (economic, social, or other forms of **value**). The canvas ties together the "who and how" and provides the "why." External to the canvas are the environmental influences (industry forces, market forces, key trends and macroeconomic forces). With the business model canvas in hand, we can now approach rethinking corporate innovation strategy and structure.

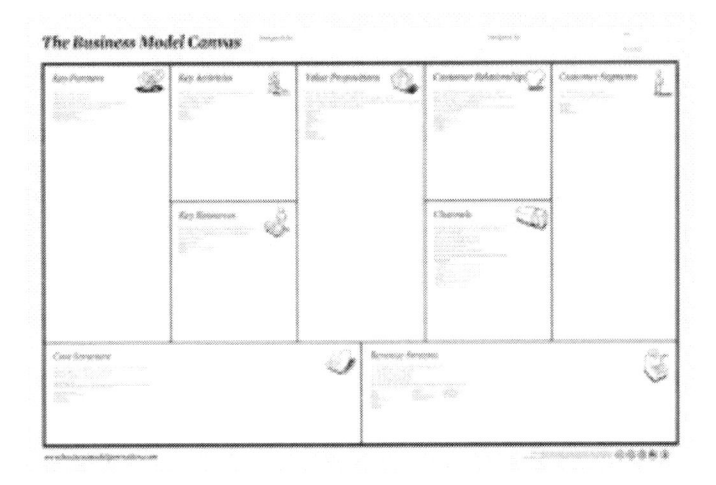

Management Innovation in the 21st Corporation

Existing companies and their operating divisions implement **known** business models. Using the business model canvas, they can draw how their organization is creating, delivering, and capturing value. A business model for an existing company or division is not filled with hypotheses, it is filled with a series of facts. Operating divisions **execute** the known business model. Plans and processes are in place, and rules, job specifications, revenue, profit and margin goals have been set. Forecasts can be based on a series of known conditions.

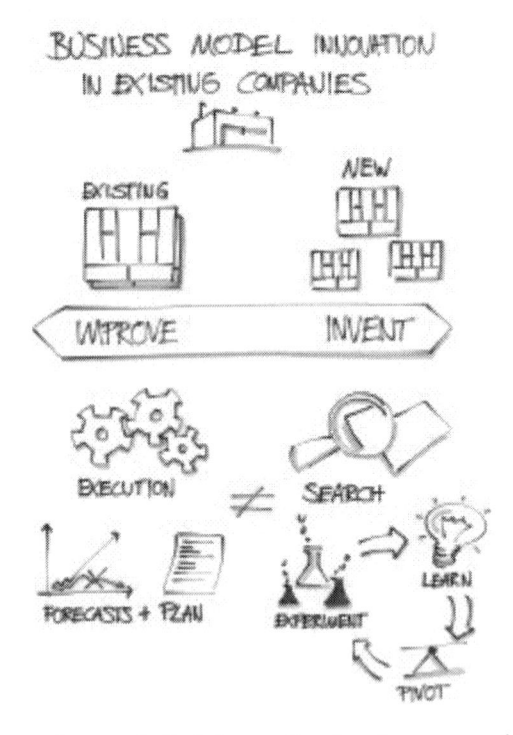

Inside existing companies and divisions, the business model canvas is used as a tool to implement and continuously **improve** existing business models incrementally. This might include new products, markets, or acquisitions.

A New Strategy for Entrepreneurship in the 21st Corporation

Yet, simply focusing on improving existing business models is not enough anymore. To assure their survival and produce satisfying growth, corporations need to **invent** new business models. This challenge requires entirely new organizational structures and skills.

This is not unlike the challenges corporations were facing in the 1920s. Companies then found that their existing strategy and structures (organizations) were inadequate to respond to a changing world. We believe that the solution for companies today is to realize that what they are facing is a strategy and structure problem, common to all companies.

Companies will need to have an organization that can do two things at the same time: executing and improving existing models and inventing – new and disruptive—business models.

We propose that corporations equipped for the challenges of the 21st century think of innovation as a sliding scale between execution and search.

1. For companies to survive in the 21st century they need to continually create a new set of businesses, by **inventing** new business models.

2. Most of these new businesses need to be created outside of the existing business units.

3. The exact form of the new business models is not known at the beginning. It only emerges after an intense business model design and search activity based on the customer development process.

4. Companies will have to maintain a **portfolio** of new business model initiatives, not unlike a venture capital firm, and they will have to accept that maybe only 1 out 10 initiatives might succeed.

5. To develop this new portfolio, companies need to provide a stable innovation funding mechanism for new business creation, one that is simply thought of as a cost of doing business.

6. Many of the operating divisions can and should provide resources to the new businesses inside the company.

7. We need a new organizational structure to manage the creation of new businesses and to coordinate the sharing of business model resources.

8. Some of these new businesses might become new resources to the existing operating units in the company or they could grow into becoming the new profit generating business units of the company's future.

Lessons Learned

Continuous disruption will be the norm for corporations in the 21st century.

Continuous innovation—in the form of new businesses—will be the path for long term corporate survival.

Current corporate organizational models are inadequate for the task.

Durant Versus Sloan

October 1, 2009 (Steve Blank)

The entrepreneur who built the largest startup in the United States is someone you probably never heard of. The guy who replaced him invented the idea of the modern corporation. Understanding the future of entrepreneurship may depend on understanding the contribution each of them made in the past.

Alfred P. Sloan

In the middle of the 20th Century Alfred P. Sloan was one of the most famous businessman in the world. Known as the "Inventor of the Modern Corporation," Sloan was president of General Motors from 1923 to 1956 when the U.S. automotive industry grew to become one of the drivers of the global economy.

If you look around the United States, it's hard to avoid Sloan. There's the Alfred P. Sloan Foundation, the Sloan School of Management at MIT, the Sloan program at Stanford, and the Sloan/Kettering Memorial Cancer Center in New York. Sloan's book, "My Years with General Motors," written 40 years ago, is still a business classic.

The Modern Corporation

Sloan is rightly credited with formalizing the idea of the modern U.S. corporation, and by extension Sloan laid the foundation for America's economic leadership in the 20th century. One guy really did all of this.

Peter Drucker wrote that Sloan was "the first to work out how to systematically organize a big company. When Sloan became president of GM in 1923 he put in place planning and strategy, measurements, and most importantly, the principles of decentralization."

Sloan realized that the traditional centralized management structures (like General Motors had in 1920) were poor fits for the management of GM's already-diverse product lines. Top management was trying to coordinate all of the operating details (sales, manufacturing, distribution, and marketing) across all the divisions and the company almost went bankrupt that year when poor planning led to excess inventory (with unsold cars piling up at dealers and the company running out of cash).

Sloan transferred responsibility down from corporate into each of the operating divisions (Chevrolet, Pontiac, Oldsmobile, Buick and Cadillac). Each of these GM divisions each focused on its own day-to-day operations and with each division general manager responsible for the division's profit and loss. Sloan kept the corporate staff small and focused on policymaking, corporate finance, and planning. Sloan had each of the divisions start systematic strategic planning.

Sloan put in place GM's management accounting system (borrowed from DuPont) that for the first time allowed the company to: 1) produce an annual operating forecast that compared each division's forecast (revenue, costs, capital requirements and return on investment) with the company's financial goals. 2) Provide corporate management with near real-time divisional sales reports and budgets that indicated when they deviated from plan. 3) Allowed management to allocate resources and compensation among divisions based on a standard set of corporate-wide performance criteria.

Finally, Sloan transformed corporate management into a real profession, establishing the standard that the professional manager is duty-bound to put the interests of the enterprise ahead of his own.

Modern Corporation Marketing

At the same time General Motors also revolutionized automotive marketing by creating multiple brands of cars, each with its own identity targeted at a specific economic bracket of American customers. The company set the prices for each of these brands from **lowest to** highest (Chevrolet, Pontiac, Oldsmobile, Buick and Cadillac). Within each brand there were several models at different price points.

The idea was to keep customers coming back to General Motors over time to upgrade to a better brand as they became wealthier. Finally, GM created the notion of perpetual demand within brands by continually obsoleting their own products yearly with new models rolled out every year. (Think of the iPod family and yearly new models.)

When Sloan took over as president of GM in 1923, Ford and its Model-T was the dominant player in the U.S. auto market with 60-percent of the U.S. car market. General Motors had 20-percent. By 1931, with the combination of superior financial management and an astute brand and product line strategy, GM had 43-percent market share to Ford's 20- percent—a lead it never relinquished.

Thanks for the History Lesson—So What?

Well thanks for the history lesson but why should you care?

If you're an entrepreneur you might be interested to know that when Sloan took over General Motors in 1923, it was already a $700 million dollar company (about $8.5 billion in sales in today's dollars).

Yet you never hear who built that company. Who founded what would become General Motors 16 years earlier in 1904? Where are the charitable foundations, business schools and hospitals named after him? What happened to him? Who was he?

The founder of what became General Motors was William (Billy) Durant. His board (led by the DuPont family) tossed him out of General Motors (for the second time) in 1920 when GM sales were $567 million (about $6 billion in today's dollars).

William Durant died managing a bowling alley in Flint Michigan in 1947.

From the day Durant was fired in 1920, and for the next half a century, American commerce would be led by an army of "Sloan-style managers."

But the spirit of Billy Durant would rise again. This time in what would become Silicon Valley.

When Big Companies Are Dead But Don't Know It

June 7, 2010 (Steve Blank)

It is a rare company that realizes it is time to fire the CEO when the financials are good but the business is fundamentally heading for a cliff. For me, I learned this lesson first hand. I had joined the board of a $200 million public company that 15 years earlier had single-handedly created an industry. The company had innovated, found a business model, grown successfully but now even as revenues continued to grow, the company was slowly but surely dying.

There's nothing harder than making radical changes when the numbers look great.

Lifecycle

The company's two co-founders had created a new technology and an innovative business strategy. The engineering co-founder had created a consumer electronics security product that created an entirely new category. The other founder, the business guy, managed to get its product legislated into consumer electronics devices. After the initial few years of technical innovation, they found their business model in licensing and over the next decade and a half grew into a $200 million company.

As the revenues grew, engineering continued to pursue sustaining innovations-incremental improvements on its core technologies.

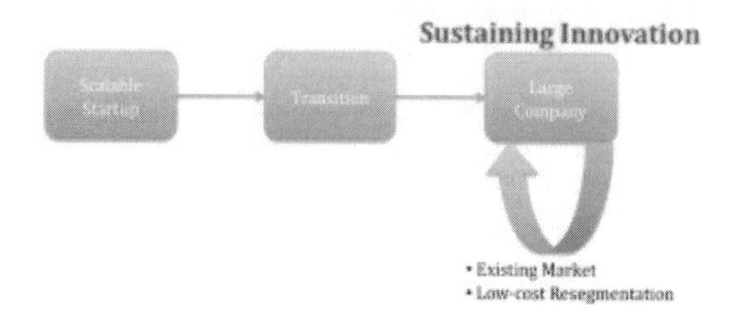

Sustaining Innovation

Scalable Startup → Transition → Large Company

- Existing Market
- Low-cost Resegmentation

At the same time its business strategy became operational execution focused on licensing and legal to collect royalties.

Execution

Over time, the co-founder responsible for the original business innovations departed. While a large loss, it wasn't fatal as the company now was executing a repeatable business model. The new CEO was promoted from inside the company and did an excellent job of running the company. Even though the company was in Silicon Valley, he ran it like it was in Kansas: no frills, no hype, no crazy expenditures, just year after year of increasing revenue and profits. And year after year, he managed to come out on top renewing the licensing contracts with Hollywood studios, who were no pushovers in negotiations. It was impressive.

We Think We Need Some Technology Advice

To their credit, the board and CEO realized that this business model couldn't continue forever. They acquired a small, innovative company in what they thought was an adjacent market. The acquisition turned out to be a culture clash of titanic proportions, kind of like the irresistible force meets the immovable object, as the great startup founder ran headlong into the excellent operating guy. Neither company really understood what it would take to integrate such different worldviews.

In the middle of this acquisition, both the board (who were finance and Hollywood executives) and the CEO realized that while they were physically in Silicon Valley, they were missing someone familiar with business innovation in technology companies.

This is when I joined the board.

Distracted

After a few months on the board trying to understand the difficulties of integrating the new acquisition, I realized that this was just a side-show. The real issue was that was that the instincts of the board and CEO were right. There were tectonic shifts happening outside the company—changes in markets, technology, platforms, regulations, etc – and outside their control.

Worse, these shifts were outside the company's control, because unlike the original co-founder, now gone, who managed to get their technology written into legislation, no one was working the same magic on the next generation of digital standards online or in the cloud.

We realized that the company had three to five years left before its licensing business would drop by half. As a board, we slowly came to the conclusion we'd have to reinvent the company, and we didn't have much time. The CEO agreed.

Reinvention

Over the next few years, the company built an internal engineering department, and expanded its business development team in search of a new strategy and new companies to acquire.

To the outside world, things still looked great; year over year, revenue and profits were still increasing.

At each board meeting, we'd hear about new products and approve new acquisitions while we were increasingly worrying about when revenues of our core product would start declining.

The world outside the company was changing faster than we could. The new strategies and acquisitions ended up as slight variations on the ones we were already executing.

We seemed to be out of big ideas.

Time for a Change

The problem was, the company needed to think like a startup again. The current team was too focused and ironically too steeped in our current business to imagine radical reinvention.

We concluded that we needed a new CEO and new board members.

There's nothing harder than changing strategy with a CEO who the board admires, with revenues seemingly increasing. Yet the consequences of ignoring the shifts in the market, technology and regulation is a going out of business strategy.

This was a tough call for the board as we liked the CEO, and he was the one who had asked us to join the board.

As one could imagine, the existing CEO didn't agree. "I've done everything you guys have asked. Our revenue is still growing and we are acquiring all the new companies."

While the CEO is the responsible executive for operating the company on a daily basis, ultimately it's the responsibility of the board of the directors to hire and fire the CEO. The board is responsible to the shareholders and all the stakeholders for the ultimate survival of the company. Our call was that it was going to take a new set of eyes to get the elephant to dance.

Postscript

The new CEO turned the company on its head, divested most of the acquisitions, made other acquisitions worth billions of dollars, refocused the company, changed out most of the board and senior management.

And he even renamed the company.

Revenue doubled in the last three years, and the market cap is approaching $4 billion as he reinvented the company.

A tough call but the right one for the shareholders.

Lessons Learned

> Just because a company is profitable doesn't mean its core businesses isn't crumbling under its feet.

> Big companies are dead long before they close the doors.

> Ultimately it's because the board of directors doesn't act in time.

> The dilemma is how to make sure that the board is not just a cheerleader for the CEO when the CEO is the primary recruiter for the board.

> Microsoft fits this description. Their failures in multiple markets is no longer just a failure of management but a failure of board governance. (Hard to fix when the major shareholder is the lifelong friend of his handpicked replacement.)

Solving the Innovator's Dilemma—Customer Development in a Big Company

August 23, 2010 (Steve Blank)

One of the ways I learn is to teach. My students ask questions I can't answer and challenge me to solve problems I never considered. At times I'll do what I consider an extension of teaching; a two-day Customer Discovery/Validation intensive session with a large corporation serious about Customer Development at my ranch on the California Coast.

My last session was with a passionate, smart, entrepreneurial team from a Fortune 100 company. (And if I told you who they were, I'd have to kill you.) Their copies of "The Four Steps" were dog-eared and marked with sticky notes. We spent two days of analyzing and exploring their customer discovery visits just completed across South America, Africa, and Asia. Learning which hypotheses survived these visits were eye-openers for all of us. We used what they learned to plan their next steps for additional Discovery, and ultimately Customer Validation.

It reminded me of the differences in Customer Discovery between a scalable startup and a big company. Here's what we observed:

It's Easier for Big Companies to Get Meetings—But It's Not Always a Blessing

When a big company calls prospective customers to set up Discovery meetings, their datebook fills up fast. Execs at higher levels than you'd expect join the meeting eager to hear what the big company has to say about their industry. That's the good news. The bad news is that the meetings become far more formal and more crowded, than one that a startup would have. This crowd actually dampens the opportunity for learning. Since the meetings attract senior execs everyone around the table waits for the big boss to speak and follows his or her lead. This stifles or shuts down the important "outlier" conversations that drive pivots and iterations in the discovery process.

Solution: try to get a blend of one-on-one meetings along with the group session. And be sure to set expectations for the meeting before it happens.

We're Not Here for a Sales Call

If someone from a large company is flying halfway around the world to visit your company, your presumption is they have something to sell you. Crucial in the Customer Discovery process is not selling… it's listening. The exploring, probing, gaining reactions is why you're there. (Of course, if someone forces a purchase order on you and you reject it, you've just failed miserably at entrepreneurship.) Disabusing the audience of the notion that the visit is a sales call is vital to the customer discovery mission. Followers of the Customer Development process know that you can't start selling until you have transformed product, customer and other hypotheses into a validated business model and sales roadmap. (Short-circuiting that process is a major "foul" that often leads to premature business models and suboptimal sales results.)

To potential customers who've never been asked for their opinion before, the purpose of a Discovery meeting can be confusing. There are business cultures where the vendor/customer interactions are limited to "here's what I have to sell, do you want to buy it."

Solution: Spend more time on the "setup" for the meeting. Tell potential customers before you meet, "We're working on an interesting product and we'd be happy to share where we are in exchange for some feedback. But we are not here for a sales call."

Getting the Customer to Talk Is Even More Challenging

There's no more important skill in Customer Discovery than "good listening." When a big company shows up, everyone expects an important formal presentation, which is hardly your Discovery mission at all. Structuring the conversation in a way that elicits feedback before you reveal the product hypothesis is essential to getting honest reactions, good or bad. Yet just reading your questions from a list is a real-turnoff. Insert them casually into a conversation and don't try too hard to get every one of them answered in every meeting.

Solution: One of our favorite hints, from a great post by Ash Maurya, is to pose problems to the group in a randomized list. "We see these three problems in your industry. Do you agree? Could you rank them in order of importance to you?" This literally forces a discussion and prioritization and is repeatable again and again. "We believe the most important features you need in a supersonic transporter are…" or "Our research tells us that female consumers most want a, b, and c."

Big Companies Are Bred for Large Scale Success
When you're doing disruptive innovation in a multi-billion dollar company, a $10 million dollar per year new product line doesn't even move the needle. So to get new divisions launched large optimistic forecasts are the norm. Ironically, one of the greatest risks in large companies is high pressure expectations to make these first pass forecasts that subvert an honest Customer Development process. The temptation is to transform the vision of a large market into a solid corporate revenue forecast—before Customer Development even begins.

Solution: Upper management needs to understand that a new division pursuing disruptive innovation is not the same as a division adding a new version of an established product. Rather, it is an organization searching for a business model (inside a company that's executing an existing one). That means you may find that revenue appears later than the plan called for, or that there are no customers or fewer than the plan suggests.

Customer Development Without Agile Engineering Is a Plan for Failure
Believing in Customer Development but still retaining waterfall development for engineering and manufacturing is a setup for problems if not outright failure. Even in a large company you can't do Customer Development without aligning some part of engineering to respond to unexpected customer needs and findings.

Solution: Get engineering buy-in by. Make sure the engineering and manufacturing plans "before" Customer Development don't look the same as "after" Customer Development.

Spend Your Way to Success Usually Results in the Opposite

Ironically large revenue goals may lead to largesse in overfunding the new division, with the implicit assumption that dollars can "buy your way to success." All the money in the world doesn't negate the painful search for a business model, or the lack of a scalable/profitable one. And new divisions in large companies operate just like startups who get overfunded—somehow their expense budgets always equal at least their funding.

Solution: Eight- and nine-digit funding before Customer Discovery is a curse not a blessing. Take the money in tranches (equivalent to VC "rounds") predicated on milestones in finding a repeatable and scalable business model.

There's an Overhead Cost to Being an Entrepreneur in a Big, Established Corporation

Large companies are just plain organized—with rules, HR, finance and more importantly, are built around process and procedures for execution. It's why so few big companies succeed at true entrepreneurship.

Solution: Assume as a given that as a new division head at least 15 percent of your time will be spent managing up and protecting down. Few in your own company will understand what you're up to.

Lessons Learned

- Customer Development in large companies has its own unique challenges.

- Some parts of being a big company make it easier, others make being a startup even riskier.

Why Innovation Dies

May 1, 2012 (Steve Blank)

Faced with disruptive innovation, you can be sure any possibility for innovation dies when a company forms a committee for an "overarching strategy."

I was reminded how innovation dies when the email below arrived in my inbox. It was well written, thoughtful and had a clearly articulated sense of purpose. You may have seen one like it in your school or company.

Skim it and take a guess why I first thought it was a parody. It's a classic mistake large organizations make in dealing with disruption.

The Strategy Committee

"Faculty and Staff:

We believe online education will become increasingly important at all levels of the educational experience. If our school is to retain its current standards in terms of access and excellence we think it is of paramount importance that we develop an overarching campus strategy that enables and supports online innovation.

We believe our Departments play an essential leadership role in the design and implementation of online offerings. However, we also want to provide guidance and support and ensure that campus goals are met, specifically ensuring that our online education efforts align with our mission, values and operational requirements.

To this end, we are convening a Strategy Committee that is charged with overseeing our efforts and accelerating implementation. The responsibilities of the group will be to provide overall direction to campus, make decisions concerning strategic priorities and allocate additional resources to help realize these priorities. Because we anticipate that most of the innovation in this area will occur at the school/unit level we underscore that the purpose of the Strategy Committee is to provide campus-level guidance and coordination, and to enable innovation. The Strategy Committee will also be responsible for reaching out to and receiving input from the President's Staff and the Faculty Senate.

The Strategy Committee will be comprised of Mark Time, Nick Danger, Ralph Spoilsport, Ray Hamberger, Audrey Farber, Rocky Rococo, George Papoon, Fred Flamm, Susan Farber, and Clark Cable.

A Policy Team, which is charged with coordinating with the schools/unit to develop detailed implementation plans for specific projects, will report to the Strategy Committee. The role of the Policy Team will be to develop a detailed strategic framework for the campus, oversee the development of shared resources, disseminate best practices, create an administrative infrastructure that provides consistent financial and legal expertise, and consult with relevant campus groups: and the Budget Office. The Policy Team will be led by two senior campus leaders, one from the academic side and one from the administration side.

We are extremely pleased that Dean Tirebiter has accepted the administrative lead role of the Policy Team. Dean Tirebiter brings to this position a deep knowledge of the online environment. He will be helping to identify a member of our Faculty to serve as the academic lead of the Policy Team.

The Strategy Committee will be meeting for a half-day retreat at Morse Science Hall in the coming weeks to begin work. We will be sending out an update to faculty and following this retreat, so stay tuned for further updates.

Sincerely,

President Peter Bergman"

We Can Figure It Out in a Meeting

The memo sounds thoughtful and helpful. It's an attempt to get all the "right" stakeholders in the room and think through the problem.

One useful purpose a university committee could have had was figuring out what the goal of going online was. It could have said, "The world expects us to lead so let's get together and figure out how we deal with online education." Our goal(s) could be:

- Looking good

- Doing good for all [or at least citizens of California]

- Doing well by our enrolled students

- Fixing our business model to fix our budget crisis

- Having a good football team—or at least filling the stadium

- Attracting donations

- Attracting faculty

- Oh and yes—building an efficient, high quality education machine

But the minute the memo started talking about a Policy Team developing detailed implementation plans, it was all over.

The problem is that the path to implementing online education is not known. In fact, it's not a solvable problem by committee, regardless of how many smart people in the room. It is an "NP complete" problem—it is so complex that figuring out the one possible path to a correct solution is computationally incalculable.

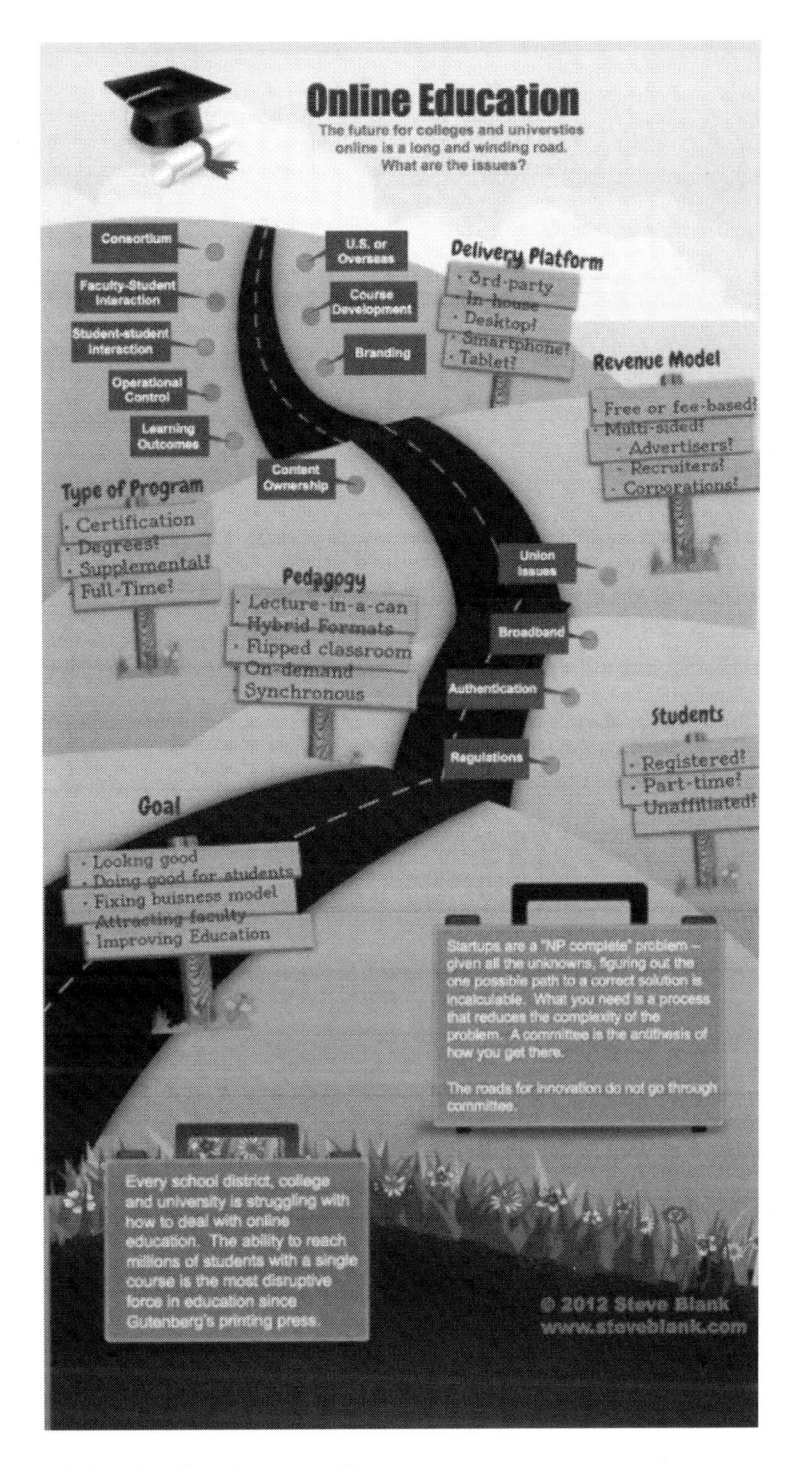

[Infographic: "Online Education – The future for colleges and universities online is a long and winding road. What are the issues?" © 2012 Steve Blank, www.steveblank.com]

Innovation Dies in Conference Rooms

The "let's put together a committee" strategy fails for four reasons:

1. Online education is not an existing market. There just isn't enough data to pick what is the correct "overarching strategy."

2. Making a single bet on a single strategy, plan or company in a new market is a sure way to fail. After fifty years, even the smartest VC firms haven't figured out how to pick one company as the winner. That's why they invest in a portfolio.

3. Committees protect the status quo. Everyone who has a reason to say "No" is represented.

4. Dealing with disruption is not solved by committee. New market problems call for visionary founders, not consensus committee members.

My bet is that there will be more people involved in this school's Strategy Committee than in the startups that find the solution.

In a perfect world, the right solution would be a one-page memo encouraging maximum experimentation with the bare minimum of rules (protecting the school's brand and the applicable laws).

Lessons Learned

- Innovation in New Markets does not come from "overarching strategies." It comes out of opportunity, chaos, and rapid experimentation.

- Solutions are found by betting on a portfolio of low-cost experiments. With a minimum number of constraints

- The road for innovation does not go through committee.

No Accounting For Startups

February 22, 2010 (Steve Blank)

Startups that are searching for a business model need to keep score differently than large companies that are executing a known business model.

Yet most entrepreneurs and their VCs make startups use financial models and spreadsheets that actually hinder their success.

Here's why.

Managing the Business

When I ran my startups our venture investors scheduled board meetings each month for the first year or two, going to every six weeks a bit later, and then moving to quarterly after we found a profitable business model.

One of the ways our VCs kept track of our progress was by taking a monthly look at three financial documents: Income Statement, Balance Sheet and Cash Flow Statement.

If I knew what I knew now, I never would have let that happen. These financial documents were worse than useless for helping us understand how well we were (or weren't) doing. They were an indicator of "I went to business school but don't really know what to tell you to measure so I'll have you do these."

To be clear—Income Statements, Balance Sheets and Cash Flow Statements are really important at two points in your startup. First, when you pitch your idea to VCs, you need a financial model showing VCs what your company will look like after you are no longer a startup and you're executing the profitable model you've found. If this sounds like you're guessing—you're right—you are. But don't dismiss the exercise. Putting together a financial model and having the founders understand the interrelationships of the variables that can make or break a business is a worthwhile exercise.

The second time you'll need to know about Income Statements, Balance Sheets and Cash Flow Statements is after you've found your repeatable and profitable business model. You'll then use these documents to run your business and monitor your company's financial health as you execute your business model.

The problem is that using Income Statement, Balance Sheets and Cash Flow Statements any other time, particularly in a startup board meeting, has the founding team focused on the wrong numbers. I had been confused for years why I had to update an income statement each board meeting that said zero for 18 months before we had any revenue.

But What Does a Business Model Have to Do With Accounting in My Startup?

A startup is a search for a repeatable and scalable business model. As a founder you are testing a series of hypotheses about all the pieces of the business model: Who are the customers/users? What's the distribution channel? How do we price and position the product? How do we create end user demand? Who are our partners? Where/how do we build the product? How do we finance the company, etc.?

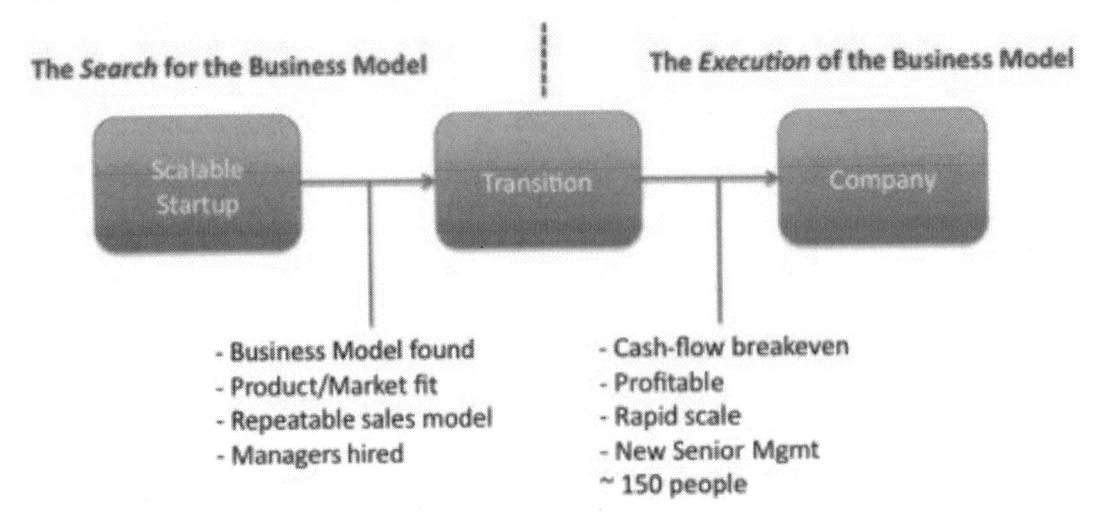

The *Search* for the Business Model | The *Execution* of the Business Model

Scalable Startup → Transition → Company

- Business Model found
- Product/Market fit
- Repeatable sales model
- Managers hired

- Cash-flow breakeven
- Profitable
- Rapid scale
- New Senior Mgmt
- ~150 people

An early indication that you've found the right business model is when you believe the cost of getting customers will be less than the revenues the customers will generate. For web startups, this is when the cost of customer acquisition is less than the lifetime value of that customer. For biotech startups, it's when the cost of the R&D required to find and clinically test a drug is less than the market demand for that drug. These measures are vastly different from those captured in balance sheets and income statements especially in the near term.

What should you be talking about in your board meeting? If you are following Customer Development, the answer is easy. Board meetings are about measuring progress measured against the hypotheses in Customer Discovery and Validation. Do the metrics show that the business model you're creating will support the company you're trying to become?

Startup Metrics

Startups need different metrics than large companies. They need metrics to tell how well the search for the business model is going, and whether at the end of that search is the business model you picked worth scaling into a company. Or is it time to pivot and look for a different business model?

Essentially, startups need to "instrument" all parts of their business model to measure how well their hypotheses in Customer Discovery and Validation are faring in the real world.

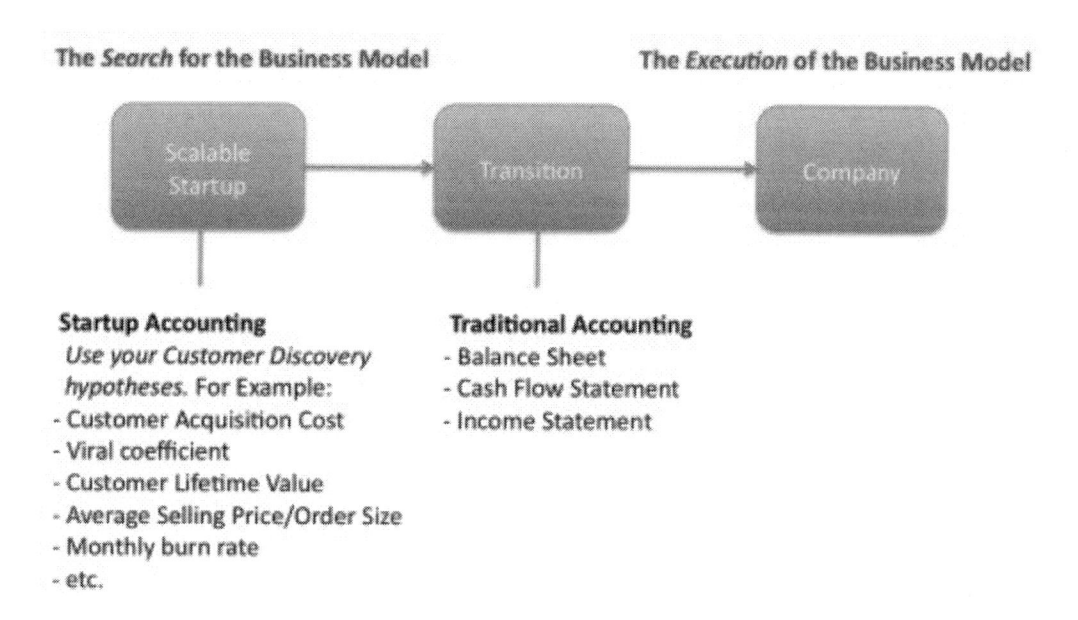

The *Search* for the Business Model → **The *Execution* of the Business Model**

Scalable Startup → Transition → Company

Startup Accounting
Use your Customer Discovery hypotheses. For Example:
- Customer Acquisition Cost
- Viral coefficient
- Customer Lifetime Value
- Average Selling Price/Order Size
- Monthly burn rate
- etc.

Traditional Accounting
- Balance Sheet
- Cash Flow Statement
- Income Statement

For example, at a minimum, a web based startup needs to understand the Customer Lifecycle, Customer Acquisition Cost, Marketing Cost, Viral Coefficient, Customer Lifetime Value, etc. Dave McClure's AARRR Model is one illustration of the web sales pipeline.

At a web startup, our board meetings were discussions of the real world results of testing our hypotheses from Customer Discovery.

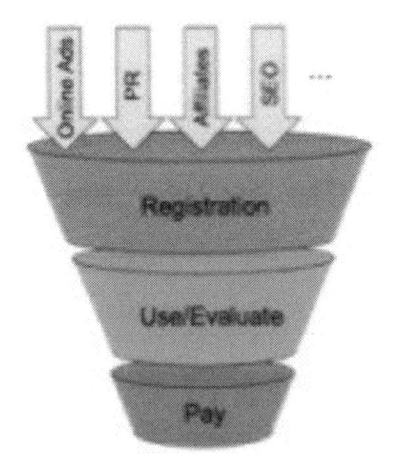

We had made some guesses about the customer pipeline and now we had a live web site. So we put together a spreadsheet that tracked these actual customer numbers every month. Every month we reported to our board progress on registrations, activations, retained users, etc. They looked like this:

User Base

- Registrations (Customers who completed the registration process during the month)

- Activations (Customers who had activity three to ten days after they registered. Measures only customers that registered during that month)

- Activation/Registrations percentage

- Retained 30+ Days

- Retained 30+/ Total Actives percentage

- Retained 90+ Days

- Retained 90+/Total Actives percentage

- Paying Customers (How many customers made purchases that month)

- Paying/(Activations + Retained 30+)

Financials
- Revenue
- Contribution Margin

Cash
- Burn Rate
- Months of cash left

Customer Acquisition
- Cost Per Acquisition Paid
- Cost Per Acquisition Net
- Advertising Expenses
- Viral Acquisition Ratio

Web Metrics
- Total Unique Visitors
- Total Page Views
- Total Visits
- PV/visit

A startup selling via a direct sales force will want to understand: average order size, Customer Lifetime Value, average time to first order, average time to follow-on orders, revenue per sales person, time to salesperson becomes effective.

Regardless of your type of business model you should be tracking cash burn rate, months of cash left, time to cash flow breakeven.

Tell Them No

If you have venture investors, work with them to agree what metrics matter. What numbers are life and death for the success of your startup? (These numbers ought to be the hypotheses you're testing in Customer Discovery and Validation.) Agree that these will be the numbers that you'll talk about in your board meeting. Agree that there will come times that the numbers show that the business model you picked is not worth scaling into a company. Then you'll all agree it's time to pivot and look for a different business model.

You'll all feel like you're focused on what's important.

Lessons Learned

- Large companies need financial tools to monitor how well they are executing a known business model.

- Income Statements, Balance Sheets and Cash Flow Statements are good large company financial monitoring tools.

- Startups need metrics to monitor how well their search for a business model is going.

- Startups need metrics to evaluate wither the business model you picked is worth scaling into a company.

- Using large company financial tools to measure startup progress is like giving the SAT to a first grader. It may measure something in the future but can only result in frustration and confusion now.

The Search For the Fountain of Youth—Innovation and Entrepreneurship in the Enterprise

June 3, 2010 (Steve Blank)

"It's not the strongest of the species that survive, nor the most intelligent, but the one that is most responsive to change."
— Charles Darwin

Companies have a fairly predictable life cycle. They start with an innovation, search for a repeatable business model, build the infrastructure for a company, then grow by efficiently executing the model.

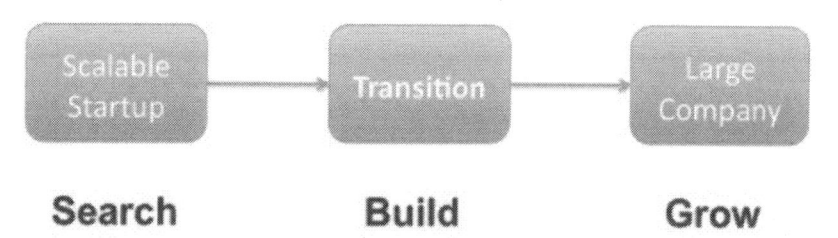

Scalable Startup → Transition → Large Company

Search   **Build**   **Grow**

Over time, innovations outside the company (demographic, cultural, new technologies, etc.) outpace an existing company's business model. The company loses customers, then revenues and profits decline and it eventually gets acquired or goes out of business. (Looking at the Dow Jones component companies over time is a graphic example of this.)

Creative Destruction

If you're an entrepreneur, you spend your time worrying about how to get out of the box on the left and move to the right. You want to start executing the business model.

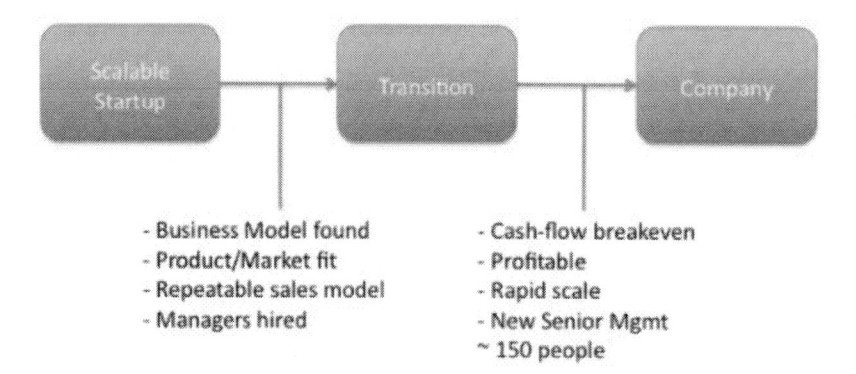

[Diagram: Scalable Startup → Transition → Company]

- Business Model found
- Product/Market fit
- Repeatable sales model
- Managers hired

- Cash-flow breakeven
- Profitable
- Rapid scale
- New Senior Mgmt
- ~150 people

Ironically, the best CEOs in the box on the right are constantly worrying not only how to execute but also how to remain innovative and entrepreneurial.

Innovation and Entrepreneurship in the Enterprise

How large companies can stay innovative and entrepreneurial has been the Holy Grail for authors of business books, business schools, consulting firms, etc. There's some great work from lots of authors in this area.

Over 15 years ago, Clayton Christensen observed that there are two types of innovative strategies for a large company— sustaining and disruptive innovation. He believed that large companies handle sustaining innovation— evolutionary changes in their markets, products, etc. valued by their existing customers—fairly well. But most large companies find it hard to deal with disruptive innovation—radical shifts in technology, customers, regulatory changes, etc, that create new markets.

Sustaining Innovation and Entrepreneurship in the Enterprise

If we use our "startup to large company," diagram, we can see that sustaining innovations occur within a large company's existing management structures. I'll offer that the diagram looks something like this.

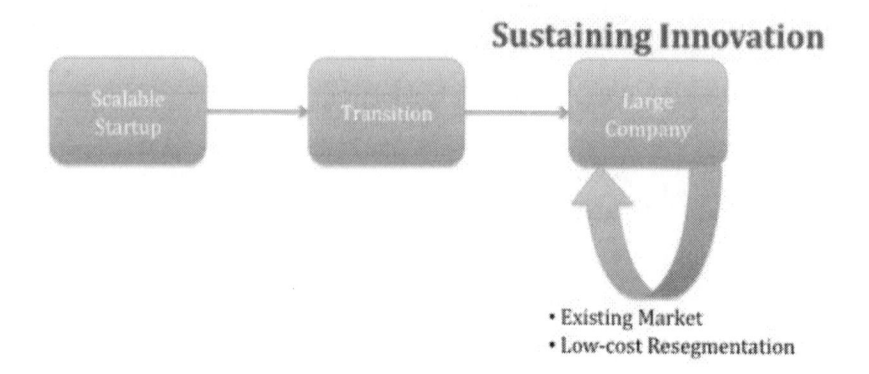

[Diagram: Scalable Startup → Transition → Large Company, with **Sustaining Innovation** arrow looping back into Large Company]

- Existing Market
- Low-cost Resegmentation

196

If you've been reading my book on Customer Development and follow my work on Market Type, this type of innovation is best for adding new products to existing markets.

Disruptive Innovation and Entrepreneurship in the Enterprise

Yet most research has shown that disruptive innovation, that is innovations that go after new markets, new customers, new technologies, etc. are best built outside a large company's existing organization.

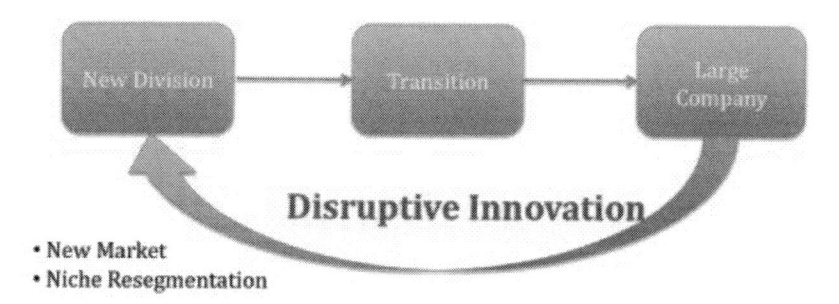

This type of organization is best for finding new niches in existing markets or creating entirely new markets. Why? Disruptive innovation in a large company is attempting to solve two simultaneous unknowns: the customer/market is unknown, and the product feature set is unknown. Just like a startup.

The diagram for managing disruptive innovation in large company looks suspiciously like starting from square one as a startup.

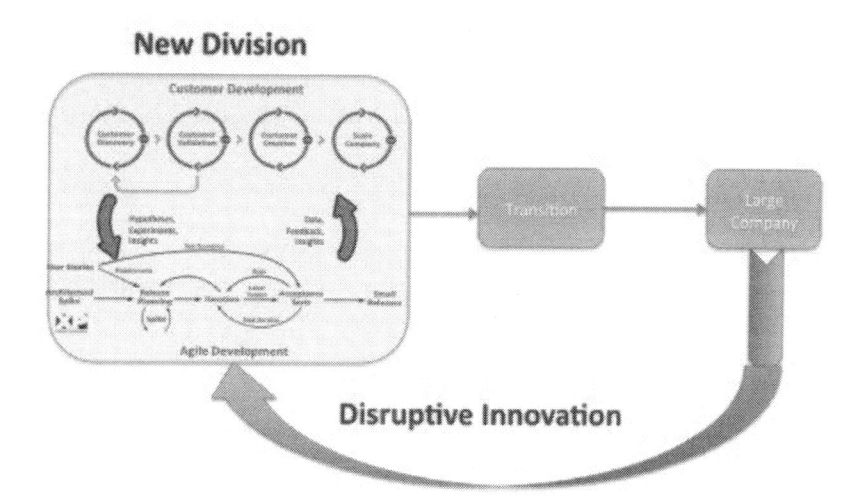

What's Missing in Innovation and Entrepreneurship in the Enterprise?

After growing past their scrappy startup roots, large companies trying to master disruptive innovation face the ultimate irony: "the Innovator's DNA" that's needed has more than likely been purged from the organization. Mastering disruptive innovation in a large company requires:

- different people
- different processes

In fact the people a large firm needs for this kind of innovation looks suspiciously like startup founders and the processes needed look like Customer Development.

Customer and Agile Development (and the Lean Startup) may be the emerging methodologies large companies need to build innovative new products.

Lessons Learned

- Innovation in large companies come in two forms: sustaining and disruptive.

- Disruptive innovation in a large company may require processes and individuals that look a lot like those in a startup.

- Customer and Agile Development may be the methodologies that large companies need to build innovative new products.

Job Titles That Can Sink Your Startup

September 13, 2010 (Steve Blank)

I had coffee with an ex student earlier in the week that reminded me yet again why startups burn through so many early VPs. And after 30 years of venture investing, we still have a hard time articulating why.

Here's one possible explanation: job titles in a startup mean something different than titles in a large company.

You Can't Always Get What You Want

I hadn't seen Rajiv in the two years since he started his second company. He had raised a seed round and then a Series A from a name brand Venture firm. I was glad to see him but it was clear over coffee that he was struggling with his first hiring failure. "I've been running our company, cycling through Customer Discovery and Validation and the board suggested that I was running out of bandwidth and needed some help in closing our initial orders. They suggested I get a VP of Sales to help."

It was deja vu all over again. I knew where this conversation was going. "Let me guess, your VCs helped you find a recruiter?"

"Yeah, and they were great. They helped me hire the best VP of Sales I could find. The recruiter verified all the references and he completely checked out. He was in the top one-percent club at (insert the name of your favorite large company here). He's been in sales for almost 15 years."

I listened as he told me the rest of the story. "I thought our new Sales VP would be out in front helping us lead Customer Validation and help us find the Pivot. That was the plan.

We had talked about it in the interview and he said he understood and agreed that's what he would do. Even when we went out to dinner before we hired him he said, he said he read "The Four Steps" and couldn't wait to try this Customer Development stuff."

"So what happened," I asked, although I was betting I could finish the conversation for him (since I had made the same mistake). "Well, he's completely lost at the job. When we ask him to call on a different group of customers all he wants to do is call on the people already in his Rolodex. When a customer throws us out he wants to get on to the next sales call and I want to talk about why we failed. He says great sales people don't do that, they just keep selling. Every time we iterate even a small part of our business model or product he gets upset. When we change the company presentation it takes him days to get up to speed to the smallest change. He's finally told us we got to stop changing everything or else he can't sell. He was supposed to be a great VP of Sales. I'm probably going to fire him and start a search for another one, but what do I do wrong?"

"Nothing," I said. "You got what you asked for. But you didn't get what you need. The problem isn't his, it's yours. You didn't need a VP of Sales, you needed something very different."

Companies Have Titles to Execute a Known Business Model

I offered that in an existing company job titles reflect the way tasks are organized to execute a known business model. For example, the role of "Sales" in an existing company means that:

1. there's a sales team executing

2. a repeatable and scalable business model

3. selling a known product to

4. a well-understood group of customers

5. using a standard corporate presentation

6. with an existing price-list and

7. standard terms, conditions and contract

Therefore the job title "Sales" in an existing company is all about execution around a series of "knowns."

Customer Validation Versus Sales

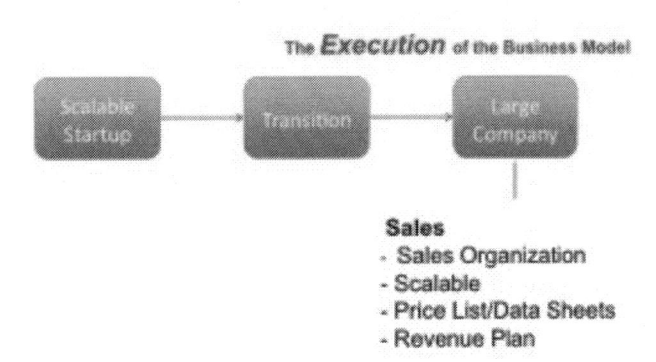

The *Execution* of the Business Model

Scalable Startup → Transition → Large Company

Sales
- Sales Organization
- Scalable
- Price List/Data Sheets
- Revenue Plan

We Use the Same Title for Two Very Different Jobs

I asked Rajiv to go through this checklist. Did he have a repeatable and scalable business model? "No." Did he have a well-understood group of customers? "No." Did he have a standard corporate presentation? "No." etc. Did he and his recruiter say any of this when they put together the job spec or interviewed candidates? "No."

Then why was he surprised the executive he hired wasn't a fit.

Startups Need Different Titles to Search For an Unknown Business Model

In a startup you need executives whose skills are 180 degrees different from what defines success in an existing company. A startup wants execs comfortable in chaos and change—with presentations changing daily, with the product changing daily, talking and with analyzing failure rather than high-fiving a success. In short, you are looking for the rare breed:

1. comfortable with learning and discovery

2. trying to search for a repeatable and scalable business model

3. agile enough to deal with daily change, operating "without a map"

4. with the self-confidence to celebrate failure when it leads to iteration and Pivots

That means the function called Sales used in a large company (and the title that goes with it, "VP of Sales") don't make sense in a startup searching for a business model. Sales implies "execution," but that mindset impedes (majorly screws-up) progress in searching for a business model. Therefore we need a different job function, job title, and different type of person. They would be responsible for Customer Validation and finding Pivots and searching around a series of unknowns. And they would look nothing like his failed VP of Sales.

Customer Validation Versus Sales

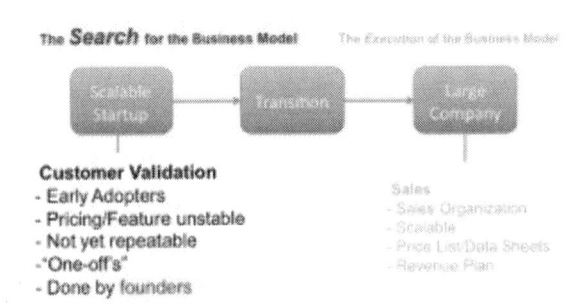

The *Search* for the Business Model | The *Execution* of the Business Model

Scalable Startup → Transition → Large Company

Customer Validation
- Early Adopters
- Pricing/Feature unstable
- Not yet repeatable
- "One-off's"
- Done by founders

Sales
- Sales Organization
- Scalable
- Price List/Data Sheets
- Revenue Plan

I suggested to Rajiv his problem was pretty simple. Since he hadn't yet found a repeatable and scalable business model, his startup did not need a "VP of Sales." The early hire he needed to help him run Customer Validation and Pivots has a very different skill set and job spec. What Rajiv needed to hire was a VP of Customer Development and part ways with his VP of Sales.

I suggested he chat with his investors and see if they agreed. "I hope they don't make me hire another "experienced" VP of Sales," he said as left.

Lessons Learned

- Companies have titles which reflect execution of known business models.

- Early stage startups are still searching for their business model.

- Individuals that excel at execution of a process rarely excel in chaotic environments.

- We burn through early VPs in startups because the job functions we are hiring for are radically different, but we are using the same titles.

- Startups need to use different titles to indicate that the search for a business model requires different skills than executing a business model.

Why Board Meetings Suck—Part 1

June 1, 2011 (Steve Blank)

"There are none so blind as those who will not see."
--Jonathan Swift

What's Wrong With Today's Board Meetings

As customer and agile development reinvent the Startup, it's time to ask why startup board governance has not kept up with the pace of innovation. Board meetings that guide startups haven't changed since the early 1900s.

It's time.

Reinventing the board meeting may offer venture-backed startups a more efficient, productive way to direct and measure their search for a profitable business model.

Reinventing the board meeting may offer angel-funded startups—which because of geography or size of investment typically don't have formal boards or directors—to attract experienced advice and investment outside of technology clusters (i.e., Silicon Valley, New York). Here's how.

Because We've Always Done It This Way

The combination of Venture Capital and technology startups is only about 50 years old. Rather than invent a new form of corporate governance, venture investors adopted the traditional board meeting structure from large corporations. Yet boards of large companies exist to monitor efficient strategy and execution of a known business model. While startups eventually get into execution mode, their initial stages are devoted to a non-linear, chaotic search for a business model: finding product/market fit to identify a product or service people will buy in droves at a sustainable, profitable pace.

In the last few years, our understanding that startups are not smaller versions of large companies, made us recognize that startups need their own tools, different from those used in existing companies: Customer Development —the process to search for a Business Model, the Business Model Canvas —the scorecard to measure progress in the search, and Agile Engineering—the tools to physically construct the product.

Yet while we've reinvented how startups build their companies, startup investors are still having board meetings like it's the 19th century.

Why Have a Board Meeting?

From a VCs point of view, there are two reasons for board meetings:

1) It's their fiduciary responsibility. Once a startup gets going, it has asymmetric information. Investors get board seats to assure themselves and their limited partners that they are duly informed about their investment.

2) Investors believe that their experience and guidance can maximize their return. Here it's the board that has asymmetric knowledge. A veteran board can bring 50- to 100- times more experience into a board meeting than a first time founder. (VCs sit on six to twelve boards at a time. Assume an average tenure of four years per board. Assume two veteran VCs per board equals 50- to 100-times more experience.)

From a founder's point of view, there are three reasons for board meetings:

1) It's an obligation that came with the check.

2) Founders who have a great board do recognize the uncanny pattern recognition skills that good VCs bring.

3) An experienced board brings an extensive network of customers, partners, help in recruiting, follow-on financing, etc.

What's Wrong With a Board Meeting?

The Wrong Metrics. Traditional startup board meetings spend an insane amount of wasted time using Fortune 100 company metrics like income statements, cash flow, balance sheet, waterfall charts. The only numbers in those documents that are important in the first year of a startup's life are burn rate and cash balance. Most board meetings never get past big company metrics to focus on the crucial startup numbers. That's simply a failure of a startup board's fiduciary responsibility.

The Wrong Discussions. The most important advice/guidance that should come from investors in a board meeting is about a startup's search for a business model: What are the business model hypotheses? What are the most important hypotheses to test now? How are we progressing validating each hypothesis? What do those numbers/metrics look like? What are the iterations and Pivots—and why?

Not Real-time. Startup board meetings occur every four to six weeks. While that's great when you showed up in your horse and buggy, the strategy-to-tactic-to implementation lag is painful at Internet speeds. And unless there's rigor in the process, because there is no formal structure for follow up, tracking what happened as a result of meeting recommendations and action items gets lost in the daily demands of everyone's work. (Of course, great VCs mix in coffees, phone calls, coaching and other non-board meeting interactions but it's ad hoc and not always done.)

Wastes Founder's Time. For the founders, "the get ready for the board meeting" drill is often a performance rather than a snapshot. PowerPoints, spreadsheets, and rehearsals consume time for materials that are used once and discarded. There are no standards for what each side (board versus management) does. What is the entrepreneur supposed to be doing? What are the board members supposed to be contributing?

The Wrong Structure. If you read advice on how to run a board meeting you'll get advice that would have felt comfortable to Andrew Carnegie or John D. Rockefeller.

In the age of the Internet why do we need to get together in one room on a fixed schedule? Why do we need to wait a month to six weeks to see progress? Why don't we have standards for what metrics VCs want to see from their early stage startup teams?

Angels in America

For angel-funded startups, life is even tougher. Data from the Startup Genome project shows that startups that have helpful mentors, listen to customers, and learn from startup thought leaders raise 7-times more money and have 3.5-times better user growth. If you're in a technology cluster like Silicon Valley, you may be able to attract ad hoc advice from experienced investors. But very little of it is formal, and almost none of it approaches the 50 to 100-times experience level of professional investors.

As there's no formal board, most of these angel/investors meetings are over coffees. And lacking a board meeting, there's no formal mechanism to get investor advice. Angel investments in mobile and web apps today are approaching the "throw it against the wall and see if it sticks" strategy.

And for startups outside of technology clusters, there's almost no chance of attracting Silicon Valley VCs or angels. Geography is a barrier to investment.

So given all this, the million dollar question is: Why in the age of the Internet haven't we adopted the tools we build/sell to solve these problems?

Lessons Learned

- Early stage board meetings are often clones of large company board meetings. That's very, very wrong.

- Angel-funded startups have no formal mechanism for experienced advice. There's a better way.

Reinventing the Board Meeting—Part 2 of 2—Virtual Valley Ventures

June 2, 2011 (Steve Blank)

"There is nothing more powerful than an idea whose time has come."
—Victor Hugo

When the Boardroom Is Bits

A revolution has taken hold as customer development and agile engineering reinvent the Startup process. It's time to ask why startup board governance has failed to keep pace with innovation. Board meetings that guide startups haven't changed since the early 1900s.

It's time for a change.

Reinventing the board meeting may allow venture-backed startups a more efficient, productive way to direct and measure their search for a profitable business model.

Reinventing the board meeting may offer angel-funded startups that don't have formal boards or directors (because of geography or size of investment) to attract experienced advice and investment outside of technology clusters (i.e. Silicon Valley, New York).

Here's how.

A Hypothesis—The Boardroom As Bits

Startups now understand what they should be doing in their early formative days is search for a business model. The process they use to guide their search is Customer Development. And to track their progress startups now have a scorecard to document their week-by-week changes—the business model canvas.

Yet even with all these tools, early stage startups still need to physically meet with advisors and investors. That's great if you can get it. But what if you can't?

What's missing is a way to communicate all this complex information and get feedback and guidance for startups that cannot get advice in a formal board meeting.

We propose that early stage startups communicate in a way that didn't exist in the 20th century—online—collaboratively through blogs.

We suggest that the founders/CEO invest one hour a week providing advisors and investors with "Continuous Information Access" by blogging and discussing their progress online in their startup's search for a business model. They would:

- Blog their Customer Development progress as a narrative
- Keep score of the strategy changes with the Business Model Canvas
- Comment/Dialog with advisors and investors on a near-real time basis

What Does This Change?

1) Structure. Founders operate in a chaotic regime. So it's helpful to have a structure that helps "search" for a business model. The "boardroom as bits" uses Customer Development as the process for the search, and the business model canvas the scorecard to keep track of the progress, while providing a common language for the discussion.

This approach offers VCs and Angels a semi-formal framework for measuring progress and offering their guidance in the "search" for a business model. It turns ad hoc startups into strategy-driven startups.

2) Asynchronous Updates. Interaction with advisors and board members can now be decoupled from the—once every six weeks, "big event"—board meeting. Now, as soon as the founders post an update, everyone is notified. Comments, help, suggestions and conversation can happen 24/7. For startups with formal boards, it makes it easy to implement, track, and follow-up board meeting outcomes.

3) Monitoring and guiding a small angel investment no longer requires the calculus to decide whether the investment is worth a board commitment. It potentially encourages investors who would invest only if they had more visibility but where the small number of dollars doesn't justify the time commitment. A board as bits ends the repetition of multiple investor coffees. It's highly time-efficient for investor and founder alike.

4) 3) Coaching. This approach allows real-time monitoring of a startup's progress and zero- lag for coaching and course-correction. It's not just a way to see how they're doing. It also provides visibility for a deep look at their data over time and facilitates delivery of feedback and advice.

5) 4) Geography. When the boardroom is bits, angel-funded startups can get experienced advice—independent of geography. An angel investor or VC can multiply their reach and/or depth. In the process it reduces some of the constraints of distance as a barrier to investment.

Imagine if a VC took $4 million (an average Series A investment) and instead spread it across 40 deals at $100,000 each in a city with a great outward-facing technology university outside of Silicon Valley. In the past they had no way to monitor and manage these investments. Now they can. The result—an instant technology cluster—with equity at a fraction of Silicon Valley prices. It might be possible to create Virtual Valley Ventures.

We Ran the Experiment
At Stanford our Lean LaunchPad class ran an experiment that showed when "the boardroom is bits" can make a radical difference in the outcome of an early stage startup.

Our students used Customer Development as the process to search for a business model. They used a blog to record their customer learning, and their progress and issues. The blog became a narrative of the search by posting customer interviews, surveys, videos, and prototypes. They used the Business Model Canvas as a scorekeeping device to chart their progress. The result invited comment from their "board" of the teaching team.

Here are some examples of how rich the interaction can become when a management team embraces the approach.

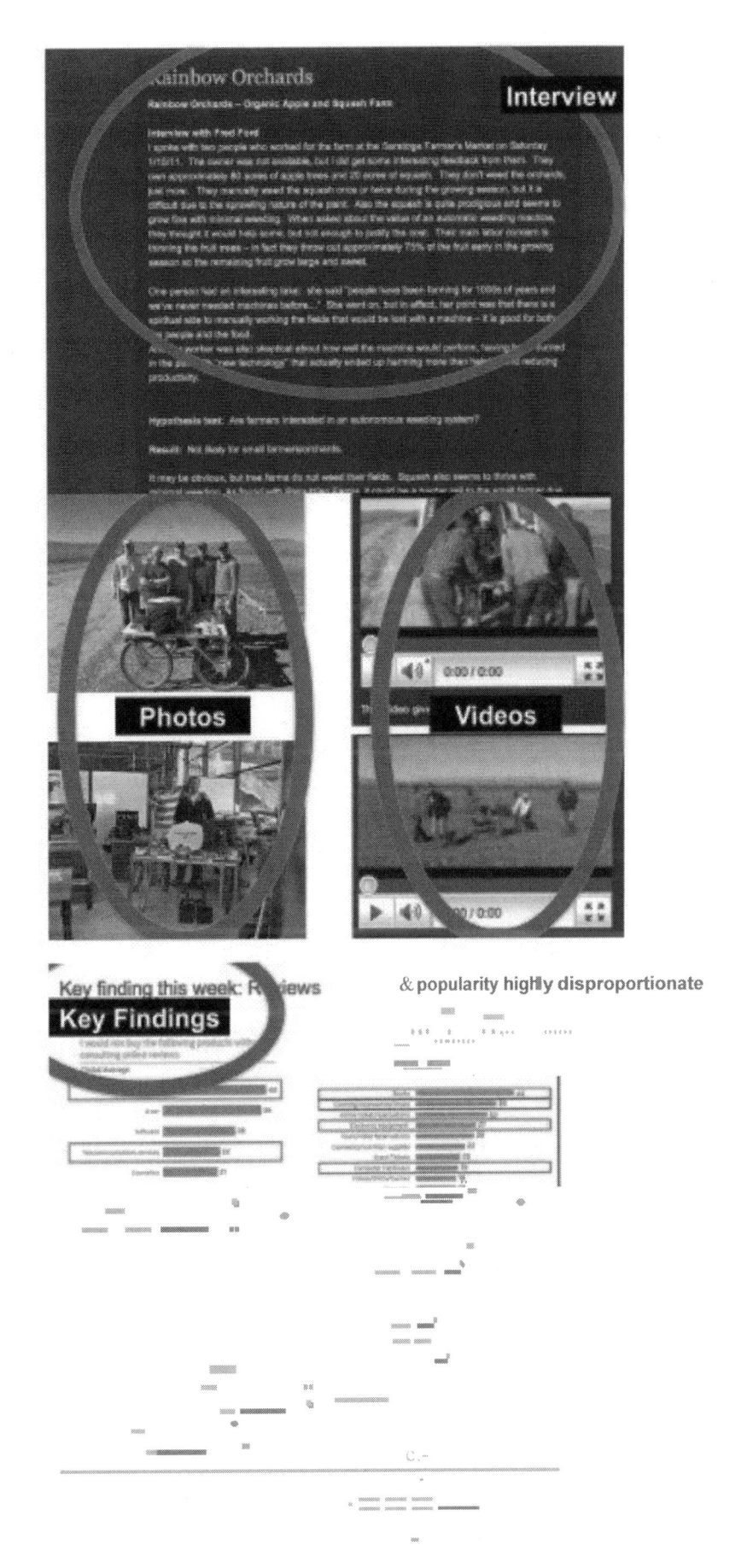

Posting credit: Ian

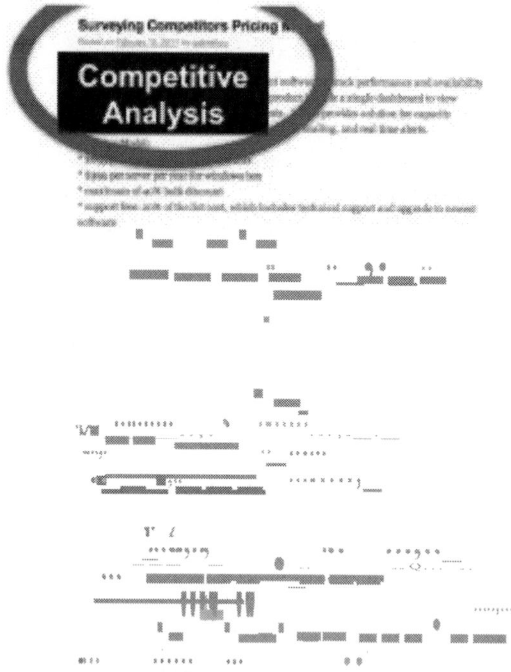
Competitive Analysis

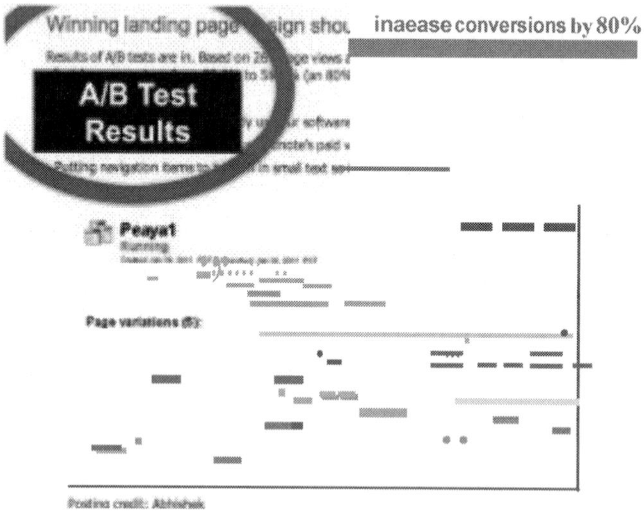
A/B Test Results
Page variations (5):
Posting credit: Abhishek

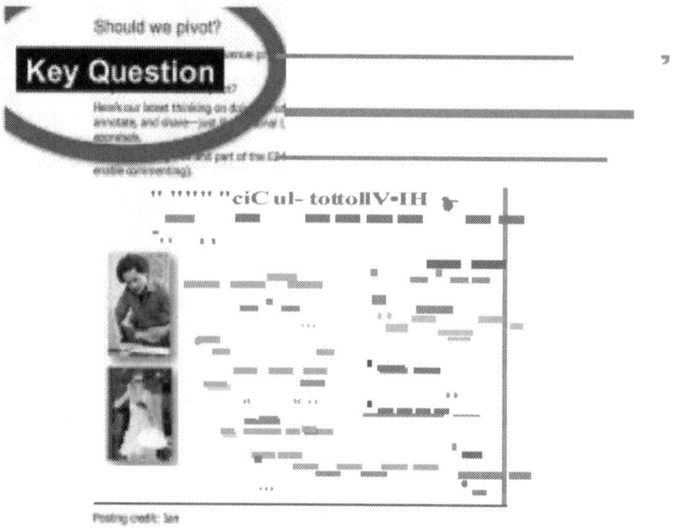
Should we pivot?
Key Question

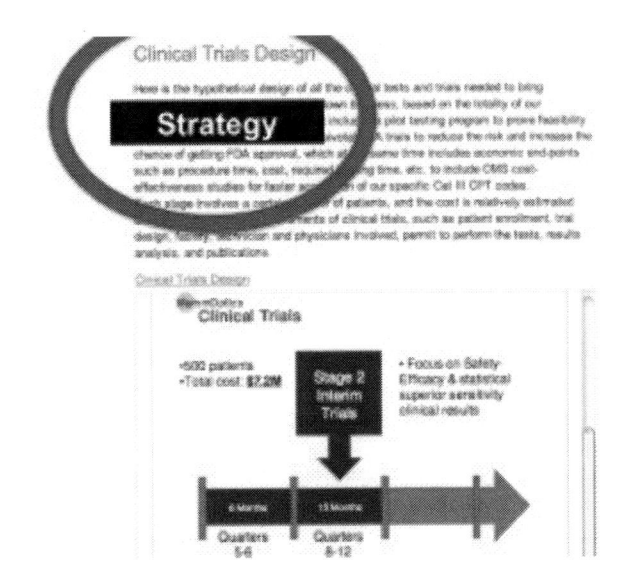

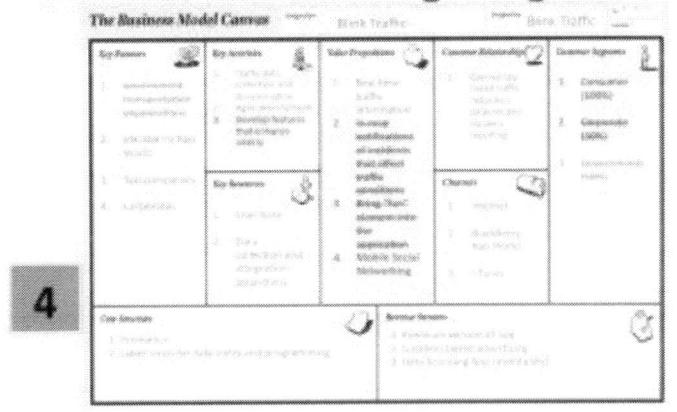

We were able to give them near real-time feedback as they posted their results. If we had been a board rather than a teaching team we would have added physical reality checks with Skype and/or face-to-face meetings.

Show Me the Money

While this worked in the classroom, would it work in the real world? I thought this idea was crazy enough to bounce off five experienced Silicon Valley VCs. I was surprised at the reaction—all of them want to experiment with it. Jon Feiber at MDV is going to try investing in startups emerging from Universities with great engineering schools outside of Silicon Valley that have entrepreneurship programs, but minimal venture capital infrastructure. (The University of Michigan is a possible first test.) Kathryn Gould of Foundation Capital and Ann Miura-Ko of Floodgate also want to try it.

Shawn Carolan of Menlo Ventures not only thought the idea had merit but seed-funded the Lean LaunchLab, a startup building software to automate and structure this process.

(More than 700 startups signed up for the Lean LaunchPad software the day it was first demoed.) Other entrepreneurs think this is an idea whose time has come and are also building software to manage their process, including Alexander Osterwalder, Groupiter, and Angelsoft. Citrix thought this was such a good idea that their Startup Accelerator has offered to provide GoToMeeting and GoToMeeting HDFaces free to participating VCs and startups.

Summary

For startups with traditional boards, I am not suggesting replacing the board meeting—just augmenting it with a more formal, interactive and responsive structure to help guide the search for the business model. There's immense value in face-to-face interaction. You can't replace body language.

But for Angel-funded companies I am proposing that a "board meeting in bits" can dramatically change the odds of success. Not only does this approach provide a way for founders to "show your work" to potential and current investors and advisors, but also it helps expand opportunities to attract investors from outside the local area.

Lessons Learned

- Startups are a search for a business model

- Startups can share their progress/get feedback in the search

- Weekly blog of the customer development narrative

- Weekly summary of the business model canvas

- Interactive comments and questions

- Skype and face-to-face when needed

- This may be a way to augment traditional board meetings

- This might be a way to rethink our notion of geography as a barrier to investments

Why Governments Don't Get Startups

September 1, 2011 (Steve Blank)

Not understanding and agreeing what "Entrepreneur" and "Startup" mean can sink an entire country's entrepreneurial ecosystem.

I'm getting ready to go overseas to teach, and I've spent the last week reviewing several countries' ambitious attempts to kick-start entrepreneurship. After poring through stacks of reports, white papers and position papers, I've come to a couple of conclusions:

1) They sure killed a ton of trees.

2) With one noticeable exception, governmental entrepreneurship policies and initiatives appear to be less than optimal, with capital deployed inefficiently (read "They would have done better throwing the money in the street.") Why? Because they haven't defined the basics:

What's a startup? Who's an entrepreneur? How do the ecosystems differ for each one? What's the role of public versus private funding?

Six Types of Startups—Pick One

There are six distinct organizational paths for entrepreneurs: lifestyle business, small business, scalable startup, buyable startup, large company, and social entrepreneur. All of the individuals who start these organizations are "entrepreneurs" yet not understanding their differences screws up public policy because the ecosystem in supporting each type is radically different.

For policy makers, the first order of business is to methodically think through which of these entrepreneurial paths they want to help and grow.

Lifestyle Startups: Work to Live Their Passion

On the California coast where I live, we see lifestyle entrepreneurs like surfers and divers who own small surf or dive shop or teach surfing and diving lessons to pay the bills so they can surf and dive some more. A lifestyle entrepreneur is living the life they love, works for no one but themselves, while pursuing their personal passion. In Silicon Valley the equivalent is the journeyman coder or web designer who loves the technology, and takes coding and U/I jobs because it's a passion.

Small Business Startups: Work to Feed the Family

Today, the overwhelming number of entrepreneurs and startups in the United States are still small businesses. There are 5.7 million small businesses in the U.S. They make up 99.7 percent of all companies and employ 50 percent of all non-governmental workers.

Small businesses are grocery stores, hairdressers, consultants, travel agents, Internet commerce storefronts, carpenters, plumbers, electricians, etc. They are anyone who runs his/her own business.

They work as hard as any Silicon Valley entrepreneur. They hire local employees or family. Most are barely profitable. Small business entrepreneurship is not designed for scale, the owners want to own their own business and "feed the family." The only capital available to them is their own savings, bank and small business loans and what they can borrow from relatives. Small business entrepreneurs don't become billionaires and (not coincidentally) don't make many appearances on magazine covers. But in sheer numbers, they are infinitely more representative of "entrepreneurship" than entrepreneurs in other categories—and their enterprises create local jobs.

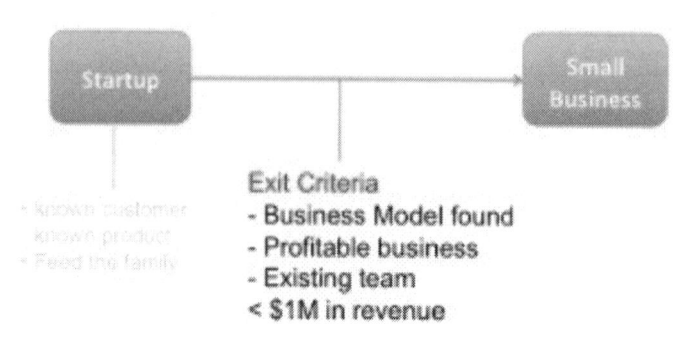

Startup → Small Business

- known customer
- known product
- Feed the family

Exit Criteria
- Business Model found
- Profitable business
- Existing team
- < $1M in revenue

216

Scalable Startups: Born to Be Big

Scalable startups are what Silicon Valley entrepreneurs and their venture investors aspire to build. Google, Skype, Facebook, Twitter are just the latest examples. From day one, the founders believe that their vision can change the world. Unlike small business entrepreneurs, their interest is not in earning a living but rather in creating equity in a company that eventually will become publicly traded or acquired, generating a multi-million-dollar payoff.

Scalable startups require risk capital to fund their search for a business model, and they attract investment from equally crazy financial investors—venture capitalists. They hire the best and the brightest. Their job is to search for a repeatable and scalable business model. When they find it, their focus on scale requires even more venture capital to fuel rapid expansion.

Scalable startups tend to group together in innovation clusters (Silicon Valley, Shanghai, New York, Boston, Israel, etc.). They make up a small percentage of the six types of startups, but, because of the outsize returns, attract all the risk capital (and press).

Just in the last few years, we've come to see that we had been building scalable startups inefficiently. Investors (and educators) treated startups as smaller versions of large companies. We now understand that's just not true. While large companies execute known business models, startups are temporary organizations designed to search for a scalable and repeatable business model.

This insight has begun to change how we teach entrepreneurship, incubate startups, and fund them.

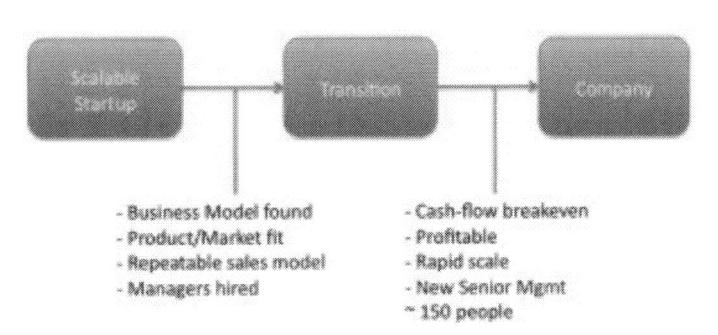

Scalable Startup → Transition → Company

- Business Model found
- Product/Market fit
- Repeatable sales model
- Managers hired

- Cash-flow breakeven
- Profitable
- Rapid scale
- New Senior Mgmt
- ~150 people

Buyable Startups: Born to Flip

In the last five years, web and mobile app startups that are founded to be sold to larger companies have become popular. The plummeting cost required to build a product, the radically reduced time to bring a product to market and the availability of angel capital willing to invest in less than a traditional VCs--$100,000 to $1 million versus $4 million on up—has allowed these companies to proliferate—and their investors to make money. Their goal is not to build a billion dollar business, but to be sold to a larger company for $5 million to $50 million.

Large Company Startups: Innovate or Evaporate

Large companies have finite life cycles. And over the last decade those cycles have grown shorter. Most grow through sustaining innovation, offering new products that are variants around their core products. Changes in customer tastes, new technologies, legislation, new competitors, etc. can create pressure for more disruptive innovation—requiring large companies to create entirely new products sold to new customers in new markets. (i.e. Google and Android). Existing companies do this by either acquiring innovative companies or attempting to build a disruptive product internally. Ironically, large company size and culture make disruptive innovation extremely difficult to execute.

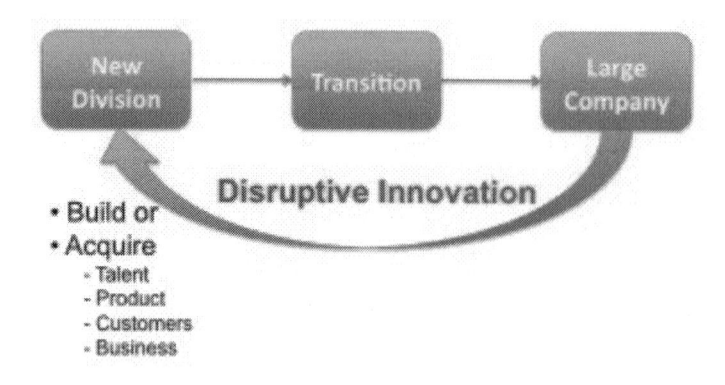

Social Startups: Driven to Make a Difference

Social entrepreneurs are no less ambitious, passionate, or driven to make an impact than any other type of founder. But unlike scalable startups, their goal is to make the world a better place, not to take market share or to create to wealth for the founders. They may be organized as a nonprofit, a for-profit, or hybrid.

So What?

When I read policy papers by government organizations trying to replicate the lessons from the valley, I'm struck how they seem to miss some basic lessons.

- Each of these six very different startups requires very different ecosystems, unique educational tools, economic incentives (tax breaks, paperwork/regulation reduction, incentives), incubators and risk capital.

- Regions building a cluster around scalable startups fail to understand that a government agency simply giving money to entrepreneurs who want it is an exercise in failure. It is not a "jobs program" for the local populace. Any attempt to make it so dooms it to failure.

- A scalable startup ecosystems is the ultimate capitalist exercise. It is not an exercise in "fairness" or patronage. While it's a meritocracy, it takes equal parts of risk, greed, vision and obscene financial returns. And those can only thrive in a regional or national culture that supports an equal mix of all those.

- Building a scalable startup innovation cluster requires an ecosystem of private not government-run incubators and venture capital firms, outward-facing universities, and a rigorous startup selection process.

- Any government that starts public financing entrepreneurship better have a plan to get out of it by building a private VC industry. If they're still publically funding startups after five to ten years they've failed.

To date, Israel is only country that has engineered a successful entrepreneurship cluster from the ground up. Its Yozma program kick-started a private venture capital industry with government funds (emulating the U.S. lesson of using SBIC funds), but then the government got out of the way.

In addition, the Israeli government originally funded 23 early stage incubators but turned them over to the VCs to own and manage. They're run by business professionals (not real-estate managers looking to rent out excess office space) and entry is not for lifestyle entrepreneurs but is a boot camp for VC funding.

Unless the people who actually make policy understand the difference between the types of startups and the ecosystem necessary to support their growth, the chance that any government policies will have a substantive effect on innovation, jobs or the gross domestic product is low.

How the iPhone Got Tail Fins
—Part 1 of 2

October 18, 2011 (Steve Blank)

It was the most advanced consumer product of the century. The industry started with its innovators located in different cities over a wide region. But within 20 years it would be concentrated in a single entrepreneurial startup cluster. At first it was a craft business, then it was driven by relentless technology innovation and then a price war as economies of scale drove efficiencies in production. When the market was finally saturated the industry reinvented itself again—one company discovered how to turn commodity products into "needs."

They opened retail outlets across the country and figured out how to convince consumers to flock to buy the newest "gotta have it" version and abandon the perfectly functional last year's model.

No, it's not Apple and the iPhone.

It was General Motors and the auto industry.

In the Beginning

At the beginning of the 20th century the auto industry was still a small hand-crafted manufacturing business. Cars were assembled from outsourced components by crews of skilled mechanics and unskilled helpers. They were sold at high prices and profits through non-exclusive distributors for cash on delivery. But by 1901, Ransom Olds invented the basic concept of the assembly line and in the next decade was quickly followed by other innovators who opened large scale manufacturing plants in Detroit—Henry Packard, Henry Leland's Cadillac, and Henry Ford with the Model A.

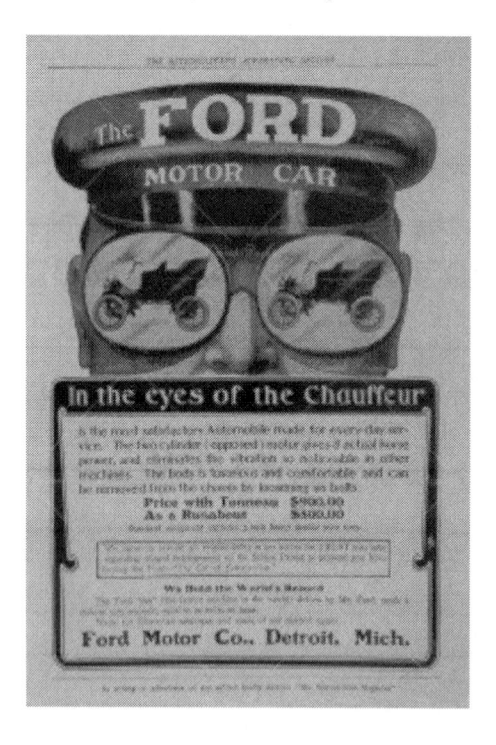

The Detroit area quickly became the place to be if you were making cars, parts for cars, or were a skilled machinist. By 1913, Ford's first conveyor belt-driven moving assembly line and standardized interchangeable parts forever cemented Detroit as the home of 20th-century auto manufacturing.

Feature Wars

The automobile industry was founded and run by technologists: Henry Ford, James Packard, Charles Kettering, Henry Leland, the Dodge Brothers, Ransom Olds. The first 25 years of the century were a blur of technology innovation—moving assembly line, steel bodies, quick dry paint, electric starters, etc. These men built a product that solved a problem—private transportation first for the elite, and then (Ford's inspiration)—transportation for the masses.

Market Saturation

Ford tried to escape the never-ending technology feature wars by becoming the low cost manufacturer. Fords River Rouge manufacturing complex—93 buildings in a 1-by-1.5-mile manufacturing complex, with 100,000 workers—vertically integrated and optimized mass production.

By 1923, through a series of continuous process improvements, Ford had used the cost advantages of economies of scale to drive down the price of the Model T automobile to $290.

When the 1920s began, there were close to a 100 car manufacturers, but the relentless drive for low cost production forced most of them out of business as they lacked capital to scale. For a brief moment, half the cars in the world were now Fords. To make matters worse, the long service life of Ford and GM cars (eight years for Ford's Model T, six years for everyone else) retarded sales of new cars. In 20 years, U.S. car ownership had risen from 0 to 80-percent of American families—the market was approaching saturation.

Now cars would have to be sold almost entirely to people who already owned a car.

The Crazy Entrepreneur

After success as a leading manufacturer of horse-drawn carriages, Billy Durant was one of the few who saw the writing on the wall and got into the car business.

Although he wasn't a technologist, he was an entrepreneur with a great eye for acquiring car companies run by technologists. His keen insight was that several carmakers combined under one company umbrella would have more growth potential than one brand on its own. Like most founders, he was great at searching for a business model but terrible at in large company execution. When his board fired him, Durant bought a competing company called Chevrolet, built it larger than his last company, and used Chevy stock to buy out his old company—General Motors—and threw out the board. Yet a few years later under his brilliant but reckless leadership GM was again on the brink of financial disaster and his new board fired him. (Durant would die penniless managing a bowling alley.)

Durant's ultimate replacement—an accountant named Alfred P. Sloan— would turn GM into the leading and most admired company in the U.S.

Relentless

Over the next decade Sloan would implement a series of innovations that would last for over half a century. And catapult General Motors from the number-two car company (with a quarter of Ford's sales) into the market leader for the next 100 years. Here's what he did:

Distributed Accounting: Unlike Ford, GM was originally a collection of separate companies. Distributed Accounting turned those fiefdoms into product divisions each of which, could be focused like Ford's mass-produced lines. But Sloan went further. He figured out how to centralize financial oversight of decentralized product lines. His CFO created standardized division sales reports and flexible accounting, and allocated resources and bonuses to the GM divisions by a uniform set of rules. It allowed GM to be ruthlessly efficient internally as well with its dealers and suppliers. It got the division general managers to fall in line with corporate goals but allowed them to run their divisions freely. GM became the prototype of the modern multidivisional company.

Car Financing: Realizing that Ford would only accept cash for car purchases, in 1919 GM formed GMAC to provide new car buyers a way to finance their purchases through debt.

Consumer Research: Ever since his days at Hyatt Roller Bearing, Sloan, and by extension GM, was relentless about getting out of the building—they had an entire department that studied consumers, dealers, suppliers. More importantly, Sloan led by example. He visited dealers and suppliers, listened to customers and was tied tightly to his head of R&D Charles Kettering.

All this would have made General Motors a well-run and well-managed company. But what they did next would make them the dominant company in the U.S. and eventually put tail-fins on the iPhone.

How the iPhone Got Tail Fins
—Part 2 of 2

October 20, 2011 (Steve Blank)

By the early 1920's General Motors realized that Ford, which was now selling the Model T for $290, had an unbeatable monopoly on low-cost automobile manufacturing. Other manufacturers had experimented with selling cars based on an image and brand. (The most notable was an ad by the Jordan Car company. But General Motors was about to take consumer marketing of cars to an entirely new level.

Market Segmentation General Motors had turned the independent car companies acquired by its founder Billy Durant into product divisions. But in a stroke of genius GM transformed these divisions into a weapon that Ford couldn't match. With the rallying cry "a car for every purse and purpose," GM positioned its car divisions (Chevrolet, Pontiac, Oldsmobile, Buick and Cadillac) so they would cover five price segments—from low-price to luxury. It targeted each of its brands (and models inside those brands) to a distinct economic segment of the population. Chevy was directly aimed at Ford—the volume car for the working masses. Pontiac came next, then Oldsmobile, then Buick. The top-of- the- line Cadillac offered luxury and prestige announcing you had finally arrived at the top of the conspicuous consumption heap. Consumers could announce their status and lives had improved by upgrading their brands.

GM had one more trick to make this happen. Within each brand, the top of the line was just a bit less expensive than the lowest priced model of the next expensive brand. The goal was to convince the consumer to spend a little more to trade up to a more prestigious brand.

Market segmentation by price was something no other automotive manufacturer had ever done. While other car companies could compete with one of GM's divisions, few had GM's capital and resources to compete simultaneously with the onslaught of car models from all five divisions.

Planned Obsolescence While market segmentation allowed GM to use its divisions to reach a wider market than Ford or Chrysler, this didn't solve the problem of market saturation. By the late 1920's, most everyone in the U.S. had a car. And cars lasted 6 to 8 years. Even worse, the market was now filled with used cars that provided even lower cost basic transportation. Sloan, the General Motors CEO, faced two seemingly unsolvable challenges:

- How do you get consumers to abandon their perfectly fine cars and buy a new one?

- How do you turn a product that competed on price and features into a need?

In another stroke of genius, GM invented the annual model change. Sloan borrowed this idea from fashion where styles changed every year and applied it to automobiles starting in the 1920s. General Motors would change the external appearance of cars every year. Sloan preferred to call it "dynamic obsolescence."

Styling and design became an integral part of GM's strategy. Sloan hired Harley Earl to set up GM's in-house styling staff. Earl would run it from 1927 to 1958.

Before Earl, cars were designed by in-house body-engineers who focused on practical issues like function, costs, features, etc. Each exterior component was designed separately to be functional—radiator, bumpers, hood, passenger compartment, etc. Some companies used third-party bodymakers to set the style, but GM was the first to take car design away from the engineers and give it to the stylists.

The concept of yearly "improvements," whether styling or incremental technology improvements, every model year gave GM an unbeatable edge in the market. (Henry Ford hated the idea. He had built Ford on economies of scale—the Ford Model T lasted for 19 years.) Smaller car makers could not afford the constant engineering and styling changes they had to make to keep competitive. GM would shut down all their manufacturing plants for a few months and literally rip out the tooling, jigs and dies in every plant and replace them with the equipment needed to make the next year's model.

GM had figured out how to take a product which solved a problem—cheap transportation—and transform it into a need. It was marketing magic that wasn't to be equaled until the next century.

By the mid-1950s, every other car company was struggling to keep up.

Mass Marketing Starting in the 1920's and continuing for the next half century, automobile advertising hit its stride. Ads emphasized brand identification and appealed to consumers' hunger for prestige and status. Advertising agencies created catchy slogans and jingles, and celebrities endorsed their favorite brands. General Motors turned market segmentation and the annual model year changeovers into national events. As the press speculated about new features, the company added to the mystique by guarding the new designs with military secrecy. Consumers counted the days until the new models were "unveiled" at their dealers.

Results

For fifty years, until the Japanese imports of the 1970s, Americans talked about the brand and model year of your car—was it a '58 Chevy, '65 Mustang, or '58 Eldorado? Each had its particular cachet, status and admirers. People had heated arguments about who made the best brand.

The car had become part of your personal identity while it became a symbol of 20th Century America.

After Sloan took over General Motors, its share of U.S cars sold skyrocketed from 12 percent in 1920, until it passed Ford in 1930, and when Sloan retired as GM's CEO in 1956, half the cars sold in the U.S. were made by GM. It would keep that 50-percent share for another 10 years. (Today, GM's share of cars total sold in the U.S. has declined to 19-percent.)

How the iPhone Got Tail Fins

Over the last five years Apple has adopted the GM playbook from the 1920s—take a product, which originally solved a problem—cheap communication—and turn it into a need.

In doing so, Apple did to Nokia and RIM what General Motors did to Ford. In both cases, innovation in marketing completely negated these firms' strengths in reducing costs. The iPhone transformed the cell phone from a device for cheap communication into a touchstone about the user's image. Just like cars in the 20th century, the iPhone connected with its customers emotionally and viscerally as it became a symbol of who you are.

The desire to line up to buy the newest iPhone when your old one works just fine was just one more part of Steve Jobs' genius—it's how the iPhone got tail fins.

It's one more reason why Steve Jobs will be remembered as the 21st-century version of Alfred P. Sloan.

V.

Startup Culture

Preparing for Chaos —the Life of a Startup

April 29, 2009 (Steve Blank)

I just finished reading Donovan Campbell's eye-opening book, "Joker One," about his harrowing combat tour in Iraq leading a Marine platoon. This book may be the Iraq war equivalent of "Dispatches" which defined Vietnam for my generation. (Both reminded me why National Service would be a very good idea.)

Campbell describes how he tried to instill in his troops the proper combat mentality. I've paraphrased his speech into the language of a startup. It's eerily similar.

Startups are inherently chaos. As a founder you need to prepare yourself to think creatively and independently, because more often than not, conditions on the ground will change so rapidly that the original well-thought-out business plan becomes irrelevant.

If you can't manage chaos and uncertainty, if you can't bias yourself for action and if you wait around for someone else to tell you what to do, then your investors and competitors will make your decisions for you and you will run out of money and your company will die.

Therefore the best way to keep your company alive is to instill in every employee a decisive mindset that can quickly separate the crucial from the irrelevant, synthesize the output, and use this intelligence to create islands of order in the all-out chaos of a startup.

Every potential startup founder should think about their level of comfort operating in chaos and uncertainty. It may not be for you.

Faith-Based Versus Fact-Based Decision Making

June 5, 2009 (Steve Blank)

I've screwed up a lot of startups on faith.

One of the key tenets of entrepreneurship is that you start your company with insufficient resources and knowledge.

Faith-Based Entrepreneurship

At first, entrepreneurship is a Faith-based initiative. There is no certainty about a startup on day-one. You make several first order approximations about your business model, distribution channels, demand creation, and customer acceptance. You leave the comfort of your existing job, convince a few partners to join you and you jump off the bridge together.

At each startup I couldn't wait to do this. No building, no money, no customers, no market? Great, sign me up. We'll build something from scratch.

You start a company on a vision; on a series of Faith-based hypotheses.

Fact-Based Execution

However, successfully executing a startup requires the company to become Fact-based as soon as it can.

Think about all the assumptions you've made to get your business off the ground. Who are the customers? What problems do they have? What are their most important problems? How much would they pay to solve them? What's the best way to tell them about our product?...

Ad infinitum. These customer and market risks need to be translated into facts as soon as possible. You can blindly continue to execute on faith that your hypotheses are correct. You'll ship your product and you'll find out if you were wrong when you run out of money.

Or you can quickly get out of the building and test whether your hypotheses were correct and turn them into facts.

In hindsight, when I was young, this where I went wrong. It's a lot more comfortable to hang on to your own beliefs than to get (or face) the facts. Because at times facts may create cognitive dissonance with the beliefs that got you started and funded.

Customer Development

This strategy of starting on faith, and quickly turning them into facts is the core of the Customer Development process.

The Startup Team

December 13, 2011 (Steve Blank)

"Individuals play the game, but teams beat the odds."
– SEAL Team saying

Over the last 40 years, technology investors have learned that the success of startups is not just about the technology, but "it's about the team."

We spent a year screwing it up in our Lean LaunchPad classes until we figured out it was about having the right team.

Startup Team Lessons Learned

During the last 12 months, we've taught 42 entrepreneurial teams with 147 students at Stanford, Berkeley, Columbia, and the National Science Foundation. (As many teams as most startup incubators.)

Get Into the Class

When I first started teaching hands-on, project/team entrepreneurship classes we'd take anyone who would apply. After awhile it became clear that by not providing an interview process we were doing these students a disservice. A good number of them just wanted an overview of what a startup was like—an entrepreneurial appreciation class (and we offer some great ones). But some of our students hadn't yet developed a passion for entrepreneurship and had no burning idea that they wanted to bring to market. Yet in class they'd be thrown into a "made up in the first week" startup team and got dragged along as a spear-carrier for someone else's vision.

Step One—Set a Bar

So as a first step we made students formally apply and interview for the Lean LaunchPad class. We were looking for entrepreneurs who had great ideas and interest in making those ideas really happen. We'd hold mixers before the first class and the students would form their teams during week one of the class.

But we found we were wasting a week or more as the teams formed and their ideas gelled.

Step Two—Apply As A Team

So next time we taught, we had the students apply to the class as a team. We hold information sessions a month or more before the classes. Here students with pre-formed teams could come and have an interview with the teaching team and get admitted. Or those looking to find other students to join their team could mix and market their ideas or join others and then interview for a spot. This process moved the team logistics out of class time and provided us with more time for teaching.

But we had been selecting teams for admission on the basis of whether they had the best ideas. We should have known better. In the classroom, as in startups, the best ideas in the hands of a B team is worse than a B idea in the hands of a world class team. Here's why:

Step Three— Hacker/Hardware/Huster, Designer, Visionary

As we taught our Lean LaunchPad classes we painfully relearned the lesson that team composition matters as much or more than the product idea. And that teams matter as much in entrepreneurial classes as they do in startups.

In a perfect world you build your vision and your customers would run to buy your first product exactly as you spec'd and built it. We now know that this "build it and they will come" is a prayer rather than a business strategy. In reality, a startup is a temporary organization designed to search for a repeatable and scalable business model. This means the brilliant idea you started with will change as you iterate and pivot your business model until you find product/market fit.

The above paragraph is worth reading a few times.

It basically says that a startup team needs to be capable of making sudden and rapid shifts—because it will be wrong a lot. Startups are inherently chaos. Conditions on the ground will change so rapidly that the original well-thought-out business plan becomes irrelevant.

And finding product/market fit in that chaos requires a team with a combination of skills.

What skills? Well it depends on the industry you're in, but generally great technology skills (hacking/hardware/science), great hustling skills (to search for the business model, customers and market), great user facing design (if you're a web/mobile app), and by having long-term vision and product sense. Most people are good at one or maybe two of these, but it's extremely rare to find someone who can wear all the hats.

It's this combination of skills is why most startups are founded by a team, not just one person.

University Silos

While building these teams are hard in the real world, imagine how hard it is in a university with classes organized as silos. Business School classes were only open to business school students. Engineering School classes were only open to engineering school students, etc. No classes could be cross-listed. This meant that you couldn't offer students an accurate simulation of what a startup team would look like. (In our business school classes we had students with great ideas but lacking the technical skills to implement it. And some of our engineering teams could have benefited from a role- model to follow as a hustler.)

So the next time we taught, we managed to ensure that the class was cross-listed and that the student teams had to have a mix of both business and engineering backgrounds.

I think we've finally got the team composition right—relearning all the lessons investors already knew.

Lessons Learned

- Finding product/market fit in startup chaos requires a team with a combination of skills.

- Hacker/Hardware, Hustler, Designer, Visionary.

- At times an A+ market (huge demand, unmet need) may trump all.

The Road Not Taken

July 23, 2009 (Steve Blank)

At Zilog I was figuring out how to cope with job burnout. And one of my conclusions was that I needed to pick one job not two. I had to decide what I wanted to do with my career—go back to ESL, try to work for the Customer, or stay at Zilog?

While it may seem like an easy choice, few people who love technology and who work on blac projects leave. These projects are incredibly seductive. Let me explain why.

National Efforts

In World War II, the U.S. put its resources behind a technical project that dwarfed anything ever built—the atomic bomb. From a standing start in 1942 the U.S. scaled up the production of U-235 and plutonium from micrograms to tens of kilograms by 1945. We built new cities in Hanford, Oak Ridge and Los Alamos and put 130,000 people to work on the project.

During the cold war, the U.S. government kept up the pace. Hundreds of thousands of people worked on developing strategic weapons, bombers, our ICBM and SLBM missile programs, and the Apollo moon program. These programs dwarfed the size that any single commercial company could do by itself. They were national efforts of hundreds of companies employing tens or hundreds of thousands of engineers.

ESL—National Technical Means of Verification

The project I was working on at ESL fit this category. The 1970's and '80's were the endgame of the cold war, and the U.S. military realized that our advantage over the Soviet Union was in silicon, software and systems. These technologies which allowed the U.S. to build sensors, stealth and smart weapons previously thought impossible or impractical, would give us a major military advantage. Building these systems required resources way beyond the scope of a single company. Imagine coming up with an idea that could work only if you had your own semiconductor fab and could dedicate its output to make specialized chips just for you. Then imagine you'd have to get some rockets and put this reconnaissance system in space—no, make that several rockets. No one laughed when ESL proposed this class of project to "the customer."

If you love technology, these projects are hard to walk away from.

The Road Not Taken

At first, I thought my choice was this: working on great technology at ESL or continuing to work on these toy-like microprocessors at Zilog.

But the more I thought about it, the choice wasn't about the hardware or systems. There was something about the energy and passion Zilog's customers had as they kept doing the most unexpected things with our products.

While I couldn't articulate at it at the time (it would take another 25 years) at ESL, the company and the customer had a known problem and were executing to building a known solution, with a set of desired specifications and PERT charts telling them what they needed to do and in what order to achieve the goal. There was a ton of engineering innovation and coordination along the way, and the project could have failed at any point. But the insight and creativity occurred at the project's beginning when the problem and solution was first being defined. Given where I was in the hierarchy, I calculated that the odds of me being in on those decisions didn't look high—ever.

In contrast, my customers at Zilog had nothing more than a set of visions, guesses and hallucinations about their customers; who they were, what they wanted to achieve and what was the right path to get there. At these startups both the problem and solution were unknown.

Startups were not just smaller versions of a large company, they were about invention, innovation and iteration - of business model, product, customers and on and on. Startups were doing discovery of the problem and solution in real-time. I could see myself doing that—soon.

Unbeknownst to me, I was facing a choice between becoming an entrepreneur or working for a large company.

I chose a path and never looked back.

"Two roads diverged in a

yellow wood, And sorry I

could not travel both

And be one traveler, long I stood

And looked down one as

far as I could To where it

bent in the undergrowth;

Then took the other, as just

as fair, And having perhaps

the better claim,

Because it was grassy and

wanted wear; Though as for

that the passing there

Had worn them really about

the same, And both that

morning equally lay

In leaves no step had

trodden black. Oh, I kept

the first for another day!

Yet knowing how way

leads on to way, I doubted if

I should ever come back.

I shall be telling this with a

sigh Somewhere ages and

ages hence: Two roads

diverged in a wood, and

I— I took the one less

traveled by,

And that has made all the difference."

— Robert Frost—The Road Not Taken—1916

Lessons Learned

- There is no "right" choice for a career.
- There's only the choice you make.
- Don't let a "career" just happen to you.
- A startup is not a smaller version of a large company.

The End of Innocence

August 24, 2009 (Steve Blank)

I love TechCrunch. If you're a startup raising money or just want to see your name online, there's not a better blog on the web. Reading this TechCrunch post made me remember the first time I saw someone confront a worldview they didn't expect.

> **TechCrunch**
> August 22, 2009
>
> "When it comes to winning in the App Store, one PR firm has discovered a dynamite strategy: throw ethics out the window."

Discovering that your worldview is wrong or mistaken can be a life-changing event. It's part of growing up but can happen at any age. What you do when it happens shapes who you'll become.

Dinner in a Strange Land

When I was in my mid 20s working at ESL, I was sent overseas to a customer site where the customers were our three-letter intelligence agencies. All of us knew who they were, understood how important this site was for our country, and proud of the work we were doing. (Their national technical means of verification made the world a safer place and hastened the end of the Soviet Union and the Cold War.)

As a single guy, I got to live in a motel-like room on the site while the married guys lived in town in houses and tried to blend in with the locals. When asked what they did, they said they worked at "the xx research facility." (Of course the locals translated that to "oh do you work for the yyy or zzz intelligence agency?")

One warm summer evening I got invited over to the house of a married couple from my company for a BBQ and after-dinner entertainment—drinking mass quantities of the local beer. The quintessential California couple, they stood out in our crowd as the engineer (in his late 20s, respected by his peers and the customer) had hair down to his shoulders, sharply contrasting with the military crew cuts of the customers and most of the other contractors.

His wife, about my age, could have been a poster child for the stereotypical California hippie surfer, with politics that matched her style—anti-war, anti-government, anti- establishment.

One of the rules in the business was that you didn't tell your spouse, girlfriend, significant other who you worked for or what you worked on—ever. It was always a welcome change of pace to leave the brown of the unchanging desert and travel into town and have dinner with them and have a non-technical conversation about books, theater, politics, travel, etc. But it was a bit incongruous to hear her get wound up and rail against our government and the very people we were all working for. Her husband would look at me out the corner of his eyes and then we'd segue the conversation to some other topic.

That evening I was there with three other couples cooking over the barbie in their backyard. After night fell we reconvened in their living room as we continued to go through the local beer. The conversation happened to hit on politics and culture, and my friend's wife innocently offered up she had lived in a commune in California. Well that created a bit of alcohol-fueled cross-cultural disconnect and heated discussion.

Until one of the other wives changed a few lives forever with a slip of the tongue.

Tell Me It Isn't True

One of the other wives asked, "Well what would your friends in the commune think of you now that your husband is working for intelligence agencies x and y?"

As soon as the words came out of her mouth, I felt time slow down. The other couples laughed for about half a second expecting my friend's wife to do so as well. But instead the look on her face went from puzzlement in processing the question, to concentration, as she was thinking and correlating past questions she had about who exactly her husband had been working for. It seemed like forever before she asked with a look of confusion, "What do you mean agencies x and y?"

The laughter in the room stopped way too soon, and the room got deathly quiet. Her face slowly went from a look of puzzlement to betrayal to horror as she realized that that the drunken silence, the dirty looks from other husbands to the wife who made the agency comment, and the wives now staring at their shoes was an answer.

She had married someone who never told her who he was really working for. She was living in a lie with people she hated. In less than a minute, her entire worldview had shattered and coming apart in front of us, she started screaming.

This probably took no more than 10 seconds, but watching her face, it felt like hours.

I don't remember how we all got out of the house or how I got back to the site, but to this day I still remember standing on her lawn staring at strange constellations in the night sky as she was screaming to her husband, "Tell me it isn't true!"

The next day the site supervisor told me that my friend and his wife had been put on the next plane out of country and sent home (sedated) along with the other couple that made the comment. By the time I came back to the United States, he was gone from the company.

It's been thirty years, but every once and awhile I still wonder what happened to the rest of their lives.

The End of Innocence

In much smaller ways I've watched my children and now my students discover that their worldview is wrong, mistaken or naive. I've watched as they realize there's no Santa Claus and Tooth Fairy; the world has injustice, hypocrisy and inequality; capitalism and politics don't work like the textbooks and money moves the system; you can't opt out of dying, and without regulation people will try to "game" whatever system you put in place.

Learning to accept the things you can't change, finding the courage to change the things you can and acquiring the common sense to know the difference, is part of growing up.

While I love TechCrunch, the post and the quote about the PR agency ("one PR firm has discovered a dynamite strategy, throw ethics out the window") left me wondering; how do PR agencies interact with TechCrunch and other blog and review sites? Is this behavior an outlier or is it the norm in the PR industry?

Or is it just someone's end of innocence?

Relentless—The Difference Between Motion And Action

November 9, 2009 (Steve Blank)

> "Never mistake motion for action."
> —Ernest Hemingway

One of an entrepreneur's greatest strengths is their relentless pursuit of a goal. But few realize how this differs from most of the population. Watching others try to solve problems reminded me why entrepreneurs are different.

Progress Report

Last week I happened to be sitting in my wife's office as she was on the phone to my daughter in college. Struggling with one of her classes my daughter had assured us that she was asking for help—and was reporting on her progress (or lack of it).

She had sent several emails to the resource center asking for help. She was also trying to set up a meeting with her professor. All good, and all part of the "when you're stuck, ask for help" heuristic we taught our kids. But the interesting part for me was learning that in spite of her efforts no one had gotten back to her.

She believed she had done all things that could be expected from her and was waiting for the result.

I realized that my daughter had confused motion with action.

This reminded me of a conversation with one of my direct reports years before my daughter was born.

Status Report

At Ardent, the marketing department was responsible for acquiring applications for our supercomputer. This required convincing software vendors to move their applications to our unique machine architecture. Not a trivial job considering our computer was one of the first parallel architectures, and our compiler required specific knowledge of our vector architecture to get the most out of it. Oh, and we had no installed customer base. I had hired the VP of marketing from a potential software partner who was responsible to get all this third party software on our computer. Once he was on board, I sat down with him on a weekly basis to review our progress with our list of software vendors.

Think Different

I still remember the day I discovered that I thought about progress differently than other people. Our conversation went like this:

Me: Jim, how are we doing with getting Ansys ported? Jim: Great, I have a bunch of calls into them.

Me: How are we doing on the Nastran port?

Jim: Wonderful, they said they'll get back to me next month. Me: How about Dyna 3D?

Jim: It's going great, we're on their list.

The rest of the progress report sounded just like this.

After hearing the same report for the nth week, I called a halt to the meeting. I had an executive who thought he was making progress. I thought he hadn't done a damn thing.

Why?

The Difference Between Motion and Action

One of Jim's favorite phrases was, "I got the ball rolling with account x." He thought that the activities he was doing—making calls, setting up meetings, etc.—was his job. In reality they had nothing to do with his job. His real job—the action—was to get the software moved onto our machine.

Everything he had done to date was just the motion to get the process rolling. And so far the motion hadn't accomplished anything. He was confusing "the accounting" of the effort with achieving the goal. But Jim felt that since he was doing lots of motion, "lots of stuff was happening." In reality we hadn't gotten any closer to our goal than the day we hired him. We had accomplished nothing—zero, zilch, nada. In fact, we would have been better off if we hadn't hired him as we wouldn't have confused a warm body with progress.

When I explained this to him, the conversation got heated. "I've been working my tail off for the last two months…" When he calmed down, I asked him how much had gotten accomplished. He started listing his activities again. I stopped him and reminded him that I could have hired anyone to set up meetings, but I had brought him in to get the software onto our machine. "How much progress have we made to that goal?" "Not much," he admitted.

Entrepreneurs Are Relentless

Jim's goal was to get other companies to put their software on an unfinished, buggy computer with no customers. While a tough problem, not an insurmountable one for an entrepreneur focused on the objective, not the process.

This was my fault. It had taken me almost two months to realize that other people didn't see the world the same way I did. My brain was wired to focus on the end-point and work backwards, removing each obstacle in my path or going around them all while keeping the goal in sight. Jim was following a different path.

Focused on the process, he defined progress as moving through a step on his to-do list, and feeling like progress was being made when he checked them off. The problem was his approach let others define the outcome and set the pace.

The difference between the two ways of thinking is why successful entrepreneurs have the reputation for being relentless. To an outsider it looks like they're annoyingly persistent. The reality is that their eyes are on the prize.

Teaching Moment

If you're not born with this kind of end-goal focus, you can learn this skill.

My wife and I called our daughter back, declared a family "teaching moment," and explained the difference between motion and action, and asked her what else she could do to get help for class. She realized that more persistence and creativity was required in getting to the right person. The next day, she was in the resource center having figured out how to get the help she needed.

Lessons Learned

- Most people execute linearly, step by step.
- They measure progress by "steps they did."
- Entrepreneurs focus on the goal.
- They measure progress by "accomplishing their goals."

Closure

November 19, 2009 (Steve Blank)

For those that know me, I'm kind of a "life is too short" kind of guy. I like to fail fast, move on, and not look back.

However, in catching up with the VP of Sales of Ardent, I was reminded one of the few times I did return for closure.

National Supercomputer Centers

For a decade starting in 1985, the National Science Foundation (NSF) established and spent a pile of money (around $50 million per year) on four supercomputing centers in the U.S.: Cornell University, University of Illinois, Urbana-Champaign, the Pittsburgh Supercomputing Center at Carnegie Mellon University, and the San Diego Supercomputer Center at the University of California at San Diego. The ostensible goal of these centers was to allow scientists and researchers access to supercomputers to simulate commercial phenomena that were too expensive, too dangerous or too time consuming to physically build.

The reality was that the U.S. Nuclear Weapons Laboratories used supercomputers to run their hydrodynamics codes for nuclear weapon design and the National Security Agency used them to decryptcodes. But with the cold-war winding down these agencies could no longer be counted on to provide Cray Research with enough business to sustain the company. Commercial applications needed to be found that could take advantage of this class of computers.

The search for commercial supercomputer applications was good news for Ardent, as this was our business as well. But bad news was that the supercomputing centers had concluded that they could justify their existence (and budget) only by buying the biggest and most expensive supercomputers Cray Research made.

We Lost the Deal

At Ardent, we were building a personal supercomputer powerful enough to run and display numerical simulations just about the time the National Science Foundation was funding these centers. I remember that the Pittsburgh Supercomputing Center had put out a request for a proposal for a supercomputer to replace the Cray X-MP they installed in 1986. In reading it, there was no doubt that it was written only in a way that Cray could respond.

I realized that given the amount of money the Supercomputing Center wanted to spend on buying the new Cray Y-MP (list price: $35 million), we could put an Ardent personal supercomputer next to every scientist and researcher connected to the university. I responded to their RFP by proposing that Ardent build the Pittsburgh Supercomputing Center a distributed supercomputing environment with hundreds of Ardent personal supercomputers rather than a monolithic Cray supercomputer.

As one could imagine this was the last thing the supercomputer center management wanted to hear. All their peers were buying Cray's, and they wanted one as well. We had support from the scientists and researchers who had bought one of our machines and were beginning to see that distributed computing would ultimately triumph, but bureaucracy marched on, and we lost the bid.

In my career I've been involved with lots of sales deals, and for some reason losing this was the one deal I never forgot. Maybe because a win here would have meant success rather than failure for the company, perhaps because I really believed we could make the impossible happen and win. For whatever reason, I hated that particular Cray that got installed in Pittsburgh.

Closure

Fast-forward 15 years. Retired for a year, I ran across an article that said, "$35 Million Dollar Supercomputer for Sale for Scrap." It was the Pittsburgh Supercomputing Center Cray Y-MP that had beaten me at Ardent. It was for sale on eBay.

I bought the Cray.

It took two semi-trailers to deliver it.

It sat in my barn next to the tractors and manure for five years. I had the only farm capable of nuclear weapons design.

Cray called two years ago and bought it back for parts for an unnamed customer still running one.

Closure.

The Elves Leave Middle Earth—Sodas Are No Longer Free

December 21, 2009 (Steve Blank)

Sometimes financial decisions that are seemingly rational on their face can precipitate mass exodus of your best engineers.

We Hired the CFO

Last week as a favor to a friend, I sat in on a board meeting of a fairly successful 3 1/2-year-old startup. Given all that could go wrong in this economy, they were doing well. Their business had just crossed cash flow breakeven, had grown past 50 employees, just raised a substantive follow-on round of financing and had recently hired a Chief Financial Officer. It was an impressive performance.

Then the new CFO got up to give her presentation—all kind of expected; Sarbanes Oxley compliance, a new accounting system, beef up IT and security, Section 409A (valuation) compliance, etc. Then she dropped the other shoe.

"Do you know how much our company is spending on free sodas and snacks?" And to answer her own question she presented the spreadsheet totaling it all up.

There were some experienced VCs in the room and I was waiting for them to "educate" her about startup culture. But my jaw dropped when the board agreed that the "free stuff" had to go.

"We're too big for that now" was the shared opinion. But we'll sell them soda "cheap."

Unintended Consequences

I had lived through this same conversation four times in my career, and each time it ended as an example of unintended consequences. No one on the board or the executive staff was trying to be stupid. But to save $10,000 or so, they unintentionally launched an exodus of their best engineers.

This company had grown from the founders, who hired an early team of superstars, many now managing their own teams. All these engineers were still heads-down, working their tails off, just as they had been doing since the first few months of the company. Too busy working, most were oblivious to the changes that success and growth had brought to the company.

The Elves Leave Middle Earth—Sodas Are No Longer Free

One day the engineering team was clustered in the snack room looking at the soda machine. The sign said, "Soda now 50 cents."

The uproar began. Engineers started complaining about the price of the soda. Someone noticed that instead of the informal reimbursement system for dinners when they were working late, there was now a formal expense report system. Some had already been irritated when "professional" managers had been hired over their teams with reportedly more stock than the early engineers had. Lots of email was exchanged about "how things were changing for the worse." A few engineers went to the see the CEO.

But the damage had been done. The most talented and senior engineers looked up from their desks and noticed the company was no longer the one they loved. It had changed. And not in a way they were happy with.

The best engineers quietly put the word out that they were available, and in less than month the best and the brightest began to drift away.

What Happened?

Startups go through a metamorphosis as they become larger companies. They go from organizations built to learn, discover and iterate, to predominantly one that can execute adroitly having found product/market fit.

Humans seem to be hard-wired for numbers of social relationships. These same numbers also define boundaries in growing an organization—get bigger than a certain size and you need a different management system. The military has recognized this for thousands of years as they built command and control hierarchies that matched these numbers.

Wake Up Call

The engineers focused on building product never noticed when the company had grown into something different than what they first joined.

The sodas were just the wake-up call.

As startups scale into a company, founders and the board need to realize that the most important transitions are not about systems, buildings or hardware. It's about the company's most valuable asset—its employees.

Great companies do this well.

Lessons Learned

- Be careful of unintended consequences when you grow.

- Recognize the transition boundaries in company size.

- Preserve and manage an Innovation Culture.

No Plan Survives First Contact With Customers—Business Plans versus Business Models

April 8, 2010 (Steve Blank)

"No campaign plan survives first contact with the enemy."
— Field Marshall Helmuth Graf von Moltke

I was catching up with an ex-graduate student at Café Borrone, my favorite coffee place in Menlo Park. This was the second of three "office hours" I was holding that morning for ex students. He and his co-founder were both PhDs in applied math who believe they can make some serious inroads on next generation search. Over coffee he said, "I need some cheering up. I think my startup is going to fail even before I get funded." Now he had my attention. I thought his technology was potentially a killer app. I put down my coffee and listened.

He said, "After we graduated we took our great idea, holed up in my apartment and spent months researching and writing a business plan. We even entered it in the business plan competition. When were done we followed your advice and got out of the building and started talking to potential users and customers." Okay, I said, "What's the problem?" He replied, "Well the customers are not acting like we predicted in our plan! There must be something really wrong with our business. We thought we'd take our plan and go raise seed money. We can't raise money knowing our plan is wrong."

I said, "Congratulations, you're not failing, you just took a three and a half-month detour." Here's why.

No Plan Survives First Contact With Customers

These guys had spent four months writing a 60-page plan with 12 pages of spreadsheets. They collected information that justified their assumptions about the problem, opportunity, market size, their solution and competitors and their team, They rolled up a five-year sales forecast with assumptions about their revenue model, pricing, sales, marketing, customer acquisition cost, etc. Then they had a five-year P&L statement, balance sheet, cash flow and cap table. It was an exquisitely crafted plan. Finally, they took the plan and boiled it down to 15 of the prettiest slides you ever saw.

The problem was that two weeks after they got out of the building talking to potential customers and users, they realized that at least half of their key assumptions in their wonderfully well-crafted plan were wrong.

Why a Business Plan Is Different Than a Business Model

As I listened, I thought about the other startup I had met an hour earlier. They also had been hard at work for the last three-and-a-half months. But they spent their time differently. Instead of writing a full-fledged business plan, they had focused on building and testing a business model.

A business model describes how your company creates, delivers and captures value. It's best understood as a diagram that shows all the flows between the different parts of your company. This includes how the product gets distributed to your customers and how money flows back into your company. And it shows your company's cost structures, how each department interacts with the others, and where your company can work with other companies or partners to implement your business.

This team had spent their first two weeks laying out their hypotheses about sales, marketing, pricing, solution, competitors, etc. and put in their first-pass financial assumptions. It took just five PowerPoint slides to capture their assumptions and top line financials.

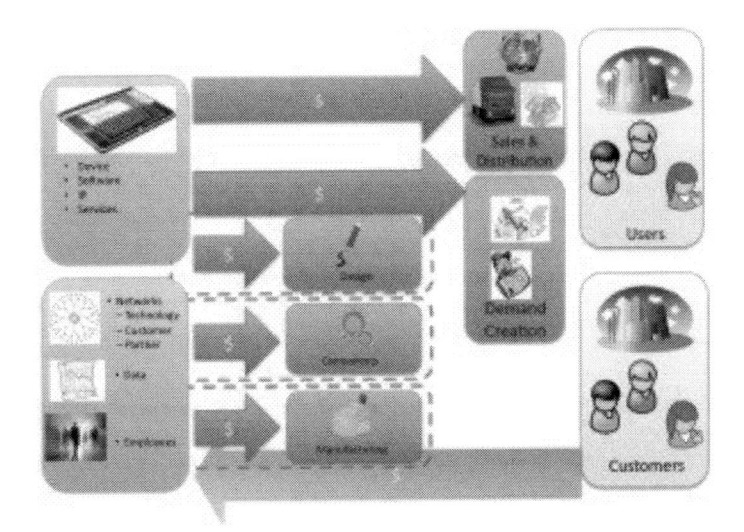

This team didn't spend a lot of time justifying their assumptions because they knew facts would change their assumptions. Instead of writing a formal business plan they took their business model and got out of the building to gather feedback on their critical hypotheses (revenue model, pricing, sales, marketing, customer acquisition cost, etc.). They even mocked up their application and tested landing pages, keywords, customer acquisition cost and other critical assumptions. After three months, they felt they had enough preliminary customer and user data to go back and write a Power Point presentation that summarized their findings.

This team had wanted to have coffee to chat about which of the four seed round offers they had received they should accept.

A Plan Is Static, A Model Is Dynamic

Entrepreneurs treat a business plan, once written as a final collection of facts. Once completed you don't often hear about people rewriting their plan. Instead it is treated as the culmination of everything they know and believe. It's static.

In contrast, a business model is designed to be rapidly changed to reflect what you find outside the building in talking to customers. It's dynamic.

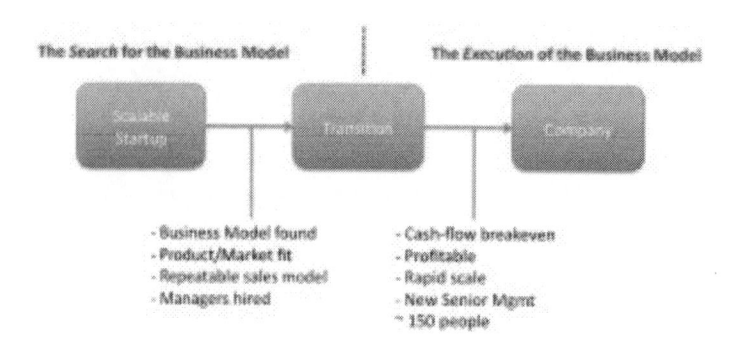

![Diagram showing The Search for the Business Model (Scalable Startup → Transition) and The Execution of the Business Model (Transition → Company). Scalable Startup: Business Model found, Product/Market fit, Repeatable sales model, Managers hired. Transition: Cash-flow breakeven, Profitable, Rapid scale, New Senior Mgmt, ~150 people.]

"So do you mean I should never have written a business plan?" asked the founder who had spent the time crafting the perfect plan. "On the contrary," I said. "Business plans are quite useful. The writing exercise forces you to think through all parts of your business. Putting together the financial model forces you to think about how to build a profitable business. But you just discovered that as smart as you and your team are, there were no facts inside your apartment. Unless you have tested the assumptions in your business model first, outside the building, your business plan is just creative writing."

Lessons Learned

- A startup is an organization formed to search for a repeatable and scalable business model.

- There are no facts inside your building, so get outside and get some.

- Draw and test the Business Model first, the Business Plan then follows.

- Few if any investors read your business plan to see if they're interested in your business

- They're a lot more interested in what you learned

The Cover-Up Culture

January 10, 2011 (Steve Blank)

In a startup, "Good news needs to travel fast, but bad news needs to travel faster." There's something about the combination of human nature (rationalization and self-deception) and large hierarchical organizations (corporations, military, government, etc.) that actively conspire to hide failure and errors. Institutional cover-ups are so ingrained that we take them for granted.

Yet for a startup a cover-up culture is death. In a startup founders and the board need to do exactly the opposite of a large company—failures need to be shared, discussed and dissected to extract "lessons learned" so a new direction can be set.

Lie to My Face

The first time I saw a corporate cover-up was as a new board member of a medium size public company. The VP of an operating division had run into trouble in product development; the product was late and getting later. The revenue plan had the new product baked into the numbers and it was clear that this division General Manager was going to crater his forecast (happens all the time, nothing new here). I knew this from talking to his people before the board meeting so none of this was a surprise. What was a surprise was the boldface lies the VP told us at the board meeting. "The product's on schedule. No problems. We'll make the numbers." The disconnect between reality and a senior executive's willingness to blatantly lie to his CEO and board just blew me away.

It would have been so much simpler for him to say, "We're screwed, and I need your help." Until I dug deeper and realized that the entire company had a "cover-up culture"— the CEO punished failure and bad news. Since only good news was rewarded (as defined by the revenue and product plan shared with Wall Street analysts), I understood why avoiding bad news and covering mistakes was the general manager's rational choice in this company. Because earlier in my career I had a board that beat me senseless when I missed a milestone.

Cover-up Or Look Like an Idiot

In large companies executives are hired and compensated for pristine and efficient execution. If you screw up, there's an unspoken assumption that you've screwed up a known process — something that was repeatable and predictable. You cover up because your screw-ups not only make you look like a failure, but everyone up the line (your boss, their boss, etc.) look like an idiot. Further, the odds are that the information you hide won't immediately be discovered or damage the company.

I mention this not because this post is about cover-ups in large companies, (I'll leave that to the experts in organizational behavior and social theory) but to contrast it with the very different kind of culture that startups need to survive.

The Cover-Up Culture: The Role of the Board

As a founder I quickly learned how open I could be with my board. A few times I had not so great investors who believed that a startup should unfold like a Harvard case study. They ignored the reality that most startups are a chaotic set of events from which founders are trying to extract a repeatable and profitable pattern. The first time I delivered bad news, I got my head handed to me. The lesson this chastened CEO took from that board meeting? Don't tell this board bad news.

In other startups I was lucky and had great investors who knew how to manage and deal with chaos. They realized that conditions change so rapidly that the original business plan hypotheses become irrelevant. These investors taught me metrics appropriate for searching for a business model, how to work with the board when I didn't make a milestone, and how we would figure out when it was time to change the strategy. I thought of these board members as partners and I shared everything with them: good, bad, and ugly.

These board members encouraged me to instill the right culture in the company. They reminded me that failures in startups tell the founders which direction not to pursue— while teaching you how to succeed. This means covering up failure in a startup was like tossing their money in the street. So instead of a cover-up culture, they encouraged a "Lessons Learned culture."

Startups: Good News Needs to Travel Fast, But Bad News Needs to Travel Faster

A key element of a "Lessons Learned" culture is rapid dissemination of information. All information, whether good or bad, must be shared rapidly. We taught our company that understanding sales losses were more important than understanding sales wins; understanding why a competitor's products were better was more important than rationalizing ways in which ours were superior. All news, but especially bad news, needed to be shared, dissected, understood, and acted on. At each weekly department and company meeting we discussed what worked and hadn't. And when we found employees who hoarded information or covered up problems we removed them. They were cultural poison for a startup.

The resulting conversations made us smarter, agile and relentless.

Lessons Learned

- Startups are built around rapid iterations of hypotheses. Most of them turn out be wrong.

- Make sure your board is not beating up on the truth.

- Build a culture of rapid dissemination of all news, good or bad.

- Founders lead by example in sharing Lessons Learned.

- Collectively analyze failures, then iterate, pivot and try again.

- A cover-up culture is death to a startup.

- Fire employees who hoard information or hide bad news.

Burnout

July 20, 2009 (Steve Blank)

If you hang around technology companies long enough, you or someone you know may experience "burnout"—a state of emotional exhaustion, doubt and cynicism. Burnout can turn productive employees into emotional zombies and destroy careers. But it can also force you to hit the pause button and perhaps take a moment to reevaluate your life and your choices.

Hitting "burnout" changed the trajectory of both ends of my career in Silicon Valley. This post is the story of the first time it happened to me.

Zilog

Zilog was my first Silicon Valley company where you could utter the customer's name in public. Zilog produced one of the first 8-bit microprocessors: the Z-80, competing at the time with Intel's 8080, Motorola 6800, and MOS Technology 6502.

I was hired as a training instructor to teach microprocessor system design for the existing Z-80 family and to write a new course for Zilog's soon to be launched 16-bit processor, the Z-8000. Given the hardware I had worked on at ESL, learning microprocessors wasn't that hard but figuring out how to teach hardware design and assembly language programming was a bit more challenging. Luckily while I was teaching classes at headquarters, Zilog's field application engineers (the technical engineers working alongside our salesmen) would work side-by-side with our large customers as they designed their systems with our chips. So our people in the field could correct any egregious design advice I gave to customers who mattered.

Customers

The irony is that Zilog had no idea who would eventually become its largest customers. Our salesmen focused on accounts that ordered the largest number of chips and ignored tiny little startups that wanted to build personal computers around these chips (like Cromemco, Osborne, Kaypro, Coleco,

Radio Shack, Amstrad, Sinclair, Morrow, Commodore, Intertec, etc.) Keep in mind this is still several years before the IBM PC and DOS. And truth be told, these early systems were laughable, at first having no disk drives (you used tape cassettes), no monitors (you used your TV set as a display), and no high-level programming languages. If you wanted your own applications, you had to write them yourself. No mainframe or minicomputer company saw any market for these small machines.

Two Jobs at Once

When I was hired at Zilog part of the deal was that I could consult for the first six months for my last employer, ESL.

Just as I was getting settled into Zilog, the manager of the training department got fired. (I was beginning to think that my hiring managers were related to redshirted guys on Star Trek.) Since the training department was part of sales no one really paid attention to the four of us. So every day I'd come to work at Zilog at 9 A.M., leave at 5 P.M., go to ESL and work until 10 P.M., 11 P.M. or later. Repeat every day, six or seven days a week.

Meanwhile, back at ESL the project I was working on wanted to extend my consulting contract, the company was trying to get me to return, and in spite of what I had done on the site, "the customer" had casually asked me if I was interested in talking to them about a job. Life was good.

But it was all about to catch up to me.

Where Am I?

It was a Friday (about three-quarters through my work week), and I was in a sales department meeting. Someone mentioned to me that there were a pile of upcoming classes heading my way, and warned me "remember that the devil is in the details." The words "heading my way" and "devil" combined in my head. I immediately responded, "well that's okay, I got it under control—as long as the devil coming at me isn't an SS-18." Given that everyone in the room knew the NATO codename for the SS-18 was SATAN, I was thinking that this was a witty retort and expected at least a chuckle from someone.

I couldn't understand why people were staring at me like I was speaking in tongues. The looks on their faces were uncomfortable. The VP of Sales gave me a funny look and just moved on with the agenda.

VP of Sales? Wait a minute… where am I?

I looked around the room thinking I'd see the faces of the engineers in the ESL M-4 vault, but these were different people. Who were these people? I had a moment of confusion and then a much longer minute of panic trying to figure out where I was. I wasn't at ESL, I was at Zilog. As I realized what I had said, a much longer panic set in. I tried to clear my head and remember what else I had said, like anything that would be really, really, really bad to say outside of a secure facility.

As I left this meeting I realized I didn't even remember when I had left ESL or how I had gotten to Zilog. Something weird was happening to me. As I was sitting in my office looking lost, the VP of Sales came in and said, "You look a bit burned out, take it easy this weekend."

"Burned out?" What the heck was that? I had been working at this pace since I was 18.

Burnout

I was tired. No, I was more than tired, I was exhausted. I had started to doubt my ability to accomplish everything. Besides seeing my housemates in Palo Alto, I had no social life. I was feeling more and more detached at work and emotionally drained. Counting the Air Force, I had been pounding out 70- and 80-hour weeks nonstop for almost eight years. I went home and fell asleep at 7 P.M. and didn't wake up until the next afternoon.

The bill had come due.

Recovery

That weekend I left the Valley and drove along the coast from San Francisco to Monterey. Crammed into Silicon Valley along with millions of people around the San Francisco Bay, it's hard to fathom that 15 air miles away was a stretch of California coast that was still rural. With the Pacific Ocean on my right and the Santa Cruz Mountains on my left, Highway 1 cut through mile after mile of farms in rural splendor. There wasn't a single stoplight along two-lane highway for the 45 miles from Half Moon Bay to Santa Cruz. Looking at the green and yellows of the farms, I realized that my life lacked the same colors. I had no other life than work. While I was getting satisfaction from what I was learning, the sheer joy of it had diminished.

As the road rolled on, it dawned on me that there was no one looking out for me. There was no one who was going to tell me, "You've hit your limit, now work less hours and go enjoy yourself." The idea that only I could be responsible for taking care of my happiness and health was a real shock. How did I miss that?

At the end of two days I realized,

- This was the first full weekend I had taken off since I had moved to California three years ago.

- I had achieved a lot by working hard, but the positive feedback I was getting just encouraged me to work even harder.

- I needed to learn how to relax without feeling guilty.

- I needed a life outside work.

And most importantly I needed to pick one job not two. I had to make a choice about where I wanted to go with my career–back to ESL, try to work for the Customer or stay at Zilog?

Lessons Learned

- No one will tell you to work fewer hours.

- You need to be responsible for your own health and happiness.

- Burnout sneaks up on you.

- Burnout is self-induced. You created it and own it.

- Recovery takes an awareness of what happened.

I've seen the Promised Land. And I might not get there with you.

January 21, 2010 (Steve Blank)

> "…I've been to the mountaintop and I've seen the Promised Land. And I might not get there with you…"
> — Martin Luther King

The startup founder who gets fired just as his/her company is growing into large company could be a cliché—if it wasn't so true—and painful.

Let's take a look at why.

Full disclosure: I've worn all the hats in this post. I've been the founder who got fired, I've been on the board as my friends got fired and I've been the board member who fired the founders.

Scalable Startups at Adolescence

In a recent post, we posited that Scalable Startups are designed to become large companies. Yet at their early stages, they are not small versions of larger established companies. They are different in every possible way—people, culture, goals, etc. Scalable startups go through a transitional form, as unique as a startup or large company, before they can grow into a large company.

```
[Scalable Startup] → [Transition] → [Company]
```

- Business Model found
- Product/Market fit
- Repeatable sales model
- Managers hired

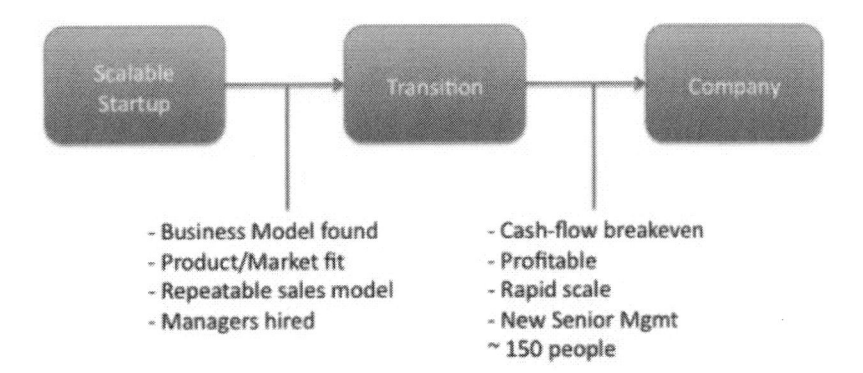

- Cash-flow breakeven
- Profitable
- Rapid scale
- New Senior Mgmt
- ~150 people

Management in the Transition

When Startups reach the Transition stage, it's time to look inward and decide whether the current CEO and executive staff are capable of scaling to a large company.

To get to this Transition stage, the company needed passionate visionaries who can articulate a compelling vision, agile enough to learn and discover in real time, resilient enough to deal with countless failures, and responsive enough to capitalize on what they learned in order to secure early customers. The good news is this team found a business model, product/market fit and a repeatable sales model.

What lies ahead, however, is a different set of challenges: finding the new set of mainstream customers on the other side of the chasm and managing the sales growth curve. These new challenges require a different set of management and leadership skills. Critical for this transition are a CEO and executive staff who are clear-eyed pragmatists, capable of crafting and articulating a coherent mission for the company and distributing authority down to departments that are all driving toward the same goal.

What's Next

By now, the board has a good sense of the skill set of the CEO and executive team as entrepreneurs. What makes the current evaluation hard is that it's based not on an assessment of what they have done, but on a forecast of what they are capable of becoming. This is the irony of successful entrepreneurial executives: their very success may predicate their own demise.

The table below helps elucidate some of the characteristics of entrepreneurial executives by stage of the company. One of the most striking attributes of founders is their individual contribution to the company, be it in sales or product development. As technical or business visionaries, they are leaders by the dint of their personal achievements. As the company grows, however, it needs less of an iconoclastic superstar and more of a leader who is mission- and goal-driven.

	Scalable Startup Entrepreneurial-Driven Learning and Discovery	Transition Mission-Oriented Management	Large Company Process-Managed Execution and Growth
CEO's Personal Contribution	Superstar	Leader	Manager of plans, goals, process, and personnel
CEO's Time Commitment	24/7	As needed	Long term 9 to 5
Planning	Opportunistic & agile	Mission- and goal-driven	Process-, and goal-driven
Process	Hates and eliminates	As needed, driven by mission	Implements and uses
Management Style	Autocratic, star system	Distributed to departments	May be bureaucratic
Span of Control	Hands-on	Mission-driven, synchronized	Distributed down the organization
Focus	High and passionate vision	Mission	Execution
Uncertainty/Chaos	Brings order out of chaos	Focuses on fast response	Focuses on repeatability

Leaders at this Transition stage must be comfortable driving the company goals down the organization and building and encouraging mission-oriented leadership on the departmental level. This Transition stage also needs less of a 24/7 commitment from its CEO and more of an as-needed time commitment to prevent burnout.

Planning is another key distinction. The Scalable Startup stage called for opportunistic and agile leadership. As the company gets bigger, it needs leaders who can keep a larger team focused on a single-minded mission. In this mission-centric Transition stage, hierarchy is added, but responsibility and decision-making become more widely distributed as the span of control gets broader than one individual can manage. Keeping this larger organization agile and responsive is a hallmark of mission-oriented management.

I Don't Get It—I Built This Company—I Deserve to Run It

This shift from Customer and Agile Development teams to mission-centric organization may be beyond the scope and/or understanding of a first-time CEO and team. Some never make the transition from visionary autocrats to leaders. Others understand the need for a transition and adapt accordingly. It's up to the board to decide which group the current executive team falls into.

This assessment involves a careful consideration of the risks and rewards of abandoning the founders. Looking at the abrupt change in skills needed in the transition from Customer Development to a mission-centric organization to process-driven growth and execution, it's tempting for a board to say: Maybe it's time to get more experienced executives. If the founders and early executives leave, that's okay; we don't need them anymore. The learning and discovery phase is over. Founders are too individualistic and cantankerous, and the company would be much easier to run and calmer without them. All of this is often true. It's particularly true in a company in an existing market, where the gap between early customers and the mainstream market is nonexistent, and execution and process are paramount. A founding CEO who wants to chase new markets rather than reap the rewards of the existing one is the bane of investors, and an unwitting candidate for unemployment.

Don't Fire the Founders

Nevertheless, the jury is still out on whether more startups fail in the long run from getting the founders completely out of the company or from keeping founders in place too long. In some startups (technology startups especially), product life cycles are painfully short. Regardless of whether a company is in a new market, an existing market, or a re-segmented market, the one certainty is that within three years the company will be faced with a competitive challenge. The challenge may come from small competitors grown bigger, from large companies that now find the market big enough to enter, or from an underlying shift in core technology. Facing these new competitive threats requires all the resourceful, creative, and entrepreneurial skills the company needed as a startup.

Time after time, startups that have grown into adolescence stumble and succumb to voracious competitors large and small because they have lost the corporate DNA for innovation and learning and discovery. The reason? The new management team brought in to build the company into a profitable business could not see the value of founders who kept talking about the next new thing and could not adapt to a process-driven organization. So they tossed them out and paid the price later.

Take the Money and Let Someone Else Sort It Out

In an overheated economic climate, where investors could get their investments liquid early via a public offering, merger or acquisition, none of this was their concern. Investors could take a short-term view of the company and reap their profit by selling their stake in the company long before the next crisis of innovation occurred. However, in an economy where startups need to build for lasting value, boards and investors may want to consider the consequences of losing the founder instead of finding a productive home to hibernate the creative talent for the competitive storm that is bound to come.

Instead of viewing the management choices in a startup as binary—entrepreneur-driven on Monday, dressed up in suits and processes on Tuesday—the Transition stage and mission-oriented leadership offers a middle path that can extend the life of the initial management team, focus the company on its immediate objectives, and build sufficient momentum to cross the chasm.

Lessons Learned
- Founder/Investor struggles about leadership are not about past successes—they're about who's best to lead future growth.

- Founder success in the Startup stage is not a predictor for success in the next stages.

- Few founders make great large company execs.

- The exceptions, Gates, Jobs, Ellison, etc., are founders who grew into large company executives while retaining founder instincts.

The Peter Pan Syndrome–The Startup to Company Transition

September 20, 2010 (Steve Blank)

One of the ironies of being a startup is that when you are small no one can put you out of business but you. Paradoxically, as your revenues and market share increase the risk of competitors damaging your company increases.

Often the cause is the inability to grow the startup past the worldview of its founders.

We're Getting Our Butts Kicked

One of my ex-engineering students helped start a six-year old company headquartered in Los Angeles that sells to government agencies. (They had funded this company themselves after their last networking company got acquired.) While he had designed a good part of the product, he now found himself the titular head of sales and marketing. We usually catch up when he's in town, but this time he said he was bringing his co-founder.

"We're trying to solve a puzzle in sales. We're not sure you know anything about our market but we sure would like to talk it through. We're suddenly getting our butts kicked in our sales to the government."

I knew their business fairly well. They were the darlings of the three-letter agencies in Washington. Their equipment was used almost everywhere. And for the last few years they couldn't make and deliver their product fast enough. Last year they had done over $50 million in sales. Now, over lunch I heard that for the first time sales were getting tougher. It even looked as if they might not make this year's sales forecast.

"What's changed?" I asked. "Well things were going great last year, but now we're competing for larger orders and for the first time we have to go through competitive bids with formal Request For Proposals— RFP's

Fortune 100 companies who never had a product in this space are saying that they can deliver what we can. We know that's not true, but we're getting our butts kicked. They're also bundling in services and other products we don't have and can't offer. We even lost a few orders we didn't even know were out for bid."

He's a Nice Guy

Trying to understand a bit more about their sales process, I asked them to tell me why their sales were so easy for the last few years. My student looked almost blissful when he described the process, "Oh, customers found our product by word of mouth. We solve a really hard and important problem. We'd give a demo, they'd bring their boss over, jaws would drop, and we'd get an order. We'd install the system, more people could see what it would do and then we'd get more orders. Doing all those demos took up a lot of my travel time so I hired someone from one of the customers as our Washington salesperson." Hmm, a hint.

My student had always struck me as very smart, driven, articulate, and a "nice guy." His co-founder seemed to have the same temperament. I ventured a question, "Is your sales head a nice guy?" "Why yes, he fits perfectly into our company culture." And he then went into a long soliloquy about their company culture of respect, ethics, compatibility, mission, etc., etc.

"So do your competitors have the same culture?"

The Peter Pan Syndrome

There was a bit of a pause as he thought, and said, "I don't exactly know, but I'd guess not. They're mostly multi-billion dollar companies who've been around a long time and they seem a lot tougher and willing to do anything to get an order. They even put things in their RFP responses that I bet aren't true."

It was about then that I remembered that one of the key reasons that these entrepreneurs had funded the company themselves was that they didn't want any VCs on their board. "Our VCs screwed us in our last company, and now that we could afford it we don't need them." So far they hadn't seemed to suffer. But now I was curious. "Any killer sales people on your board of directors?" They listed a couple of world-class engineering professors and a retired customer who had pointed them to some key early sales. But it dawned on me what they might be missing.

A Killer Sales Culture

"My first observation is that you guys don't even know what you don't know," I suggested. "Large procurements for government agencies are being played out on level you aren't participating in. There's a game going on around you that you don't even know about."

So far they hadn't got up and left so I continued. "I think the root cause is that you two are 'nice guys.'" Your company needs to grow up—not in a way that changes your entire company culture, but enough to realize that the world outside your offices doesn't match your idealistic view of how things should operate. The question is whether you are willing to accept that some part of how you sell may have to change."

My ex-student asked, "Are you suggesting we hire a new Washington salesperson?" "Actually, no. Not yet," I offered. Of all cities, Washington had an abundance of seasoned sales people who could teach them how the game was played. Turning to my student, "I think you need to go to Washington, hire one or more of these grizzled sales veterans as consultants and have them teach you what you need to know. If you are going to compete in Federal procurements, your company is going to have to grow up to play on another level, and eventually you are going to have to hire a team that can play that game.

"But first you need to become a domain expert. Spend a year in Washington."

Lessons Learned

- When the big guys discover your market you need to recognize their game.

- You don't have to play by their rules, but to understand what they are.

- Then you need to develop a strategy that lets you compete.

- Otherwise they will eat your lunch.

You'll Be Dead Soon—Carpe Diem

November 30, 2011 (Steve Blank)

"Remembering that I'll be dead soon is the most important tool I've ever encountered to help me make the big choices in life. Because almost everything—all external expectations, all pride, all fear of embarrassment or failure—these things just fall away in the face of death, leaving only what is truly important."
— Steve Jobs

Watching an entrepreneur fail is sad, but watching them fail from a lack of nerve is tragic.

Excitement
At the beginning of this year Bob, one of my ex-students was in entrepreneurial heaven. He had an idea for a new class of enterprise software insight-as-a-service based on big data web analytics as a Cloud/SaaS (Software As a Service) application.

Bob had taken to heart the business model canvas and Customer Development lessons. After graduating he put together a prototype and had quickly marked through Customer Discovery, iterating his product with the help of CIOs and Fortune 1000 IT departments.

I had made one of the introductions to a Fortune 100 CIOs so I got to hear his progress from both him and the CIO.

Takeoff
After 90 days, things seemed to be moving at startup speed. Bob had a backlog of users wanting to try his application, and the corporate IT people

who were trying his early prototype said, "It's crude, we hate the user interface, it's missing lots of features—but we'll kill you if you try to take it away from us."

pointed a VC who followed the space to the CIO who was testing the prototype. The VC told me the CIO wouldn't get off the phone. He kept telling him he couldn't remember when he had seen an enterprise software product with so much promise. The VC checked with other IT users and heard the same reaction. It was a "gotta use it, don't take it away, we'll have to buy it" product. After a demo and lunch, the VC (who normally did later stage deals) wrote my ex-student a check for a seed round. Life couldn't be better.

I followed Bob's progress in bits and pieces from updates from the CIO, the VC and his emails and blogs. He seemed to be on the fast track to startup success. But pretty soon a few worrying warning signs appeared.

The first thing that I noticed was that Bob couldn't seem to find a co-founder. I wasn't close enough to know if he wasn't really looking for one, but given the early success he was having, it seemed a bit odd. But the next thing really got me concerned. Bob started hiring second-rate developers. At best they were B-players.

Stall

A month went by, and the product stopped getting better. The U/I still sucked, and new features had stopped appearing. The next month, the same thing. I got a call from my CIO friend asking, "What was going on?" He said, "It was a great prototype, we would have loved to deploy it company-wide, and I hate to let it go, but it looks like Bob's company just lost interest in developing it. I'm going to dump it and look for a substitute." So I called Bob and suggested we grab a coffee.

I asked him how things were going and got the update on how the earlyvangelists were using the product. As I had heard, they were ecstatic. But Bob said he was worried he hadn't found the right customer segment yet. "I'm not sure I can get all of these guys to pay me big bucks," he said. "That's why I stopped coding, and I'm spending all my time out in the field still talking to more customers." "What does your VC say you ought to be doing?" I asked. "Oh, he hasn't had much time for me, his firm almost never does seed deals. It turns out I was an exception." Oh, oh.

The conversation was starting to make the hair on the back of my neck stand up. Bob had gotten to a place most founders never do—his product was a "gotta have it for people with big budgets." He should have been back rapidly coding, iterating and finding out what feature set would get him to paying customers.

Instead, he had produced barely three weeks of progress in the last five months. His prototype was rapidly wearing out its welcome.

A Lack of Nerve
When I pressed Bob on this he admitted, "No I guess my engineers aren't very good. But I hired guys who were cheap because I wasn't sure if my hypotheses were right. Didn't you tell us to test our hypotheses first?" Now it was my time to be surprised. "Bob, you've validated your hypotheses better than any startup I've ever seen. You found that out in the first month. You got customers begging you to finish the product so they could buy it. You should have been hiring world-class talent and building something these CIOs will pay for. It's not too late. It's time to grab them by the throat and go for it."

I wasn't ready for the answer. "Steve, I've been reading all about premature scaling and making sure everything is right before I go for it. I want to be sure I get all of this right. I'm afraid I'll run out of money."

I thought I'd make one more run at it. "Bob," I said. "Few entrepreneurs get the first time response you have from an early product. At your rate, you're going to burn through your cash trying to get it perfect. It's a startup. You'll never have perfect information. You're sitting on a gold mine. Grab the opportunity!"

I got a blank stare.

We made some more small talk and shook hands as he left.

Bob was in the wrong business, not the wrong market. He wanted certainty, comfort, and security.

I stared at my coffee for a long time.

VI.

On-the-Job Training—The Best Way to Learn

Entrepreneurship Is Hard But You Can't Die

September 4, 2012 (Steve Blank)

We Sleep Peaceably In Our Beds At Night Only Because Rough Men Stand Ready To Do Violence On Our Behalf

Everyone has events that shape the rest of their lives. This was one of mine.

I've never been shot at. Much braver men I once worked with faced that every day. But for a year and a half I saw weapons of war take off every day with bombs hanging under the wings. It never really hit home until the day I realized some of the planes didn't come back.

Life in a War Zone

In the early 1970s, the U.S. was fully engaged in the war in Vietnam. Most of the fighter planes used to support the war were based in Thailand, or from aircraft carriers (or for some B-52 bombers, in Guam). I was 19, in the middle of a hot war learning how to repair electronics as fast as I could. It was everything life could throw at you at one time with minimum direction and almost no rules.

It would be decades before I would realize I had an unfair advantage. I had grown up in a home where I learned how to live in chaos and bring some order to my small corner of it. For me a war zone was the first time all those skills of shutting out everything except what was important for survival came in handy. But the temptations in Thailand for a teenager were overwhelming: cheap sex, cheap drugs (a pound of Thai marijuana for twenty dollars, heroin from the Golden Triangle that was so pure it was smoked, alcohol cheaper than soda). I saw friends partying with substances in quantities that left some of them pretty badly damaged. At a relatively young age, I learned the price of indulgence and the value of moderation.

What a Great Job

But I was really happy. What a great job—you work hard, party hard, get more responsibility and every once in awhile get to climb into fighter plane cockpits and turn them on. What could be better?

Near the beginning of the year when I was at an airbase called Korat, a new type of attack aircraft showed up—the A-7D Corsair. It was a single seat plane with modern electronics (I used to love to play with the Head Up Display). And it was painted with a shark's mouth. This plane joined the F-4s and F-105 Wild Weasels (who went head-to-head with surface-to-air missiles) and EB-66's reconnaissance aircraft all on a very crowded fighter base.

While the electronics shop I worked in repaired electronic warfare equipment for all the fighter planes, I had just been assigned to 354th Fighter Wing so I took an interest in these relatively small A-7D Corsairs (which had originally been designed for the Navy).

He's Not Coming Back

One fine May day, on one of my infrequent trips to the flight line (I usually had to be dragged since it was really hot outside the air-conditioned shop), I noticed a few crew chiefs huddled around an empty aircraft spot next to the plane I was working on. Typically there would have been another of the A-7s parked there. I didn't think much of it as I was crawling over our plane trying to help troubleshoot some busted wiring. But I started noticing more and more vans stop by with other pilots and other technicians— some to talk to the crew chief, others just to stop and stare at the empty spot where a plane should have been parked. I hung back until one of my fellow techs said, "Let's go find out what the party is about."

We walked over and quickly found out it wasn't a party—it was more like a funeral. The A-7 had been shot down over Cambodia. And as we found out later, the pilot wasn't ever coming home.

An Empty Place on the Flight Line

While we were living the good life in Thailand, the Army and Marines were pounding the jungle every day in Vietnam. Some of them saw death up close. 58,000 didn't come back—their average age was 22.

Everyone shook their heads about how sad. I heard later from "old-timers" who had come back for multiple tours "Oh, this is nothing you should have been here in…" and they'd insert whatever year they had been around when some days multiple planes failed to return. During the Vietnam War, around 9,000 aircraft and helicopters were destroyed. Thousands of pilots and crews were killed.

It's Not a Game

I still remember that exact moment—standing in the bright sun where a plane should be, with the ever present smell of jet fuel, hearing the engines of various planes taxing and taking off with the roar and then distant rumble of full afterburners—when all of a sudden all the noise and smells seemed to stop—like someone had suddenly turned off a switch. And there I had a flash of realization and woke up to where I was. I suddenly and clearly understood this wasn't a game. This wasn't just a big party. We were engaged in killing other people and they were equally intent on killing us. I turned and looked at the pilots with a growing sense of awe and fear and realized what their job—and ours—was.

That day I began to think about the nature of war, the doctrine of just war, risk, and the value of National Service.

Epilogue
Captain Jeremiah Costello and his A-7D was the last attack aircraft shot down in the Vietnam War.

Less than ninety days later the air war over Southeast Asia ended.

For the rest of my career when things got tough in a startup (being yelled at, working until I dropped, running out of money, being on both ends of stupid decisions, pushing people to their limits, etc.), I would vividly remember seeing that empty spot on the flightline. It put everything in perspective.

Entrepreneurship is hard but you can't die.

Careers Start by Peeling Potatoes

November 23, 2012 (Steve Blank)

Listening to my the family talk about dividing up the cooking chores for this Thanksgiving dinner, including who would peel the potatoes, reminded me that most careers start by peeling potatoes.

KP—Kitchen Patrol

One of the iconic punishments in basic training in the military was being threatened by our drill instructors of being assigned to KP—Kitchen Patrol—as a penalty for breaking some rule. If you got assigned to KP you were sent to the base kitchen and had to peel potatoes all day for all the soldiers on the base. It was tedious work but to my surprise I found that it wasn't the dreadful experience our drill instructors made it out to be.

But working in the mess hall, the real eye-opener was the inside look at the workings of something I took for granted—how do you cook three meals a day for 10,000 people at a time. Peeling potatoes was a small bit in the thousands of things that had to go right every day to keep 10,000 of us fed.

One my first career lessons: stop taking for granted finished goods and appreciate the complexity of the system that delivered them.

Solutions From Hands On

When I got to my first airbase my job was lugging electronics boxes on and off fighter planes under the broiling hot Thailand sun, to bring them into the technicians inside the air-conditioned shop, to troubleshoot and fix. The thing we dreaded hearing from the techs was, "this box checks out fine, it must be a wiring problem." Which meant going back to the aircraft trying to find a bent pin in a connector or short in a cable or a bad antenna. It meant crawling over, under and inside an airplane fuselage the temperature of an oven. Depending on the type of aircraft (F-4s, F-105s or A-7s—the worst), it could take hours or days to figure out where the problem was.

A few months later, I was now the guy in the air-conditioned shop telling my friends on the flight-line, "the box was fine, must be a cable." Having just been on the other side I understood the amount of work that phrase meant. It took a few weeks of these interactions, but it dawned on me there was a gap between the repair manuals describing how to fix the electronics and the aircraft manuals telling you the pin-outs of the cables—there were no tools to simplify finding broken cables on the flightline. Now with a bit more understanding of the system problem, it didn't take much thinking to look at the aircraft wiring diagrams and make up a series of dummy connectors with test points to simplify the troubleshooting process. I gave them to my friends, and while the job of finding busted aircraft cabling was still unpleasant it was measurably shorter.

My next career lesson: unless I had been doing the miserable, hot and frustrating job on the flightline, I would never have known this was a valuable problem to solve.

Up From the Bottom

My startup career started on the bottom, installing process control equipment inside auto assembly plants and steel mills (in awe of the complexity of the systems that delivered finished products). Wrote technical manuals and taught microprocessor design (to customers who knew more than I did). Worked weeks non-stop responding to customer Requests For Proposals (RFPs). Designed tradeshow booths, spent long nights at shows setting them up, and long days inside them during the shows.

Over ten long years, I wrote corporate brochures (making legal, finance and sales happy), and sales presentations (treading the line between sales, marketing, truth, and competition), and data sheets, web sites and competitive analyses, press releases (getting a degree in creative writing without being an English major) and flew to hundreds of customer meetings on red-eyes at a drop of a hat (making sales guys rich and gaining a huge appreciation for their skills).

Partnered with engineering trying to understand what customers really wanted, needed and would pay for, versus what we could actually build and deliver (and learning the difference between a simply good engineer and working in the presence of sheer genius). In the sprint to first customer ship, slept under the desk in my office the same nights my engineering team was doing the same.

Each of those crummy, tedious, exhausting jobs made me understand how hard they were. Each made me appreciate the complexity of the systems (with people being the most valuable) that make up successful companies. It made me understand that they were doable, solvable and winnable.

It took me a decade to work my way up to VP of Marketing and then CEO. By that time, I knew what each job in my department meant because I had done every one of them. I knew what it took to get these jobs done (and screw them up), and I now pushed the people who worked for me as hard as I had worked.

Career Lessons Learned

- Winning at entrepreneurship is for practitioners, not theorists.

- Building a company in all its complexity is computationally unsolvable.

- There's no shortcut for getting your hands dirty. Reading stories about the success of Facebook or blogs about the secrets of SEO might make you feel smarter, but it's not going to make you more skilled.

- Unless you've had a ton of experience (which includes failing) in a broad range of areas, you're only guessing.

- Great careers start by peeling potatoes.

SuperMac War Story 6: Building The Killer Team—Mission, Intent and Values

April 9, 2009 (Steve Blank)

> If you don't know where you're going,
> how will you know when you get there?

At the same time we were educating the press, we began to educate our own marketing department about what exactly we were supposed to be doing inside the company. During the first few weeks I asked each of my department heads what they did for marketing and the company. When I asked our trade show manager she looked at me like I was the house idiot and said, "Steve, don't you know that my job is to set up our trade show booth?" The other departments in marketing gave the same answers; the product-marketing department said their job was to write data sheets. But my favorite was when the public relations manager said, "we're here to write press releases and answer the phone in case the press calls."

If these sound like reasonable answers to you, and you are in a startup/small company, update your resume.

Titles Are Not Your Job

When I pressed my staff to explain why marketing did trade shows, or wrote press releases or penned data sheets, the best I could get was "why, that's our job." It dawned on me that we had a department full of people who were confusing their titles with what contribution they were supposed to be making to the company. While their titles might be what their business cards said, titles were not their job—at least in any marketing department I was running.

Titles are not the same as what your job is. This is a big idea.

Department Mission Statements—What am I Supposed to Do Today?
It wasn't that we somehow had inherited dumb employees. What I was actually hearing was a failure of management. No one had sat the marketing department down and defined what our department Mission (with a capital "M") was.

Most startups put together a corporate mission statement because the CEO remembered seeing one at their last job, or the investors said they needed one. Most companies spend an inordinate amount of time crafting a finely honed corporate mission statement for external consumption and then do nothing internally to actually make it happen. (And to this day, I can't remember if we even had a corporate mission statement.) What I'm about to describe here is quite different.

What was missing in SuperMac marketing was anything in writing that gave the marketing staff daily guidance on what they should be doing. The first reaction from my CEO was, "that's why you're running the department." And yes, we could have built a top-down, command-and-control hierarchy. But what I wanted was an agile marketing team capable of operating independently without day-to-day direction.

So what we needed to do was to craft a Departmental Mission statement that told everyone why they come to work, what they need to do, and how they will know they have succeeded. And it was going to mention the two words that SuperMac marketing needed to live and breathe: revenue and profit.

Five Easy Pieces—The Marketing Mission
After a few months of talking to customers, talking to our channel and working with sales we defined the marketing Mission (our job) was to:

"Help Sales deliver $25 million in sales with a 45-percent gross margin. To do that we will create end-user demand and drive it into the sales channel, educate the channel and customers about why our products are superior, and help Engineering understand customer needs and desires. We will accomplish this through demand-creation activities (advertising, PR, tradeshows, seminars, web sites, etc.), competitive analyses, channel and customer collateral (white papers, data sheets, product reviews), customer surveys, and market requirements documents.

This year, marketing needs to provide sales with 40,000 active and accepted leads, company and product name recognition over 65-percent in our target market, and five positive product reviews per quarter. We will reach 35-percent market share in year one of sales with a headcount of 20 people, spending less than $4,000,000.

- Generate end user demand (to match our revenue goals)

- Drive that demand into our sales channels

- Value price our products to achieve our revenue and margin goals (create high-value)

- Educate our sales channel(s)

- Help engineering understand customer needs"

That was it. Two paragraphs, Five bullets. It didn't take more.

Working to the Mission

Having the mission in place meant that our marketing team could see that what mattered was not what their business card said, but how much closer did their work move our department to completing the mission. Period.

It wasn't an easy concept for everyone to understand.

Building the Team

My new Director of Marketing Communications turned the Marcom departments into a mission-focused organization. Her new tradeshow manager quickly came to understand that their job was not to set up booths. We hired union laborers to do that. A trade show was where our company went to create awareness and/or leads. And if you ran the tradeshow department you owned the responsibility of awareness and leads. The booth was incidental. I couldn't care less if we had a booth or not if we could generate the same amount of leads and awareness by skydiving naked into a coffee cup.

The same was true for PR. My new head of Public Relations quickly learned that my admin could answer calls from the press. The job of Public Relations at SuperMac wasn't a passive "write a press release and wait for something to happen activity." It wasn't measured by how busy you were, it was measured by results. And the results weren't the traditional PR metrics of number of articles or inches of ink. I couldn't care less about those. I wanted our PR department to get close and personal with the press and use it to generate end user demand and then drive that demand into our sales channel. (The Potrero benchmark strategy was one component of this creating end user demand through PR.) We were constantly creating metrics to see the effects of different PR messages, channels and audiences on end-user purchases.

The same was true for the Product Marketing group. I hired a Director of Product Marketing who in his last company had run its marketing and then went out into the field and became its national sales director. He got the job when I asked him how much of his own marketing material his sales team actually used in the field. When he said, "about ten percent," I knew by the embarrassed look on his face I had found the right guy. And our Director of Technical Marketing was superb at understanding customer needs and communicating them to engineering.

Teaching Mission Intent—What's Really Important

With a great team in place, the next step was recognizing that our Mission statement might change on the fly. "Hey, we just all bought into this Mission idea and now you're telling us it can change?!"

We introduced the notion of Mission intent. What is the company goal behind the mission. In our case, it was to sell $25 million in graphics boards with 45-percent gross margin. The idea of intention is that if employees understand the thinking behind the mission, they can work collaboratively to achieve it.

But we recognized that there would be time marketing would screw up, making the mission obsolete (i.e. we might fail to deliver 40,000 leads). Think of intention as the answer to the adage, "When you are up to your neck in alligators it's hard to remember you were supposed to drain the swamp." For example, our mission said that the reason why marketing needed to deliver 40,000 leads and 35-percent market share, etc, was so that the company could sell $25 million in graphics boards at 45-percent gross margin.

What we taught everyone is that the intention is more enduring than the mission. ("Let's see, the company is trying to sell $25 million in graphics boards with 45-percent gross margin. If marketing can't deliver the 40,000 leads what else can we do for sales to still achieve our revenue and profitability?") The mission was our goal, but based on circumstances it may change, but the Intent was immovable.

When faced with the time pressures of a startup, too many demands and too few people, we began to teach our staff to refer back to the five Mission goals and the Intent of the department. When stuff started piling up on their desks, they learned to ask themselves, "Is what I'm working on furthering these goals? If so, which one? If not, why am I doing it?"

They understood the mission intent was our corporate revenue and profit goals.

Core Values

Even after we had Mission and Intent down pat, one of the things that still drove me crazy was when we failed to deliver a project for sales on time or we missed a media deadline, everyone in my department had an excuse. (Since a large part of marketing was as a service organization to sales, our inability to deliver on time meant we weren't holding up our end of the mission.) I realized that this was a broken part of our culture, but couldn't figure out why. And one day it hit me that when deadlines slipped, there were no consequences.

And with no consequences, we acted as if schedules and commitments really didn't matter. I heard a constant refrain of, "The channel sales brochure was late because the vendor got busy and they couldn't meet the original deadline." Or, "the January ad had to be moved into February because my graphic artist was sick but I didn't tell you assuming it was okay." Or, "we're going to slip our product launch because the team thought they couldn't get ready in time." We had a culture that had no accountability, and no consequences – instead there were simply shrugged shoulders and a litany of excuses.

This had to change. I wanted a department that could be counted on delivering. One day I simply put up a sign on my door that said, "No excuses accepted." And I let the department know what I meant was we were all going to be "accountable."

What I didn't mean was "deliver or else." By accountable I meant, "we agreed on a delivery date, and between now and the delivery date, it's okay if you ask for help because you're stuck, or something happened outside of your control. But do not walk into my office the day something was due and give me an excuse. It will cost you your job." That kind of accountable.

And, "since I won't accept those kind of excuses, you are no longer authorized to accept them from your staff or vendors either." The goal wasn't inflexible dates and deadlines, it was no surprises and collective problem solving. After that, we spent a lot more time working together to solve problems and remove obstacles in getting things done on-time.

Over time, accountability, execution, honesty and integrity became the cornerstones of our communication with each other, other departments and vendors.

- We wouldn't give excuses for failures, just facts and requests for help.
- We wouldn't accept excuses for failures, just facts, and offer help.
- Relentless execution.
- Individual honesty and integrity.

That was it. Four bullets. It defined our culture.

Why Do It

By the end of the first year our team had jelled. It was a department willing to exercise initiative, had the judgment to act wisely, and an eagerness to accept responsibility.

I remember at the end of a hard week my direct reports came into my office just to talk about the weeks little victories. And there was a moment as they shared their stories, that they all began to realize that our company (one that had just come off of life support) was beginning to kick the rear of our better-funded and bigger competitors.

We all marveled in the moment.

What Did I Learn So Far?

- Push independent execution of tasks down to the lowest possible level

- Give everyone a shared Mission Statement: why they come to work, what they need to do, and how they will know they have succeeded.

- Share Mission Intent for the big picture for the Mission Statement

- Build a team comfortable with independent Mission execution

- Agree on Core Values to define your culture

SuperMac War Story 8: Cats and Dogs—Admitting a Mistake

April 23, 2009 (Steve Blank)

At SuperMac, I thought I was a good VP of marketing; aggressive, relentless and would take no prisoners—even with my peers inside the company. But a series of Zen-like moments helped me move to a different level that changed how I operated. It didn't make my marketing skills any worse or better, but moved me to play forever on a different field.

Zen Moment #1- Admitting a Mistake and Asking for Help

Up until this point in my career I had one response anytime I screwed something up: blame someone else. The only variable was how big the screw-up was—that made a difference in whom I blamed. If it was a very big mistake, I blamed the VP of Sales. "This marketing campaign didn't work? It was a brilliant strategy but Sales screwed it up." (My own lame defense here for this behavior is that sales and marketing are always cats and dogs in startups. Historically, these were two guys with high testosterone. They hit each other with baseball bats until one of them dropped.)

This first Zen moment happened at a SuperMac exec staff meeting. I was asked to explain why a marketing program that cost $150,000 bucks literally generated nothing in revenue for the company. I still remember that I was gearing up to go into my 'I'm going to blame the sales guy' routine. Since our sales guy was a good street fighter, I knew the ensuing melee would create enough of a distraction that no one would talk about my marketing debacle. My brain had queued up the standard, "It's all Sales's fault," but instead, what came out of my mouth was, "You know, I really screwed this marketing campaign up, making it successful is important for the company, and I need all your help to fix it." You could have heard a pin drop. It was so out of character, people were shocked. Some stammered out, "Can you say that again?"

Our president picked up on the momentum and asked me what I needed from the rest of the exec team to fix this debacle. I replied: "This is really important for our success as company and I'm really at a loss why customers didn't respond the way we expected. Anybody else got some other ideas?"

From there, the conversation took a different trajectory. It was uncomfortable for some people, because it was new ground—I was asking for help—wanting to do what was right for the company.

It was definitely a "Zen moment" for me in terms of my career. From then on when I screwed up, not only did I own up to it, I asked for help. This behavior had an unintended consequence I couldn't have predicted: when others started volunteering to help me solve a problem, finding a solution became their goal as well.

Soon one or two others execs tested the waters by making a small tentative "ask" as well. When they discovered that the sky didn't fall and they still had their jobs, our corporate culture took one more step toward a more effective and cohesive company.

Ownership and Teamwork not turf.

When Microsoft Threatened to Sue Us Over the Letter "E"

August 20, 2012 (Steve Blank)

By 1997 E.piphany was a fast growing startup with customers, revenue and something approaching a repeatable business model. Somewhere that year we decided to professionalize our logo (you should have seen the first one). With a massive leap of creativity we decided that it should it should have our company name and the letter "E" with a swoop over it.

1997 was also that year that Microsoft was in the middle of the browser wars with Netscape. Microsoft had just released Internet Explorer 3, which for the first time was a credible contender. With the browser came a Microsoft logo.

And with that same massive leap of creativity Microsoft decided that their logo would have their product name and the letter "E" with a swoop over it.

One of E.piphany's product innovations was that we used this new fangled invention called the browser and we ran on both Netscape and Microsoft's. We didn't think twice about it.

That is until the day we got a letter from Microsoft's legal department claiming similarity and potential confusion between our two logos.

They demanded we change ours.

I wish I still had their letter. I'm sure it was both impressive and amusing.

I had forgotten all about incident this until this week when Doug Camplejohn, E.piphany's then VP of Marketing somehow had saved what he claims was my response to Microsoft's legal threat and sent it me. It read:

Response Letter to Bill Gates

Dear Bill,

We are in receipt of your lawyer's letter claiming Microsoft's ownership of the look and feel of the letter "e." While I understand Microsoft's proprietary interest in protecting its software, I did not realize (until the receipt of your ominous legal missive) that one of the 26 letters in the English language was now the trademarked property of Microsoft. Given the name of your company, claiming the letter "e" is an unusual place to start. I can understand Microsoft wanting exclusive rights to the letter 'M" or "W", but "e"? I can even imagine a close family member starting your alphabet collection by buying you the letters "B" or "G" as a birthday present. Even the letters "F" "T" or "C" must be more appealing right now then starting with "e." In fact, considering Microsoft's financial health and legal prowess you may want to consider buying a symbol rather than a letter. Imagine the value of charging royalties on the use of the dollar "$" sign. I understand the legal complaint refers to the similarities of our use of "e" in the Epiphany corporate logo to the "e" in the Internet Explorer logo. Given that the name of my company and the name of your product both start with the same letter, it doesn't take much imagination to figure out why we both used the letter in our logos, but I guess it has escaped your lawyers.

As to confusion between the two products, it is hard for me to understand why someone would confuse a $250,000 enterprise software package (with which we require a customer to buy $50,000 of Microsoft software: NT, SQL Server and IIS), with the free and ever present Internet Explorer.

Given that Microsoft sets the standard for most things in the computer industry, I hope we don't open the mail next week and find Netscape suing us for using the letter "N," quickly followed by Sun's claim on "J." Perhaps we can submit all 26 letters to some sort of standards committee for arbitration. Come to think of it, starting with "e" is another brilliant Microsoft strategy. It is the most common letter in the English language.

Steve Blank

Epilogue

Given later that year Microsoft ended up being a large multi-million dollar E.piphany customer, all I can assume is that cooler heads prevailed (more than likely our new CEO), and this letter was never sent and the threatened lawsuit never materialized.

Ironically, since the turn of the century Microsoft has done great things for entrepreneurs. Their BizSpark and DreamSpark programs have become the best corporate model of how a large company can successfully partner with startups and students worldwide.

But I am glad we helped keep the letter E in the public domain.

Nuke 'em 'Till They Glow—Quitting My First Job

July 12, 2010 (Steve Blank)

I started working when I was 14 (I lied about my age) and counting four years in the Air Force I've worked in 12 jobs. I left each one of them when I was bored, ready to move on, got fired, or learned as much as I could.

There was only one job that I quit when I feared for my life.

Life Is Good

The Vietnam War had just ended and I was out of the Air Force back in college living in Ann Arbor Michigan. Colors other than olive green or camouflage slowly seeped back in my life as "Yes sir, and no sir" faded away. Unlike my previous attempt at college as a pre-med, four years working with electronics convinced me that perhaps I ought to study engineering.

Civilian life was good, the government was paying my tuition and I got a college work/study job in the University of Michigan physics department. After a few weeks, the Physics lab staff realized I knew something about repairing electronics (you try fixing a sodium-iodide scintillation detector without a manual). I got asked, "Would you like to work at the nuclear reactor?" I thought they were joking. "The university has its own nuclear reactor?"

Oh man, something really new to learn. "Heck yes, sign me up."

Nuclear Reactors on Campus

Starting in 1953, the U.S. built over a 150 research reactors. Much smaller than the 500-1,500 megawatt nuclear reactors that generate electricity, by the late 1960s, these 1 to 10 megawatt reactors were in 58 U.S. universities.

In addition, 40 foreign countries got research reactors in exchange for a commitment to not develop nuclear weapons. (But these reactors used weapons-grade Uranium-235 for their cores, and by the late 1970s we realized it wasn't a good idea to be shipping highly enriched uranium overseas.)

My first day in the reactor electronics lab I got a lecture from the health physics department. I was given a film-badge (a dosimeter to measure whole body radiation) and taught how to use the hand and foot monitors (to prevent radioactive contamination from spreading outside the containment dome).

Scram

Lots of things could go wrong in a nuclear reactor—loss of cooling, power failure, jammed control rods, reactor power excursions, etc. While a reactor failure can't create a nuclear explosion, if its core is uncovered long enough it can generate enough heat to melt itself, with all kind of nasty consequences (see Three Mile Island and Chernobyl). To "scram" a reactor means an emergency shutdown by inserting neutron-absorbing control rods into the core. This stops the nuclear chain reaction. My job in the reactor electronics lab was to rebuild the reactor "scram system."

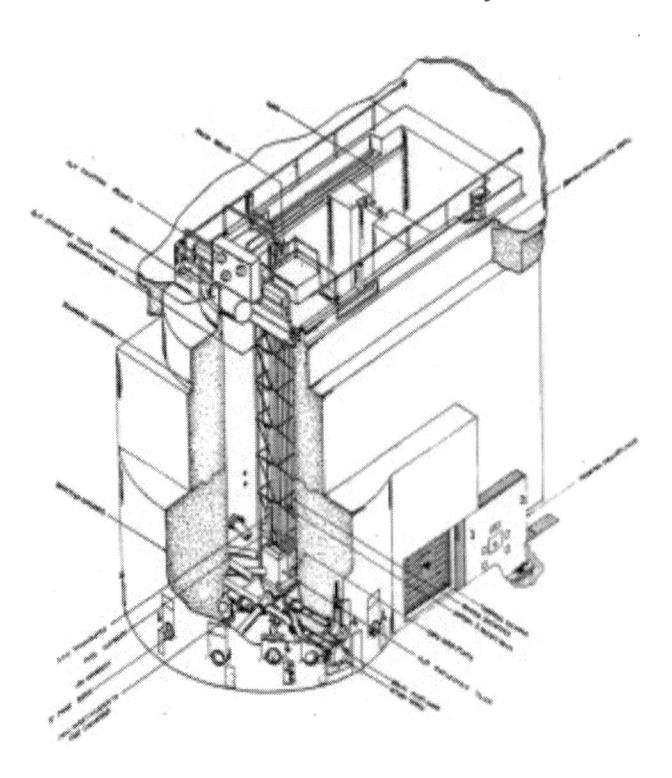

Ford Nuclear Reactor at the Phoenix Lab

The scram system had three parts: the mechanical part (the control rod drives and electromagnetic latches), the electronic part (comparators circuits and trip logic), and the sensors (to measure neutron flux, core temperature, pool water level, etc.).

The 20-year old electronics in our existing scram system were based on vacuum tubes and had the annoying habit of scramming the reactor every time a thunderstorm was nearby. And summertime in the Midwest has lots of thunderstorms. The Nuclear Regulatory Commission had approved a transistorized version of the electronics. My job was to build the approved design, retrofit it into the existing power supplies and integrate it with the existing mechanical systems and sensors.

But first I was going to see the reactor.

Cerenkov Radiation

Over time I would get used to visiting the reactor, but the first visit was awe-inspiring. Entering the containment building through the air lock, my eyes took a few seconds to adjust to the dim light. The first thing I saw was a gigantic mural of the earth rising over the moon painted on the side of the dome.

After another few seconds I realized that the mural was illuminated by an unearthly blue glow coming from what looked like a swimming pool below it. My eyes followed the source of the light down to to the pool and there I first saw the 2 MW nuclear reactor in the bottom of the swimming pool—

and it was generating its own light. When I could tear my eyes from the pool I noticed that in the far end of the building was a glass wall separating a room bathed in red light, where the reactor operators sat at their console. The lab manager let me stand there for a while as I caught my breath. Hollywood couldn't have set the scene better.

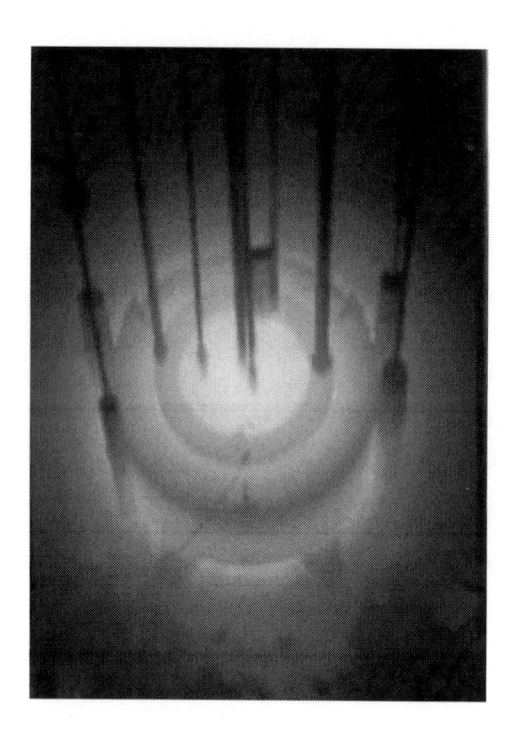

As we walked towards the pool, I learned that the bright blue light was Cerenkov radiation from the reactor core (electrons moving faster than the speed of light in water polarizing the water molecules, which when they turned back to their ground state, emitted photons). We briefly walked across a bridge that spanned the pool and stood directly over the core of the reactor. Wow. They were going to pay me for this?

Dose Roulette

Over the next few weeks, as I began work on the scram system, I got to know the control room operators and others on the staff. Most of them were ex-Navy reactor technicians or officers. They had been around nukes for years and were bemused to find an ex-Air Force guy among them.

One of their weekly rituals was to read the bulletin board for the results of the dosimeter readings. Since most of my time was spent outside the containment dome my radiation exposure numbers were always zero. But there was a bizarre culture of "you're not a real man until you glow in the dark" among the ex-Navy crew. They would celebrate whoever got the highest dose of the week by making them buy the beer for the rest.

After spending the last four years around microwaves, I had become attuned to things that you couldn't see but could hurt you. In the Air Force I had watched my shop mates not quite understand that principle. On the flightline they would test whether a jamming pod was working by putting their hand on the antenna. If their hand felt warm they declared it was. When I tried to explain that the antenna wasn't warm, but it was the microwaves cooking their hand, they didn't believe me. There were no standards for microwave protection. (I always wondered if the Air Force would ever do a study of the incidence of cataracts among radar technicians.)

You Buy the Beer

In a few months I had the new scram system ready for debugging. This required connecting the new electronics to the neutron detectors in the pool that monitored the core. We timed this for the regular downtime when used fuel elements were swapped out and they had lowered the pool water level for easier installation. I remember standing on the bridge right over the reactor core watching as the reactor techs remotely connected up the cables to my electronics. I leaned over the bridge to get a better look. By now the reactor was so familiar that I didn't think twice of where I was standing.

A week later as I was about to enter the dome, I heard someone congratulate me and ask when I was going to buy the beer. They were pointing to the Health/Safety printout on the wall. In one week I had managed to get close to my annual allowable radiation dose (around 5 rems).

In my mandatory talk with the safety officer to figure out where I got exposed, I remembered hanging out over the core on the bridge. The heavy water in the pool was both a moderator and a radiation shield. With the pool level lowered I shouldn't have been on the bridge. I had been in the wrong place at the wrong time.

"Don't do it again" was his advice.

Career Choices

That week I finished up the installation and resigned from the lab. While the radiation dose I received was unlikely to affect my health, the cumulative effect of four years of microwaves and the potential for more unexpected "winning the dosimetery lottery" convinced me to consider alternate jobs in electronics.

In some sense, my career in startups was steered by deciding to avoid future jobs with gamma rays or high-power microwaves.

But I sure learned a lot about nuclear reactors.

Postscript: a year and a half after I left, the power reactor at Three Mile Island had a core meltdown. For years I would worry and wonder if I had wired my scram system correctly.

Lessons Learned

- Things you can't see can hurt you (microwaves, gamma rays, toxic bosses).

- No job is worth your health.

- If it seems dangerous or stupid it probably is.

- Rules and regulations won't stop all possible mistakes.

- No one but you will tell you it's time to quit.

Lying on Your Resume

July 30, 2012 (Steve Blank)

> "It's not the crime that gets you, it's the cover-up."
> — Richard Nixon on Watergate

Getting asked by reporter about where I went to school made me remember the day I had to choose whether to lie on my resume.

I Badly Want the Job

When I got my first job in Silicon Valley it was through serendipity (my part) and desperation (on the part of my first employer). I really didn't have much of a resume—four years in the Air Force, building a scram system for a nuclear reactor, a startup in Ann Arbor Michigan but not much else.

It was at my second startup in Silicon Valley that my life and career took an interesting turn. A recruiter found me, now in product marketing and wanted to introduce me to a hot startup making something called a workstation. "This is a technology-driven company and your background sounds great. Why don't you send me a resume and I'll pass it on." A few days later I got a call back from the recruiter. "Steve, you left off your education. Where did you go to school?"

"I never finished college," I said.

There was a long silence on the other end of the phone. "Steve, the VP of Sales and Marketing previously ran their engineering department. He was a professor of computer science at Harvard and his last job was running the Advanced Systems Division at Xerox PARC. Most of the sales force were previously design engineers. I can't present a candidate without a college degree. Why don't you make something up."

I still remember the exact instant of the conversation. In that moment, I realized I had a choice. But I had no idea how profound, important, and lasting it would be. It would have been really easy to lie, and what the heck the recruiter was telling me to do so. And he was telling me that, "no one checks education anyway." (This is long before the days of the 'net.)

My Updated Resume

I told him I'd think about it. And I did for a long while. After a few days I sent him my updated resume and he passed it on to Convergent Technologies. Soon after I was called into an interview with the company. I can barely recall the other people I met, (my potential boss the VP of Marketing, interviews with various engineers, etc.) but I'll never forget the interview with Ben Wegbreit, the VP of Sales and Marketing.

Ben held up my resume and said, "You know you're here interviewing because I've never seen a resume like this. You don't have any college listed and there's no education section. You put 'Mensa' here—" pointing to the part where education normally goes. "Why?" I looked back at him and said, "I thought Mensa might get your attention."

Ben just stared at me for an uncomfortable amount of time. Then he abruptly said, "Tell me what you did in your previous companies." I thought this was going to be a storytelling interview like the others. But instead the minute I said, "My first startup used CATV coax to implement a local-area network for process control systems (which 35 years ago pre- Ethernet and TCP/IP was pretty cutting edge). Ben said, "Why don't you go to the whiteboard and draw the system diagram for me." Do what? Draw it? I dug deep and spent 30 minutes diagramming trying remember headends, upstream and downstream frequencies, amplifiers, etc. With Ben peppering me with questions I could barely keep up. And there was a bunch of empty spaces where I couldn't remember some of the detail.

When I was done explaining it I headed for the chair, but Ben stopped me.

"As long as you're at the whiteboard, why don't we go through the other two companies you were at." I couldn't believe it, I was already mentally exhausted, but we spent another half hour with me drawing diagrams and Ben asking questions. First talking about what I had taught at ESL— (as carefully as I could). Finally, we talked about Zilog microprocessors, making me draw the architecture (easy because I had taught it) and some sample system designs (harder).

Finally I got to sit down. Ben looked at me for a long while not saying a word. Then he stood up and opened the door signaling me to leave, shook my hand and said, "Thanks for coming in." WTF? That's it? Did I get the job or not?

That evening I got a call from the recruiter. "Ben loved you. In fact, he had to convince the VP of Marketing who didn't want to hire you. Congratulations."

Epilogue

Three and a half years later, Convergent was now a public company and I was a Vice President of Marketing working for Ben. Ben ended up as my mentor at Convergent (and for the rest of my career), my peer at Ardent and my partner and co-founder at Epiphany. I would never use Mensa again on my resume, and my education section would always be empty.

But every time I read about an executive who got caught in a resume scandal, I remember the moment I had to choose.

Lessons Learned

- You will be faced with ethical dilemmas your entire career.

- Taking the wrong path is most often the easiest choice.

- These choices will seem like trivial and inconsequential shortcuts—at the time.

- Some of them will have lasting consequences.

- It's not the lie that will catch up with you, it's the cover-up.

- Choose wisely.

VII.

An Entrepreneur in the Family

Lies Entrepreneurs Tell Themselves

June 15, 2009 (Steve Blank)

Watching my oldest daughter graduate high school this week made me think about what it was like raising a family and being an entrepreneur.

Convergent Technologies

When I was in my 20s, I worked at Convergent Technologies, a company that was proud to be known as the "Marine Corps of Silicon Valley." It was a brawling "take no prisoners," work hard, party hard, type of company, the founders coming out of the DEC (Digital Equipment Corporation) and Intel culture of the 1960s and '70s. As an early employee I worked all hours of the day, never hesitated to jump on a "red-eye" plane to see a customer at the drop of a hat, and I did what was necessary to make the company a winner. I learned a lot at Convergent, going from product marketing manager in a small startup to VP of Marketing of the Unix Division as it became a public company. Two of my role models for my career were in this company. (And one would become my mentor and partner in later companies.) But this story is not about Convergent. It's about entrepreneurship and family.

Like most 20-somethings, I modeled my behavior on the CEO in the company. His marketing and sales instincts and skills seemed magical and he built the company into a $400 million OEM supplier, ultimately selling the company to Unisys. But his work ethic was legendary. Convergent was a six-day a week, 12-hour day company. Not only didn't I mind, but I couldn't wait to go to work in the morning and would stay until I dropped at night. If I did go to social events, all I would talk about was my new company. My company became the most important thing in my life.

But the problem was that I was married. Uh oh.

What's More Important—Me or Your Job?

If you're a startup founder or an early employee, there may come a time in your relationship that your significant other/spouse will ask you the "what's more important?" question. It will come after you come home at 2 a.m. after missing a dinner/movie date you promised to make. Or you'll hear it after announcing one morning that weekend trip isn't going to happen because you have a deadline at work. Or if you have kids, it will get asked when you've missed another one of their plays, soccer games, or school events because you were too busy finishing that project or on yet another business trip. At some point your significant other/spouse's question will be, "What's more important, me and your family or your job?"

I remember getting the question after missing yet another event my wife had counted on me attending. When she asked it, I had to stand there and actually think about it. And when I answered, it was "my job." We both then realized our marriage was over. Luckily we had no kids, minimal assets, and actually held hands when we used the same lawyer for the divorce, but it was sad. If I had been older, wiser, or more honest with myself, I would have understood that my wife and family should have been the most important thing in my life.

Lies Entrepreneurs Tell Themselves

Part of my problem was that my reality distortion field encompassed my relationships. In hindsight, I had convinced myself that throwing myself into work was the right thing to do because I succumbed to the four big lies entrepreneurs tell themselves about work and family:

- I'm only doing it for my family.

- My spouse "understands."

- All I need is one startup to "hit" and then I can slow down or retire.

- I'll make it up by spending "quality time" with my wife/kids.

None of these were true. I had thrown myself into a startup because work was an exciting technical challenge with a fixed set of endpoints and rewards. In contrast, relationships were messy, non deterministic (i.e. emotional rather than technical) and a lot harder to manage than a startup.

The Reality

If it was up to my wife she wouldn't have had me working the hours I was working and would rather have me home. She didn't sign up for my startup, she had signed up for me.

While she stuck it out for seven years, she had no connection to the passion and excitement that was driving me; all she saw was a tired and stressed entrepreneur when I got home.

At this point in my career, I had hit a couple of successful startups as a low level exec, making enough to remodel our kitchen, but not the big "hit" that made us so much money I could slow down or retire. And even if it did, startups are like a gambling addiction—if I had been honest, I would have had to admit I would probably be doing many of them.

"Quality time" with the wife or kids is a phrase made up by guilty spouses. My relationship wasn't going to be saved by one great three-day weekend after 51 weekends at work. A great vacation with my wife wasn't going to make up for being AWOL from home the rest of the year.

Summary

For the next few years, I licked my wounds and threw myself into two more startups. Over time I began to recognize and regret the tradeoffs I had made between work and relationships. I realized that if I ever wanted to get married again and raise a family, my life/work balance needed to radically change.

Epitaph for an Entrepreneur

June 18, 2009 (Steve Blank)

Raising our kids and being an entrepreneur wasn't easy. Being in a startup and having a successful relationship and family was very hard work. But entrepreneurs can be great spouses and parents.

This post is not advice, nor is it recommendation of what you should do, it's simply what my wife and I did to raise our kids in the middle of starting multiple companies. Our circumstances were unique and your mileage will vary.

Biological Clocks

After Convergent and now single again, I was a co-founder of my next two startups: MIPS and Ardent. I threw myself into work and worked even more hours a day. And while I had great adventures, by the time I was in my mid-30s I knew I wanted a family. (My friends noticed that I was picking up other people's babies a lot.) I didn't know if I was ready, but I finally could see myself as a father.

I met my wife on a blind date, and we discovered that not only did we share the same interests but we were both ready for kids. My wife knew a bit about startups. Out of Stanford Business School, she went to work for Apple as an evangelist and then joined Ansa Software, the developer of Paradox, a Mac-database.

Product Launch

Our first daughter was born about four months after I started at SuperMac. We ended up sleeping in the hospital lounge for five days as she ended up in intensive care. Our second daughter followed 14-and-a-half months later.

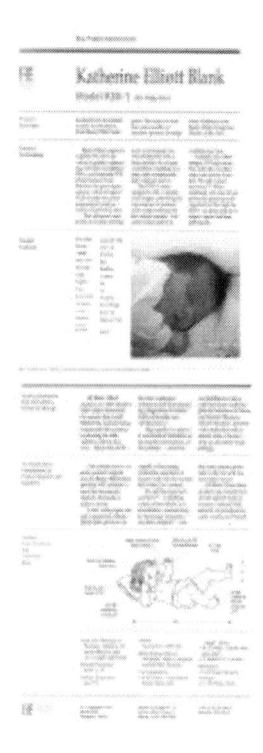

Family Rules

My wife and I agreed to a few rules upfront and made up the rest as went along. We agreed I was still going to do startups, and probably more than most spouses, she knew what that meant. To her credit she also understood that meant that child-raising wasn't going to be a 50/50 split; I simply wasn't going to be home at 5 P.M. every night.

In hindsight, this list looks pretty organized but in reality we made it up as we went along, accompanied with all the husband and wife struggles of being married and trying to raise a family in Silicon Valley. Here are the some of the rules that evolved that seemed to work for our family:

- We would have a family dinner at home most nights of the week. Regardless of what I was doing, I had to be home by 7 P.M. (My kids still remember Mom secretly feeding them when they were hungry at 5 P.M. but eating again with Dad at 7 P.M.) But we would use dinner time to talk about what they did at school, have family meetings, etc.

- Put the kids to bed. Since I was already home for dinner it was fun to help give them their baths, read them stories, and put them to bed. I never understood how important the continuity of time between dinner through bedtime was until my kids mentioned it as teenagers.

Act and be engaged. My kids and wife had better antenna than I thought. If I was home but my head was elsewhere and not mentally engaged they would call me on it.

So I figured out how to split the flow of the day in half. I would work 10 hours a day in the office, come home, and then…

Back to work after the kids were in bed. What my kids never saw is that as soon as they were in bed, I was back on the computer and back at work for another four or five hours until the wee hours of the morning.

Weekends were with and for my kids. There was always some adventure on the weekends. I think we must have gone to the zoo, beach, museum, picnic, amusement park, etc., 100 times.

Half a day work on Saturday. While weekends were for my kids, I did go to work on Saturday morning. But my kids would come with me. This had two unexpected consequences; my kids still remember that work was very cool. They liked going in with me and they said it helped them understand what dad did at "work." Second, it set a cultural norm at my startups, first at SuperMac as the VP of Marketing, then at Rocket Science as the CEO and at E.piphany as President. (Most Silicon Valley startups have great policies for having your dog at work but not your kids.)

Long vacations. We would take at least a three-week vacation every summer. Since my wife and I like to hike, we'd explore national parks around the U.S. (Alaska, Wyoming, Colorado, Washington, Oregon, Maine.) When the kids got older our adventures took us to Mexico, Ecuador, India, Africa, and Europe. The trips gave them a sense that the rest of the country and the world was not Silicon Valley and that their lives were not the norm.

Never miss an event. As my kids got older, there were class plays, soccer games, piano and dance performances, birthdays, etc. I never missed one if I was in town, sometimes even if it was in the middle of the day. (And I made sure I was in town for the major events.)

- Engage your spouse. I asked my wife to read and critique every major presentation and document I wrote. Everything she touched was much better for it. What my investors never knew is that they were getting two of us for the price of one. (And one of us actually went to business school.) It helped her understand what I was working on and what I was trying to accomplish.

- Have a Date-Night. We tried hard to set aside one evening a week when just the two of us went out to dinner and/or a movie.

- Get your spouse help. Early on in our marriage we didn't have much money but we invested in childcare to help my wife. While it didn't make up for my absences it offloaded a lot.

- Traditions matter. Holidays, both religious and secular, weekly and yearly, were important to us. The kids looked forward to them and we made them special.

- Travel only if it needed me. As an executive it was easy to think I had to get on a plane for every deal. But after I had kids I definitely thought long and hard before I would jump on a plane. When I ran Rocket Science our corporate partners were in Japan (Sega), Germany (Bertelsmann) and Italy (Mondadori) and some travel was unavoidable. But I probably traveled 20-percent of what I did when I was single.

- Document every step. Like most dads I took thousands of photos. But I also filmed the girls once a week on the same couch, sitting in the same spot, for a few minutes—for 16 years. When my oldest graduated high school, I gave her a time-lapse movie of her life.

"Live to Work" or "Work to Live"?

When I was in my 20s, the two concepts that mattered were "me" and "right now." As I got older I began to understand the concept of "others" and "the future." I began to realize that working 24/7 wasn't my only goal in life.

As a single entrepreneur I had a philosophy of "I live to work"—nothing was more exciting or important than my job. Now with kids it had become, "I work to live." I still loved what I did as an entrepreneur but I wasn't working only for the sheer joy of it, I was also working to provide for my family and a longer term goal of retirement and then doing something different. (The irony is when I was working insane hours, it was to make someone else wealthy. When I moderated my behavior, it was when they were my startups.)

Work Smarter Not Harder

As I got older I began to realize that how effective you are is not necessarily correlated with how many hours you work. My ideas about Customer Development started evolving around these concepts. Eric Ries' astute observations about engineering and Lean Startups make the same point. I began to think how to be effective and strategic rather than just present and tactical.

Advice From Others

As my kids were growing up I got a piece of advice that stuck with me all these years.

The first was when our oldest daughter was six-months old, and a friend was holding her. She looked at the baby then looked at me and asked, "Steve, do you know what your most important job with this baby is?" I guessed, "Take care of her?" No. "Love her?" No. "Okay, I give up, what is my most important job." She answered. "Steve, your job is teaching her how to leave." This was one of the most unexpected things I ever heard. This baby could barely sit up and I have to teach her how to leave?

My friend explained, "Your kids are only passing through. It will seem like forever but it will be gone in a blink of an eye. Love them and care for them but remember they will be leaving. What will they remember that you taught them?"

For the next 18 years, that thought was never far from my mind.

What Will Your Epitaph Say?

At some point I had heard two aphorisms, which sounded very trite when I was single but took on a lot more meaning with a family.

- This life isn't practice for the next one. I started to realize that some of the older guys who I had admired as role models at work had feet of clay at home. They had chosen their company over family and had kids who felt abandoned by their dads for work— and some of these kids have turned out less than optimally. I met lots of other dads going through the "could-have, would-have, should-have" regrets and reflections of the tradeoffs they had made between fatherhood and company building. Their regrets were lessons for me.

- What will your epitaph say? When our kids were babies I was still struggling to try to put the work/life balance in perspective. Someone gave me a thought that I tried to live my live my life around. He asked me, when you're gone would you rather have your gravestone say, "He never missed a meeting." Or one that said, "He was a great father." Holding my two kids on my lap, it was a pretty easy decision.

I hope I did it right.

Know When to Hold Them, Know When to Fold Them, Know When to Walk Away

When my last startup, E.piphany went public in the dot.com boom, I was faced with a choice: start company number nine, or retire.

I looked at my kids and never went back.

Thanks to my wife for being a great partner. It takes two.

Unintended Lessons

September 28, 2009 (Steve Blank)

Last week I drove my daughter on an East Coast college tour (1500 miles, eight colleges in six days). We started in North Carolina eating BBQ and enjoying the Southern culture, went through Washington, D.C., checking out the shopping in Georgetown, saw beautiful horse country in Pennsylvania and upstate NY, and headed down into the bays and coves of Connecticut filled with sailboats.

We had some great conversations in the car, but one stuck in my mind. It was something I never thought about, and when I first heard it I thought it was a terrible thing to have taught her. She said, "Dad, one of the great things you and Mom did was never tell us how much things cost."

Whoa, when I first heard her say that, I thought she meant that we raised a spoiled kid who had and an unlimited sense of entitlement. For a minute it was a pretty depressing thought for a parent. But on further questioning what came out was a bit more interesting and rewarding.

She said, "Dad what I meant was that growing up we loved when we traveled. And I remember staying in everything from little motels to big hotels and resorts, from National parks in Alaska to trips in India. And as kids we never had any idea which was cheap and which was expensive. Now that I'm older, I'm starting to know what things cost. And I realize you guys never told us we had to enjoy something any more or less because of the price. It made me realize that the goal is not to get the most expensive things, but to go and get what you enjoy."

It was a lesson we never intended to consciously teach.

It made me wonder how many other lessons we taught without knowing.

Thanksgiving Day

November 26, 2009 (Steve Blank)

On Thanksgiving Day in the United States, families gather from across the country to spend time with each other and feast on a traditional turkey dinner.

Since our kids were little, our Thanksgiving tradition was to head to Hawaii with friends and eat Thanksgiving dinner under the palm trees to the sound of the waves next to the warm ocean. (Imuturkey can't be beat if you're trying to exceed any rational amount of salt intake.) This year, with the kids grown, their choice was to fly up from Southern California and spend the holidays at our ranch. My brother and sister in-law, niece and nephew are here, and we're all going to spend Thanksgiving morning creating a new tradition—an extended family scavenger hunt that will take us across the ranch trails. Hopefully we won't run into any wildlife bigger than us (other than our assortment of rattlesnakes, rabbits, deer, bobcats, wild boar, and mountain lions). Our friends who run the state park surrounding our ranch will join all of us for Thanksgiving dinner.

So no post today on entrepreneurship, Secret History of Silicon Valley, Customer Development, Lean Startups, etc. Just a reflection on my family and hopes for our children.

A Few Thoughts for Thanksgiving

- On this day it's hard not to be grateful and give thanks for the things that matter— family, friends, our health, and feel blessed for all the things that have come to us. It's harder to remember that we have no perpetual rights to them, they aren't our due, but they're gifts. We try our best to give back to our community and country and always wonder—is it enough?

- We've taken the kids to enough places in the world to realize the United States still remains a country of opportunity and hope. For all its flaws, America is still a beacon of liberty and justice. My parents were immigrants who came through Ellis Island with nothing but the clothes on their backs—but they believed in the American dream. They worked hard their entire lives so their children could have a better life. Each year I teach hundreds of students from around the world who come to America to pursue their version of this same dream.

This year as American families face economic hardships (one out of eight Californians are unemployed), we remember that as a nation we are still a generous people, willing to share and give to others less fortunate than ourselves—both at home and abroad. I hope we managed to teach our children compassion and charity for others. And as they find their own way in life, they will continue to give back to others.

I'm grateful to those who serve our country and remember that people sleep peaceably in their beds at night only because rough men stand ready to do violence on their behalf. I hope our children remember that freedom needs to be earned and that they too find their way to serve their country.

The Seven Days of Christmas

December 24, 2009 (Steve Blank)

I'm sitting next to the fireplace in my favorite chair listening to holiday music, looking at the ocean and making occasional attempts to "help" get ready for Christmas dinner. We went for a hike checking out our new trail signs and playing "spot the bobcat." Our kids are home for the school break, some friends are visiting from the East Coast and we have everything for the holidays but snow on the California coast.

My kids are now almost the age I was long ago at another Christmas.

So This Is Christmas

As a 20-year old in Thailand in the middle of the chaos of the Vietnam War, my days were filled being an infinitesimal part of the synchronized machinery of maintaining, arming, and launching row after row of fighter planes parked in their revetments—F-105 Wild Weasels, F-4s, A-7s, as well AC-130 Spectre gunships.

There was something both awe-inspiring and incongruous watching fighter planes with bombs on the wing racks take off two at a time. They would accelerate down the runway with full afterburners with sound you could feel in your chest, climb steeply banking sharply to avoid the towering thunderstorms and seem to fly through double rainbows so bright and beautiful they looked painted on the sky.

While I spent most of my time in an air-conditioned avionics shop, my forays out to the flight-line forever made the smell of JP-4 (jet fuel) an integral part of my life. I still associate the kerosene odor with the ballet-like choreography and precision of hundreds of bomb loaders, pod loaders, start-carts, maintenance crews and the cacophonous sound of dozens of jet engines and fighters purposefully taxiing to the runway. As I look out of the window from a seat of a commercial airplane and see the fuel trucks and baggage carts scurry about, the smell of jet fuel still makes me remember somewhere else.

R&R

Halfway through my tour of duty I got to go on vacation—what the military called R&R (rest and recreation). All my buddies went to Bangkok or somewhere equally exotic. I decided to go to Ann Arbor Michigan to see my girlfriend. Normally, you got five days off and then it was time to forget civilian life and get back to the war. Somehow (lost in the mist of time, or perhaps it was because my R&R would occur over the Christmas holidays) I managed to make my R&R seven days.

One day, I was in the middle of Thailand and the next I was hoping space-available military flights to snowbound Michigan.

So This Is Christmas

To my girlfriend, Christmas was the high-point of her year. Getting off the plane I was in a jet-lagged daze, standing out with very short-hair in a '70s college town, as she met me by the gate reminding me that having me back was her best Christmas present. As soon as we left the airport we began a seven-day frenzy of a full-immersion Christmas. (All of this was new for me, as I was raised by a single mother who never celebrated holidays-secular or religious, including events like birthdays.)

I still remember some of the things we did; making wrapping paper by tie-dying plain tissue paper, baking Christmas cookies and Gingerbread men and fruitcake. We made our own Christmas ornaments. I even believe, given how little money we had, we made each other our presents. We went caroling in the snow and had Christmas dinner with friends.

Yet with all of that holiday activity the one thing I still remember, the one thing I can still feel after almost 40 years, was regardless of the adventures you have, how important coming home to a family was.

Of all the goals I set in my life coming home to a family was the one I set standing in the snow that Christmas.

Duality of Man

On the flight back I had plenty of time to think of the contradictions of war with the messages of peace, the imperfections of man and the limits of reason.

VIII.

VC Confidential

Is Your VC Founder Friendly?

June 15, 2010 (Steve Blank)

The role of a founding CEO in a startup searching for a business model is radically different than a CEO building and growing a company. Some VCs get it, others may not. So if you're the founder of a startup, you may want to consider who you take money from.

Is Your VC Founder Friendly?

How do you figure out which VC firm is best for you? Here are five questions to consider.

1. What startup stage do they typically invest in?

2. Do they "get" Customer Development?

3. Who do they have as advisors?

4. How many of their founders are still with their company?

5. Will they tailor your vesting to your contribution as a founder?

What Startup Stage Do They Invest In?

Ask potential investors which stage they invest in.

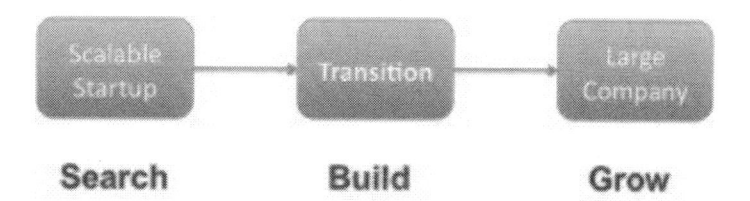

Search → Build → Grow
(Scalable Startup → Transition → Large Company)

Certain VCs, like the new class of Super-Angels and small VC funds, specialize in the early stage of a startup where you are searching for a business model. And some larger funds that specialize in later stage deals may have a partner or two who likes to invest at this stage. (Some VCs invest solely on technology breakthroughs and assume they'll find a market later.)

Early stage investors have different insights than those investing in a later stage. They understand that now is not the time to hire a senior VP of Sales to start to scale the sales force or to look for a finance department to create income statements that say zero each month. These VCs are skilled in helping you search for the business model.

If they haven't done many early deals before a business model is found, ask them why they are interested in you? Is it for your technology? Your potential business model?

Do They Get Customer Development?

For a founder there's nothing worse than searching for a business model day after day and then sitting in a board meeting with a VC who asks about some detail of year five of your revenue plan.

Ask potential investors, how will they measure progress for the company and you as a CEO? Do they have metrics and a methodology they use for early stage companies that differs from companies that have already found a business model? Have they heard about Customer Development? Lean Startups? Can they tell you what you should be doing in Customer Discovery and Customer Validation? If not, do they have a better methodology?

Who Do They Hang With?

Investors who have successful ex-founders who you can call for advice, grab a coffee with or get on your advisory board is a good sign (and a sign that their ex-founders still like them).

VCs who have ex-CEOs who took over from the founder and built the startup into a multi-$100 million company can give great advice about your growing company's infrastructure, but if you are still searching for your first customer, they may not be much help. (In fact, unless they've been founders themselves, they usually provide bad advice.) VCs with formerly high-ranking government officials and Fortune 1000 CEOs as advisors may be wonderful to help you grow your company in a later stage but not helpful now. (Unfortunately the odds of you being the CEO at this future stage are pretty low.)

How Many of Their Founders Are Still With Their Company?

Most early stage VCs are betting on the founders to both deliver the product and to find the business model. At this stage, firing the founder is not a strategy, it's an act of desperation.

By the time the company gets to the build-stage (the Transition) what differentiates VCs is how many turn the founders into builders versus relying on bringing in new, more experienced management to lead the transition. As a founder, you should ask: What percentage of the firm's companies still have founders as the CEOs? In any active role? If the number is less than 25-percent, you may want to think twice. Ask to talk to some of the founders who are no longer with their startups. I'll bet you get some interesting stories.

Will the VC Tailor Your Vesting to Your Contribution?

Most founders don't make it past the build stage in a startup. Almost invariably the new CEO will comes in and complain about how disorganized the place is and then does a wonderful job in putting policies and procedures in place. Yet none of this would be possible if the founder hadn't created the company in the first place. Typical vesting of your stock is over a four-year period, yet the founder's contribution is heavily weighted to the first few years.

Over the years, I've become a bigger and bigger believer in some sort of accelerated vesting for the founders tied to finding the business model. There have been suggestions of a different class of stock for founders on Startup Company Lawyer and good general advice in VentureHacks.

All these suggestions are written as if you had a choice of who to take money from. Most of the time you'll take whatever check will cash. But if you do have a choice, asking these questions will keep you from being surprised in a board meeting.

Lessons Learned

- What phase of the company lifecycle are you?

- What phase do your VCs typically invest in?

- What type of advisors does your VC have?

- What percentage of this firm's former founders are still running their companies?

- What metrics are they going to use to measure progress in a board meeting?

'Lessons Learned' — A New Type of Venture Capital Pitch

November 12, 2009 (Steve Blank)

I joined the board of Cafepress.com when it was a startup. It was amazing to see the two founders, Fred Durham and Maheesh Jain, build a $100 million company from coffee cups and T-shirts.

But Cafepress's most memorable moment was when the founders used a "Lessons Learned" VC pitch to raise their second round of funding and got an eight-digit term sheet that same afternoon.

Here's how they did it.

Fail Fast and Cheap

Fred and Maheesh had started nine previous companies in six years. Their motto was: "Fail fast and cheap. And learn from it." Cafepress literally started in their garage and was another set of experiments only this time it caught fire. They couldn't keep up with the orders.

Tell the Story of the Journey

The company got to a point where additional capital was needed to expand just to keep up with the business (a warehouse/shipping center collocated with UPS, etc). Rather than a traditional VC pitch, I suggested that they do something unconventional and tell the story of their journey in Customer Discovery and Validation. The heart of the Cafepress presentation is the "Lessons Learned from our Customers" section.

Their presentation looked like this:

- Market/Opportunity
- Lessons Learned Slide 1
- Lessons Learned Slide 2
- Lessons Learned Slide 3
- Why We're Here

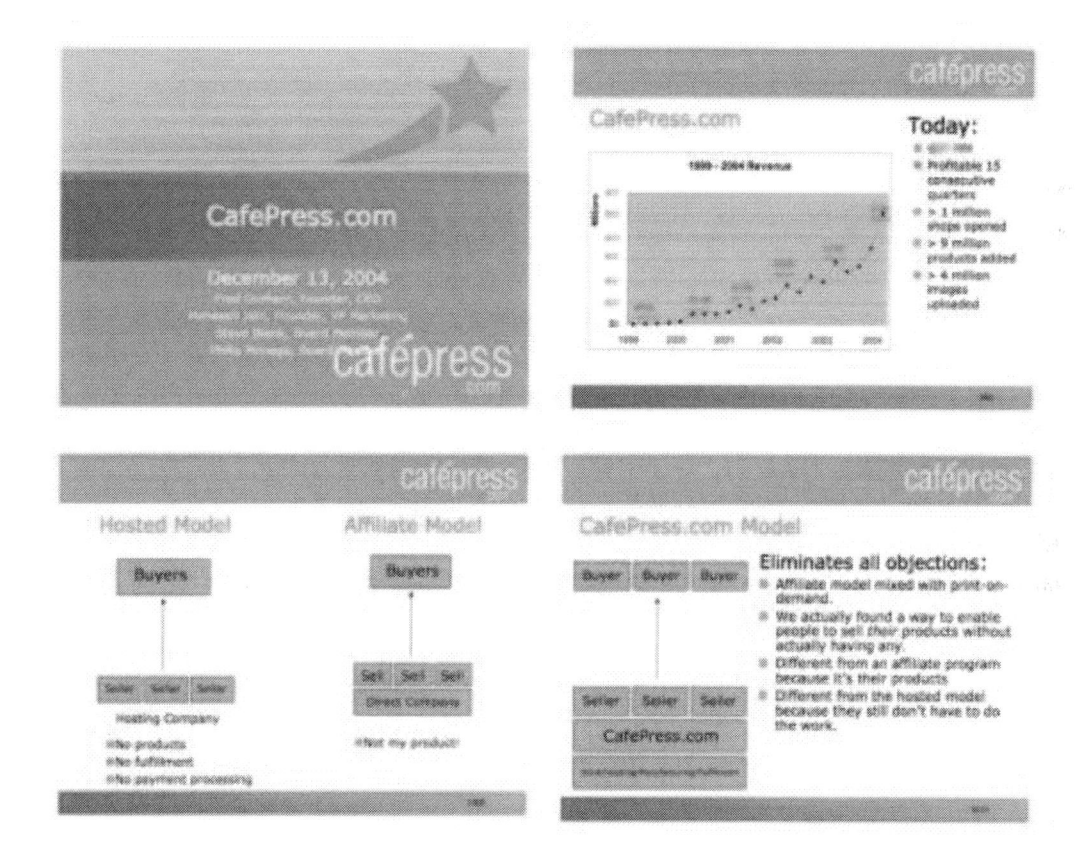

Telling the Cafepress Customer Discovery and Customer Validation story allowed Fred and Maheesh to take the VCs on their journey year by year.

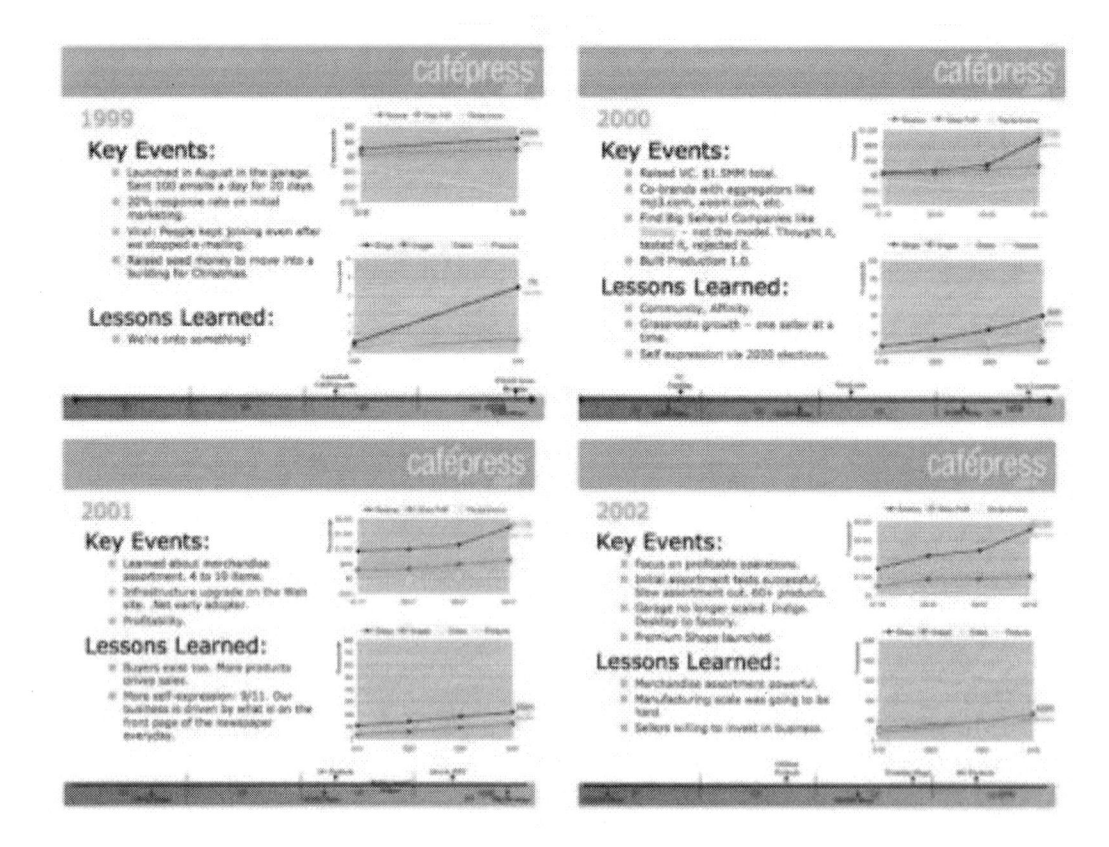

After these slides, these VCs recognized that this company had dramatically reduced risk and built a startup that was agile, resilient and customer-centric.

The presentation didn't have a single word about Lean Startups or Customer Development. There was no proselytizing about any particular methodology, yet the results are compelling.

The VC firm delivered a term sheet for an eight-digit second round that afternoon. Your results may vary.

Steel In Their Eyes—Why VCs Should Be Startup CEOs

November 1, 2011 (Steve Blank)

"A man who carries a cat by the tail learns something he can learn in no other way."

— Mark Twain

Venture Capitalists who are serious about turning their firms into more than one-fund wonders may want to have their associates actually start and run a company for a year. Running a company is distinctly different from simply having operating experience—(working in bus dev, sales, or marketing). None of that can compare with being the CEO of a startup facing a rapidly diminishing bank account, your best engineer quitting, working until 10 P.M. and rushing to the airport and catching a red-eye for a "Hail Mary" close of a customer, with your board demanding you do it faster.

Today, you can start a web/mobile/cloud startup for $500,000 and have money left over. Every potential early-stage Venture Capitalist should take a year and do it before he or she makes partner.

Here's why.

———

Venture capital as a profession is less than half a century old.

Over time, venture firms realized that the partners in the firms needs a variety of skills:

- People skills (ability to recognize patterns of success in individuals and teams)

- Market/technology acuity (patterns of success, domain expertise)

- Rolodex/dealflow (deal sourcing/ability to make connections for the portfolio)

- Board skills (Startup coaching, mentoring, strategy, operational/growth)

- Fund raising skills

Some of these skills are learned in school (finance), some are innate aptitudes (people skills), some are learned pattern recognition skills (shadowing experienced partners, hard won success and failures of their own), and some are learned by having operating experience. But none of them are substitutes for having started and run a company.

How to Become a VC

Early-stage Venture Capital firms grow their partnerships in different ways, some hire:

- partners from other firms

- associates and put them on a long career path

- venture/operating partners to get them into new industries

- an executive who had startup "operating experience"

- rarely a startup founder/CEO

In surveying my VC friends, I was surprised about the strong and diverse opinions. The feedback varied from:

- ".. because culture is such an important part of who we are, we will probably never hire a partner from another firm. The idea of bolting on someone from another firm is somewhat antithetical to who we are. We think that our venture partner role is the most likely path to general partner."

- ".".we have a partner-track associates program. We want to find someone who has a lot of consumer internet product experience as either product manager, founder, VP Product, etc. with three to seven years of experience."

- "…we do not even try to train new partners. We bring people into our firm who have learned how to be VCs at the partner level somewhere else and have demonstrated their talent in boardrooms alongside of us. We completely and totally punt on the idea of 'training a VC.' It's an ugly and painful process and I don't want to be part of it."

- "…if they don't have operating experience, the odds of them knowing what they're talking about in a board meeting for the first five years is low.."

Carrying the Cat by the Tail

When I finally became a CEO it was after I had spent my career working my way up the ladder in marketing in startups. I did every low-level job there was, at times sleeping under my desk (engineering was doing the same). By the time I was running a company, having some junior employee tell me why they couldn't do something because of "how hard it was" didn't get much sympathy from me. I knew how hard it was because I had done it myself. Startups are hard.

What running a company would do is give early-stage VCs a benchmark for reality, something most newly-minted partners sorely lack. They would learn how a founding CEO turns their money into a company which becomes a learning, execution and delivery engine. They would learn that a CEO does it through the people—the day-to-day of who is going to do what, how you hold people accountable, how teams communicate, and more importantly, who you hire, how you motivate and get people to accomplish the seemingly impossible. Further, they'd experience first hand how, in a startup, the devil is in the details of execution and deliverables.

My hypotheses is simple: what most VCs lack is not brains or rolodex or people skills—but hands-on experience as a startup CEO—knowing what it's like trying to make a payroll while finding sufficient customers while you're building the product. Sure, a year as a CEO won't make them an expert, but it will change them quicker than 10 years in the boardroom.

Does It Matter?
There's a school of thought that says the skill set of a great early-stage VC—awesome people skills, curiosity, likable, etc.—versus the attributes of a great entrepreneur— pattern recognition, tenacity, etc. may not have much overlap. Early stage investing is not a spreadsheet, quantitative driven exercise, nor is it about technology—it is a deal business and people drive the deals. And while having experience as a startup CEO may make you a better board member, it may not substantively contribute to your career as an early stage investor—which depend on many more important skills.

Steel in Their Eyes
Ten years ago starting a company required millions of dollars and first customer ship took years. Now it's possible to build a company, ship product and get tens of thousands of customers in a year with less than $500,000. For venture firms who want to groom/grow associates or operating execs into partners (rather than hiring proven partners), here's my suggestion:

1. Have them start as an analyst (search for dealflow and people, due diligence)

2. Then take a year as a product manager in a startup in the firm's portfolio

3. Then come back as an associate for a year—shadowing board and partner meetings

4. Then take a year and $250,000 – $500,000 to start and run a mobile/web/cloud company. See what it's really like on the other side of that boardroom table

5. Then return as a partner

This process will create a new generation of venture capital partners, ones who have been battle tested in the trenches of a startup, hardened by hiring and firing, tempered by making a payroll and losing orders, and will never forget it's all about the people.

These VCs would return to their firms with steel in their eyes. They'd be relentless about accountability from board meeting to board meeting with laser like focus on the one or two issues that matter. They would understand the CEO-VC-board dynamic in a way that few who hadn't lived it could. They'd be ruthless in their choice of people and teams, looking for those few who have natural curiosity, a passion to win, and who won't take no for answer.

Lessons Learned

Venture Capital is still a "craft business."

Early stage VCs should have startup CEO experience.

It can now be gained cheaply and quickly.

It will give them perspective and edge that would take a decade to learn.

Raising Money Using Customer Development

November 5, 2009 (Steve Blank)

Getting "funded" is the holy grail for most entrepreneurs. Unfortunately, in early stage startups the drive for financing hijacks the corporate DNA and becomes the raison d'etre of the company. Chasing funding versus chasing customers and a repeatable and scalable business model is one reason startups fail.

Companies using the Customer Development model can increase their credibility, valuation and probability of getting a first round of funding by presenting their results in a "Lesson Learned" venture pitch.

It should go without saying that this post is not advice, nor is it recommendation of what you should do, it's simply my observation of how companies using Customer Development positioned themselves to successfully raise money from venture investors.

Product Development—Getting Funded as the Goal

In a traditional product development model, entrepreneurs come up with an idea or concept, write a business plan and try to get funding to bring that idea to fruition. The goal of their startup in this stage becomes "getting funded." Entrepreneurs put together their funding presentation by extracting the key ideas from their business plan, putting them on PowerPoint/Keynote and pitching the company—until they get funded or exhausted.

What Are Early Stage VCs Really Asking?

When you are presenting to a VC there are two conversations going on—the one you are presenting and the one that investors are thinking as they are listening to your presentation. (If they're not busy looking at their BlackBerrys/iPhones.)

A VC listening to your presentation is thinking, "Are you going to blow my initial investment, or are you going to make me a ton of money? Are there customers for what you are building? How many are there? Now? Later?" Is there a profitable business model?

Can it scale?" And finally, "Is this a team that can build this company?"

The Traditional VC Pitch

Entrepreneurs who pursue the traditional product development model don't have customer data to answer these questions. Knowing this venture firms have come up with a canonical checklist of what they would like to see. A typical pitch to a venture firm might cover:

- Technology/Product
- Team
- Opportunity/Market
- Customer Problem
- Business Model
- Go to Market Strategy
- Financials

Given that the traditional pitch has no hard customer metrics (and VCs don't demand them), you get funded on the basis of intangibles that vary from firm to firm: Do you fit the theme of thesis of the venture firm? Did the VCs like your team? Do they believe you have a big enough vision and market? Did the partner have a good or bad day, etc. Tons of advice is available on how to pitch, present and market your company. Tons of advice is available on how to pitch, present and market your company.

I believe all this advice is wrong. It's akin to putting lipstick on a pig. The problem isn't your pitch, it's your fundamental assumption that you can/should get funded without having real customer and product feedback. No amount of learning how to get a VC meeting or improving your VC demo skills will fix the lack of concrete customer data. You might as well bring your lucky rabbit's foot to the VC meeting.

Customer Development—Getting Funded After You Find a Repeatable Model

In contrast, if you are following a Customer Development process you have a greater chance of getting listened to, believed and funded.

Just as a refresher. The first step in Customer Development was Customer Discovery; extracting hypotheses from the business plan and getting the founders out of the building to test the hypotheses in front of customers. Your goal was to preserve your cash while you turned these guesses into facts and searched for a repeatable and scalable sales model. Your proof that you have a business rather than a hobby comes from customer orders or users for your buggy, unfinished product with a minimum feature set.

If you're following Customer Development, you are now raising money because even with this first rev of the product you think you've found product/market fit and you want to scale.

What VCs Really Want But Don't Know How to Ask For or Get

Mike Maples at Maples Investments observes that the quality of pitches from entrepreneurs get better as you climb the "Hierarchy of Proof."

1. On the bottom, and least convincing are statements about your "idea."

2. Next are hypothesis—"I think customers will care about x or y."

3. Better are facts from customers—"We interviewed 30 customers with 20 questions."

4. Even better is "Customer Validation"—"We just got $50,000 from a customer" or "We got 100,000 users spending x minutes on our site."

5. Finally, if you're ever so lucky—"Everyone's buying in droves and we're here because we need money to scale and execute."

If you've actually been doing Customer Development at a minimum, you're at step 3 or 4. If not, you don't have enough data for a VC presentation. Get out of the building, get some more customer feedback, spin your product, and go back and read the book.

"Lessons Learned"—A New Type of VC Pitch

A Customer Development fundraising presentation tells the story of your journey in Customer Discovery and Validation. While your presentation will cover some of the same ground as the traditional VC pitch, the heart of the presentation is the "Lessons Learned from our Customers" section. The overall presentation looks something like this:

- Market/Opportunity
- Team
- Lessons Learned Slide 1
- Lessons Learned Slide 2
- Lessons Learned Slide 3
- Why We're Here

Here's What We Thought, What We Did, What We Learned

- "Here's What We Thought."
- "Here's What We Did."
- "Here's What Happened."
- A Progress Graph

Here's What We Thought is you describing your initial set of hypotheses. Here's What We Did allows you to talk about building the first-pass of the products minimum feature set. Here's What Happened is the not so surprising story of why customers didn't react the way you thought they would. A Progress Graph on the right visually shows how far you've come (in whatever units of goodness you're tracking—revenue, units, users, etc.).

Telling the Customer Discovery and Customer Validation story this way allows you to take VCs on your journey through all the learning and discovery you've done. After three of these slides, smart VCs will recognize that by iterating on your assumptions you have dramatically reduced risk—on your nickel, not theirs. They will realize that you have built a startup that's agile, resilient, and customer-centric.

Your presentation doesn't have a single word about Lean Startups or Customer Development. There is no proselytizing about any particular methodology, yet the results are compelling.

This is a radical departure from a traditional VC pitch. It will blow the minds of 70 to 80- percent of investors. The others will throw you out of their office.

Guaranteed Funding—Not

Will this type of presentation guarantee you funding? Of course not. Even if you have the worlds best Lessons Learned slides you might find out that your particular market (i.e. consumer Internet) might have a really, really high bar of achievement for funding.

In fact, just trying to put three Lessons Learned slides together showing tangible progress will make most startups realize how hard really doing Customer Development is.

Try it.

How Scientists and Engineers Got It Right, and VCs Got It Wrong

July 25, 2011 (Steve Blank)

Scientists and engineers as founders and startup CEOs is one of the least celebrated contributions of Silicon Valley.

It might be its most important.

———-

ESL, the first company I worked for in Silicon Valley, was founded by a PhD in Math and six other scientists and engineers. Since it was my first job, I just took for granted that scientists and engineers started and ran companies. It took me a long time to realize that this was one of Silicon Valley's best contributions to innovation.

Cold War Spin Outs

In the 1950s the groundwork for a culture and environment of entrepreneurship were taking shape on the east and west coasts of the United States. Each region had two of the finest research universities in the United States, Stanford and MIT, which were building on the technology breakthroughs of World War II and graduating a generation of engineers into a consumer and cold war economy that seemed limitless. Each region already had the beginnings of a high-tech culture, Boston with Raytheon, Silicon Valley with Hewlett Packard.

However, the majority of engineers graduating from these schools went to work in existing companies. But in the mid 1950s, the culture around these two universities began to change.

Stanford—1950s Innovation

At Stanford, Dean of Engineering/Provost Fred Terman wanted companies outside of the university to take Stanford's prototype microwave tubes and electronic intelligence systems and build product volumes for the military. While existing companies took some of the business, often it was a graduate student or professor who started a new company. The motivation in the mid-1950s for these new startups was a crisis—we were in the midst of the Cold War, and the United States military and intelligence agencies were rearming as fast as they could.

Why It's "Silicon" Valley

In 1956, entrepreneurship as we know it would change forever. At the time it didn't appear earthshaking or momentous. Shockley Semiconductor Laboratory, the first semiconductor company in the valley, set up shop in Mountain View. Fifteen months later, eight of Shockley's employees (three physicists, an electrical engineer, an industrial engineer, a mechanical engineer, a metallurgist and a physical chemist) founded Fairchild Semiconductor. (Every chip company in Silicon Valley can trace their lineage from Fairchild.)

The history of Fairchild was one of applied experimentation. It wasn't pure research, but rather a culture of taking sufficient risks to get to market. It was learning, discovery, iteration and execution. The goal was commercial products, but as scientists and engineers the company's founders realized that at times the cost of experimentation was failure. And just as they don't punish failure in a research lab, they didn't fire scientists whose experiments didn't work. Instead the company built a culture where when you hit a wall, you backed up and tried a different path. (In 21st century parlance, we say that innovation in the early semiconductor business was all about "pivoting" while aiming for salable products.)

The Fairchild approach would shape Silicon Valley's entrepreneurial ethos: In startups, failure was treated as experience (until you ran out of money).

Scientists and Engineers as Founders

In the late 1950s, Silicon Valley's first three IPOs were companies that were founded and run by scientists and engineers: Varian (founded by Stanford engineering professors and graduate students,) Hewlett Packard (founded by two Stanford engineering graduate students), and Ampex (founded by a mechanical/electrical engineer). While this signaled that investments in technology companies could be very lucrative, both Shockley and Fairchild could only be funded through corporate partners—there was no venture capital industry. But by the early 1960s, the tidal wave of semiconductor startup spinouts from Fairchild would find a valley with a growing number of U.S. government-backed venture firms and limited partnerships.

A wave of innovation was about to meet a pile of risk capital.

For the next two decades venture capital invested in things that ran on electrons: hardware, software and silicon. Yet the companies were anomalies in the big picture in the U.S.—there were almost no MBAs. In 1960s and '70s, few MBAs would give up a lucrative career in management, finance or Wall Street to join a bunch of technical lunatics. So the engineers taught themselves how to become marketers, sales people and CEOs. And the venture capital community became comfortable in funding them.

Medical Researchers Get Entrepreneurial

In the 60s and 70s, while engineers were founding companies, medical researchers and academics were skeptical about the blurring of the lines between academia and commerce. This all changed in 1980 with the Genentech IPO.

In 1973, two scientists, Stanley Cohen at Stanford and Herbert Boyer at UCSF, discovered recombinant DNA, and Boyer went on to found Genentech. In 1980 Genentech became the first IPO of a venture funded biotech company. The fact that serious money could be made in companies investing in life sciences wasn't lost on other researchers and the venture capital community.

Over the next decade, medical graduate students saw their professors start companies, other professors saw their peers and entrepreneurial colleagues start companies, and VCs started calling on academics and researchers and speaking their language.

Scientists and Engineers = Innovation and Entrepreneurship

Yet when venture capital got involved they brought all the processes to administer existing companies they learned in business school—how to write a business plan, accounting, organizational behavior, managerial skills, marketing, operations, etc. This set up a conflict with the learning, discovery and experimentation style of the original valley founders.

Yet because of the Golden Rule, the VCs got to set how startups were built and managed (those who have the gold set the rules).

Fifty years later we now know the engineers were right. Business plans are fine for large companies where there is an existing market, product and customers, but in a startup all of these elements are unknown and the process of discovering them is filled with rapidly changing assumptions.

Startups are not smaller versions of large companies. Large companies execute known business models. In the real world a startup is about the search for a business model or more accurately, startups are a temporary organization designed to search for a scalable and repeatable business model.

Yet for the last 40 years, while technical founders knew that no business plan survived first contact with customers, they lacked a management tool set for learning, discovery and experimentation.

Earlier this year, we developed a class in the Stanford Technology Ventures Program (the entrepreneurship center at Stanford's School of Engineering) to provide scientists and engineers just those tools – how to think about all the parts of building a business, not just the product. The Stanford class introduced the first management tools for entrepreneurs built around the business model/customer development/agile development solution stack.

The $10 Million Photo and Other VC Stories

July 19, 2011 (Steve Blank)

While on vacation I had a phone interview with Kevin Ohannessian of Fast Company, who wanted a few "funding stories." Here are two of them. Apologies for the rambling stream of consciousness.

Throw in the Photo and You Have a Deal

When we were trying to raise money for E.piphany, my last startup, I was negotiating with a venture capital firm called Infinity Capital. They really wanted to invest, but it was the beginning of the bubble, and I wanted (what was then) an absurd valuation. All we had were six slides, and I wanted a $10 million post-money valuation. But it was my eighth startup and my partner Ben was even more experienced: ex-VC, ex-Harvard Computer Science professor, genius at building products and teams. I had sat on a board of an Electronic Design Automation company with this VC, and we had gotten to know each other. So when I wanted to start a company he wanted to fund us. We had gone back and forth with them on valuation, but this was a new firm and they wanted to close a deal with us.

After about our fifth meeting I'm in their conference room. I say, "Why can't you guys do a $10 million post money valuation?" Picking the biggest number I could think of for three founders without a product a semi-coherent idea and badly written slides. Finally they admitted, "Steve, we're a new fund; everybody will think we are idiots if we do that." I said, "All right. Can you do some other number close to my number?" So I stepped out of the room as they caucused, and they called me back in 10 minutes later and said, "So listen. We can do $9.99 million." I'm trying to play poker with the deal, and one of the partners at the time was a great photographer—the firm had big prints of his on the walls.

I was really in love with the one in the boardroom. So without thinking, when they made me that offer, trying to keep a straight face, I reached behind me, grabbed the photo off the wall and slammed it on the desk, and said, "If you throw this photo in, you got the deal!"

The $10 Million Photo

The look on their face was utter astonishment. I was thinking it was because I was being creative by throwing the photo in, but then I noticed that this cloud of dust was settling around me. I turn around and looked at the wall and it turned out the photo had been bolted into the drywall. And there was now a hole – I literally ripped a part of their boardroom wall off as I was accepting the offer. Without missing a beat, they said, "Yes, you can have the photo. But we're going to have to deduct $500 to repair our wall." And I said, "Deal." And that's how E.piphany got its Series A.

Invest in the Team

Before we closed our Series A with Infinity, I had called on Mohr, Davidow Ventures, the firm which had funded my last company, Rocket Science. The senior partner at the time was Bill Davidow, a marketing legend and a hero of mine who had also funded other Enterprise software companies. I went in and pitched Bill the idea about how to automate the marketing domain. He gave me 15 minutes, then as politely as he could do it, walked me out the door and said, "Stupidest idea I ever heard, Steve. Enterprise software means across the Enterprise. Marketing is just one very small department." As he was walking me out, I remember as I physically crossed the threshold of the door that: A) He was right, and B) I figured out how to solve the problem of making our product useful across the entire enterprise. So E.piphany went from a bad idea to a good idea by being thrown out by a VC who gave me advice that made the company. He has reminded me since, "Sometimes you invest in the idea, but you should always be investing in the people. If I would've remembered who you were, I would've known you would figure it out."

(Kleiner Perkins would do the Series B round for E.piphany. After our IPO Infinity's and Kleiner Perkins' investment in Epiphany would be worth $1 billion dollars to each of them.) I still have the photo.

IX.

Steve's Favorite Posts

When It's Darkest Men See the Stars

November 24, 2010 (Steve Blank)

> "When It's Darkest, Men See the Stars."
> — Ralph Waldo Emerson

This Thanksgiving, it might seem that there's a lot less to be thankful for. One out of ten of Americans is out of work. The common wisdom says that the chickens have all come home to roost from a disastrous series of economic decisions including outsourcing the manufacture of America's physical goods. The United States is now a debtor nation to China and that the bill is about to come due. The pundits say the American dream is dead and this next decade will see the further decline and fall of the West and in particular of the United States.

It may be that all the doomsayers are right. But I don't think so.

Let me offer my prediction. There's a chance that the common wisdom is very, very wrong. That the second decade of the 21st century may turn out to be the West's and in particular the United States' finest hour.

I believe that we will look back at this decade as the beginning of an economic revolution as important as the scientific revolution in the 16th century and the industrial revolution in the 18th century. We're standing at the beginning of the entrepreneurial revolution. This doesn't mean just more technology stuff, though we'll get that. This is a revolution that will permanently reshape business as we know it and more importantly, change the quality of life across the entire planet for all who come after us.

There's Something Happening Here, What it Is Ain't Exactly Clear

The story to date is a familiar one. Over the last half a century, Silicon Valley has grown into the leading technology and innovation cluster for the United States and the world. Silicon Valley has amused us, connected (and separated us) as never before, made businesses more efficient and led to the wholesale transformation of entire industries (bookstores, video rentals, newspapers, etc.).

Wave after wave of hardware, software, biotech and cleantech products have emerged from what has become "ground zero" of entrepreneurial and startup culture. Silicon Valley emerged by the serendipitous intersection of:

- Cold War research in microwaves and electronics at Stanford University,

- a Stanford Dean of Engineering who encouraged startup culture over pure academic research,

- Cold War military and intelligence funding driving microwave and military products for the defense industry in the 1950s,

- a single Bell Labs researcher deciding to start his semiconductor company next to Stanford in the 1950s which led to

- the wave of semiconductor startups in the 1960s and 70s,

- the emergence of venture capital as a professional industry,

- the personal computer revolution in 1980s,

- the rise of the Internet in the 1990s and finally

- the wave of internet commerce applications in the first decade of the 21st century.

The pattern for the valley seemed to be clear. Each new wave of innovation was like punctuated equilibrium — just when you thought the wave had run its course into stasis, a sudden shift and radical change into a new family of technology emerged.

The Barriers to Entrepreneurship

While startups continued to innovate in each new wave of technology, the rate of innovation was constrained by limitations we only now can understand. Only in the last few years do we appreciate that startups in the past were constrained by:

1. long technology development cycles (how long it takes from idea to product),

2. the high cost of getting to first customers (how many dollars to build the product),

3. the structure of the venture capital industry (a limited number of VC firms each needing to invest millions per startups),

4. the expertise about how to build startups (clustered in specific regions like Silicon Valley, Boston, New York, etc.),

5. the failure rate of new ventures (startups had no formal rules and were a hit or miss proposition),

6. the slow adoption rate of new technologies by the government and large companies.

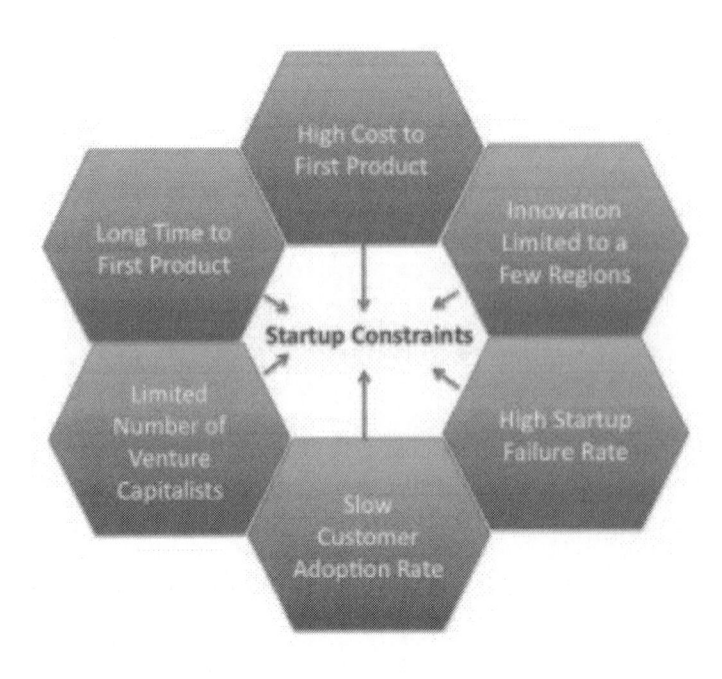

The Democratization of Entrepreneurship

What's happening is something more profound than a change in technology. What's happening is that all the things that have been limits to startups and innovation are being removed. At once. Starting now.

Compressing the Product Development Cycle

In the past, the time to build a first product release was measured in months or even years as startups executed the founder's vision of what customers wanted. This meant building every possible feature the founding team envisioned into a monolithic "release" of the product. Yet time after time, after the product shipped, startups would find that customers didn't use or want most of the features. The founders were simply wrong about their assumptions about customer needs. The effort that went into making all those unused features was wasted.

Today startups have begun to build products differently. Instead of building the maximum number of features, they look to deliver a minimum feature set in the shortest period of time. This lets them deliver a first version of the product to customers in a fraction on the time.

For products that are simply "bits" delivered over the web, a first product can be shipped in weeks rather than years.

Startups Built For Thousands Rather than Millions of Dollars

Startups traditionally required millions of dollars of funding just to get their first product to customers. A company developing software would have to buy computers and license software from other companies and hire the staff to run and maintain it. A hardware startup had to spend money building prototypes and equipping a factory to manufacture the product.

Today open source software has slashed the cost of software development from millions of dollars to thousands. For consumer hardware, no startup has to build their own factory as the costs are absorbed by offshore manufacturers.

The cost of getting the first product out the door for an Internet commerce startup has dropped by a factor of a ten or more in the last decade.

The New Structure of the Venture Capital Industry

The plummeting cost of getting a first product to market (particularly for Internet startups) has shaken up the venture capital industry. Venture capital used to be a tight club clustered around formal firms located in Silicon Valley, Boston, and New York. While those firms are still there (and getting larger), the pool of money that invests risk capital in startups has expanded, and a new class of investors has emerged. New groups of VCs, super angels, smaller than the traditional multi-hundred million dollar VC fund, can make small investments necessary to get a consumer internet startup launched. These angels make lots of early bets and double-down when early results appear. (And the results do appear years earlier than in a traditional startup.)

In addition to super angels, incubators like Y Combinator, TechStars and the 100-plus others worldwide like them have begun to formalize seed-investing. They pay expenses in a formal three-month program while a startup builds something impressive enough to raise money on a larger scale.

Finally, venture capital and angel investing is no longer a U.S. or Eurocentric phenomenon. Risk capital has emerged in China, India and other countries where risk taking, innovation and liquidity is encouraged, on a scale previously only seen in the U.S.

The emergence of incubators and super angels have dramatically expanded the sources of seed capital. The globalization of entrepreneurship means the worldwide pool of potential startups has increased at least ten fold since the turn of this century.

Entrepreneurship as Its Own Management Science

Over the last ten years, entrepreneurs began to understand that startups were not simply smaller versions of large companies. While companies execute business models, startups search for a business model. (Or more accurately, startups are a temporary organization designed to search for a scalable and repeatable business model.)

Instead of adopting the management techniques of large companies, which too often stifle innovation in a young start up, entrepreneurs began to develop their own management tools. Using the business model/customer develoment/agile development solution stack, entrepreneurs first map their assumptions (their business model) and then test these hypotheses with customers outside in the field (customer development) and use an iterative and incremental development methodology (agile development) to build the product. When founders discover their assumptions are wrong, as they inevitably will, the result isn't a crisis, it's a learning event called a pivot—and an opportunity to change the business model.

The result, startups now have tools that speed up the search for customers, reduce time to market and slash the cost of development.

Consumer Internet Driving Innovation

In the 1950s and '60s, U.S. Defense and Intelligence organizations drove the pace of innovation in Silicon Valley by providing research and development dollars to universities, and purchased weapons systems that used the valley's first microwave and semiconductor components. In the 1970s, 80s, and 90s, momentum shifted to the enterprise as large businesses supported innovation in PCs, communications hardware and enterprise software. Government and the enterprise are now followers rather than leaders. Today, it's the consumer—specifically consumer Internet companies—that are the drivers of innovation. When the product and channel are bits, adoption by tens and hundreds of millions users can happen in years versus decades.

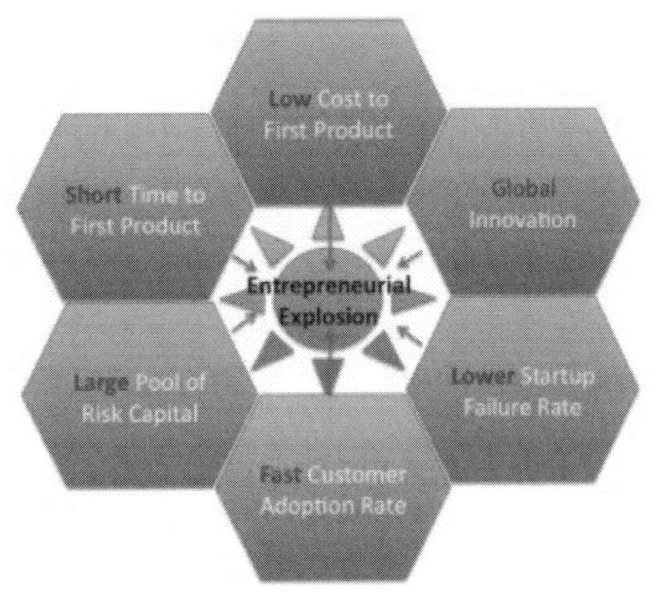

The Entrepreneurial Singularity
The barriers to entrepreneurship are not just being removed. In each case they're being replaced by innovations that are speeding up each step, some by a factor of ten. For example, for Internet commerce startups the time needed to get the first product to market has been cut by a factor of ten, the dollars needed to get the first product to market cut by a factor of ten, the number of sources of initial capital for entrepreneurs has increased by a factor of ten, etc.

And while innovation is moving at Internet speed, this won't be limited to just internet commerce startups. It will spread to the enterprise and ultimately every other business segment.

When It's Darkest Men See the Stars
The economic downturn in the United States has had an unexpected consequence for startups—it has created more of them. Young and old, innovators who are unemployed or underemployed now face less risk in starting a company. They have a lot less to lose and a lot more to gain.

If we are at the cusp of a revolution as important as the scientific and industrial revolutions what does it mean? Revolutions are not obvious when they happen. When James Watt started the industrial revolution with the steam engine in 1775 no one said, "This is the day everything changes." When Karl Benz drove around Mannheim in 1885, no one said, "There will be 500 million of these driving around in a century." And certainly in 1958, when Noyce and Kilby invented the integrated circuit, the idea of a quintillion (10 to the 18th) transistors being produced each year seemed ludicrous.

Yet it's possible that we'll look back to this decade as the beginning of our own revolution. We may remember this as the time when scientific discoveries and technological breakthroughs were integrated into the fabric of society faster than they had ever been before. When the speed of how businesses operated changed forever. As the time when we reinvented the American economy and our Gross Domestic Product began to take off and the U.S. and the world reached a level of wealth never seen before. It may be the dawn of a new era for a new American economy built on entrepreneurship and innovation.

One that our children will look back on and marvel that when it was the darkest, we saw the stars.

Philadelphia University Commencement Speech

May 17, 2011 (Steve Blank)

I am honored to be with you as we gather to celebrate your graduation from Philadelphia University.

While I teach at Stanford and Berkeley, to be honest... this is the closest I've ever gotten to a college graduation.

I realize that my 15 minutes up here is all that's between you and the rest of your life, so if I can keep you awake, I'm going to share four short stories from my life.

My first story is about finding your passion.

My parents were immigrants. Neither of them had been to college—my mother graduated from high school but my father left school after the seventh grade. Still, like many immigrants, they dreamed that someday their children would go to college. Unfortunately that was their dream, but it wasn't mine.

I ended up at Michigan State because I got a scholarship. Once I got there, I was lost, unfocused and had no idea of who I was and why I was in school. I hated school.

One day my girlfriend said, "You know some of us are working hard to stay here. But you don't seem to care. Why don't you find out what you really want to do?"

That was the moment I realized I, not anyone else, was in charge of my life.

I took her advice. I dropped out of Michigan State University after the first semester. In the middle of a Michigan winter, I stuck out my thumb and hitchhiked to Miami, the warmest place I could think of.

I had no idea what would be at the end of the highway. But that day I began a pattern that I still follow: stick out your thumb and see where the road takes you.

I managed to find a job at the Miami International Airport loading racehorses onto cargo planes. I didn't like the horses, but the airplanes caught my interest.

Airplanes were the most complicated things I had ever seen. Unlike other kids who were fans of the pilots, I was in awe of the electronics technicians in charge of the planes' instruments. I would hang around the repair shop just helping out wherever I could. I didn't know anything, so I didn't get paid.

But soon some technician took me under his wing and gave me my first tutorial on electronics, radar and navigation. I was hooked. I started taking home all the equipment manuals and would read them late into the night.

For the first time in my life, I found something I was passionate about.

And the irony is that if I hadn't dropped out, I would never have found this passion, the one that began my career. If I hadn't discovered something I truly loved to do, I might be driving a cab at the Miami airport.

My life continued to follow this same pattern. I'd pursue my curiosity, volunteer to help, and show up a lot. Again and again, the same thing would happen – people would notice that I cared, and I'd get a chance to learn something new.

Now that you paid for your degree, I'm going to let you in on a secret. It's your curiosity and enthusiasm that will get you noticed and make your life interesting—not your grade point average.

But at the time, as excited as I was, I couldn't see how my passion for airplanes and avionics could ever get me anywhere. Without money, or a formal education, how could I learn about them?

The answer turned out to be a war.

My second story is about Volunteering and Showing Up.

In the early 1970s, as some of you might remember, our country was in the middle of the Vietnam War—and the Air Force was happy to have me.

I enlisted to learn how to repair electronics. The Air Force sent me to a year of military electronics school. While college had been someone else's dream, learning electronics had become mine.

After electronics school, when most everyone else was being sent overseas to a war-zone, I was assigned to one of the cushiest bases in the Air Force, right outside of Miami.

My first week on the base, our shop chief announced: "We're looking for some volunteers to go to Thailand." I still remember the laughter and comments from my fellow airmen. "You got to be kidding… leave Miami for a war in Southeast Asia?"

Others wisely remembered the first rule in the military: never volunteer for anything. Listening to them, I realized they were right. Not volunteering was the sane path of safety, certainty, and comfort.

So I stepped forward, raised my hand – and I said, "I'll go."

Once again, I was going to see where the road would take me. Volunteering for the unknown, which meant leaving the security of what I knew and would continually change my life.

Two weeks later, I was lugging heavy boxes across the runway under the broiling Thailand sun. My job was to replace failed electronic warfare equipment in fighter planes as they returned from bombing missions over North Vietnam.

As I faced yet another 110-degree day, I did consider that perhaps my decision to leave Miami might have been a bit hasty. Yet every day I would ask, "Where does our equipment come from… and how do we know it's protecting our airplanes?"

The answer I got was, "Don't you know there's a war on? Shut up and keep doing what you're told."

Still I was forever curious. At times continually asking questions got me in trouble, once it almost sent me to jail, but mostly it made me smarter.

I wanted to know more. I had found something I loved to do, and I wanted to get better at it.

When my shift on the flightline was over, my friends would go downtown drinking. Instead, I'd often head into the shop and volunteer to help repair broken jammers and receivers. Eventually, the shop chief who ran this 150-person shop approached me and asked, "You're really interested in this stuff, aren't you?" He listened to me babble for a while, and then walked me to a stack of broken electronic equipment and challenged me troubleshoot and fix them.

Hours later when I was finished, he looked at my work and told me, "We need another pair of hands repairing this equipment. As of tomorrow, you no longer work on the flightline." He had just given me a small part of the electronic warfare shop to run.

People talk about getting lucky breaks in their careers. I'm living proof that the "lucky breaks" theory is simply wrong. You get to make your own luck. 80-percent of success in your career will come from just showing up. The world is run by those who show up…not those who wait to be asked.

Eighteen months after arriving in Thailand, I was managing a group of 15 electronics technicians.

I had just turned 20 years old.

My third story is about Failure and Redemption

After I left the military, I ended up in Palo Alto, a town south of San Francisco. Years later this area would become known as Silicon Valley.

For a guy who loved technology, I was certainly in the right place.

Endlessly curious, I went from startups in military intelligence to microprocessors to supercomputers to video games.

I was always learning. There were times I worried that my boss might find out how much I loved my job, and if he did, he might make me pay to work there. To be honest, I would have gladly done so. While I earned a good salary, I got up and went to work every day not because of the pay, but because I loved what I did.

As time went on, I was a co-founder or member of the starting team for six high-tech startups.

With every startup came increasing responsibility. I reached what I then thought was the pinnacle of my career when I raised tens of millions of dollars and became CEO of my seventh startup, a hot new video game company. My picture was in all the business magazines and made it onto the cover of Wired magazine. Life was perfect.

And then one day it wasn't.

It all came tumbling down. We had believed our own press, inhaled our own fumes, and built lousy games. Customers voted with their wallets and didn't buy our products. The company went out of business. Given the press we had garnered, it was a pretty public failure.

We let our customers, our investors, and our employees down. While it was easy to blame it on others—and trust me at first I tried—in the end it was mostly a result of my own hubris, the evil twin of entrepreneurial passion and drive.

I thought my career and my life were over. But I learned that in Silicon Valley, honest failure is a badge of experience.

In fact, unlike in the movies, most startups actually fail. For every Facebook and Zynga that make the press, thousands just never make it at all.

All of you will fail at some time in your career—or in love, or in life.

No one ever sets out to fail. But being afraid to fail means you'll be afraid to try. Playing it safe will get you nowhere.

As it turned out, rather than run me out of town on a rail, the two venture capital firms that had lost $12 million in my failed startup actually asked me to work with them.

During the next couple years (and much humbler), I raised more money and started another company, one that was lucky enough to go public in the dot.com bubble.

In 1999, with the company's revenue north of $100 million. I handed the keys to a new CEO and left. I had married a wonderful woman and together we had two young daughters.

I decided that, after 20 years of working 24/7 in eight startups, I wanted to go home and watch my kids grow up.

Which brings me to my last story—there's a pattern here.

When I retired, I found myself with lots of time to think.

I began to reflect about my career and what had happened in my 21 years with startups in Silicon Valley.

I was all alone in a ski cabin with the snow falling outside. With my wife and daughters out on the slopes all day, I started to collect my thoughts by writing what I had hoped would become my memoirs.

Eighty pages later, I realized that I had some great stories as an entrepreneur and a failed CEO. But while writing them was a great catharsis, it was quickly becoming clear that I'd even have to pay my wife and kids to read the stories.

But the more I thought about what I had done, and what other entrepreneurs had tried, I realized something absurdly simple was staring at me. I saw a repeatable pattern that no else had ever noticed.

Business schools and investors were treating new companies like they were just small versions of large companies. But it struck me that startups were actually something totally different. Startups were actually like explorers—

searching for a new world, where everything (customers, markets, prices)—were unknown and new.

These startups needed to be inventive as they explore, trying new and different things daily. In contrast, existing companies, the Wal-Marts and McDonalds, already had road maps, guidebooks and playbooks—they already know their customers, markets, and prices. To succeed, they just need to do the same thing every day.

Now it would have been easy to say, "Nah, this can't be right—every smart professor at Harvard and Wharton and Stanford believes something different." In fact, in your lives this will happen to you.

You will have a new idea, and people will tell you, "That can't be right because we've always done it this way."

Ignore them. Be persistent. Never give up. Innovation comes from those who see things that other don't.

As a retired CEO, I had a lot of free time. So I was often invited to be a guest lecturer at the business school at Berkeley. They thought I could tell stories about what it was like to start a company. I was generous with my time, and I showed up a lot.

But I began to nag the head of the department about this new idea I had… one that basically said that everything you learn about starting new companies in business schools was wrong. I thought that there was a better a way to teach and manage startups than the conventional wisdom of the last 40 years. And to their credit, Berkeley's Business School and then Stanford's Engineering School let me write and teach a new course based on my ideas.

Now, a decade later, that course called Customer Development is the basis of an entirely new way to start companies.

If you're in a technology company or build a web or mobile application, it's probably the only way to start a company.

How did this happen? By showing up a lot and questioning the status quo.

These days I write a weekly blog about entrepreneurship. At the end of each post, I conclude with lessons learned—a kind of Cliff Notes of my key takeaways. So in case you haven't been listening, that's how I'll finish up today.

- Be forever curious.

- Volunteer for everything.

- Show up a lot.

- Treat failure as a learning experience.

- Live life with no regrets.

- Remembering there is no undo button.

Congratulations again to you all, and thank you very much.

Requiem For A Roommate

October 18, 2010 (Steve Blank)

> And, when he shall die, Take him and cut him out in little stars,
>
> And he will make the face of Heaven so fine
>
> That all the world will be in love with night
>
> And pay no worship to the garish sun.
>
> — William Shakespeare

Last week I had my "public servant" hat on in my official capacity as a California Coastal Commissioner. Walking out after a 13-hour hearing, one of my fellow commissioners asked, "Why on earth do we do this?" As I got back to the hotel, I found myself wondering the same thing. Whatever got me interested in public service and non-profits? As I tried to unwind, I turned on the hotel TV and caught part of an old movie, "The Big Chill."

It reminded me that I volunteer my time because of a gift I had received my first year in college.

Unshakable Certainty

I had never been outside of New York so, to me, Michigan seemed like a foreign country. On the first day of college I wandered down my dorm hall introducing myself and met Michael Krzys, the guy who would one day be the best man at my wedding, making a salad on the floor of his room. I provided the bowl and as we started talking, I was fascinated that he was from Adrian, Mich., a quintessential small town in the Midwest. He was equally curious about someone who grew up in New York. As we got to know each other, I pretty quickly I realized that I had met my match, someone with even more curiosity, creativity, and a wry sense of humor. As best friends our freshman year, we did all the crazy things that first year college students do (things I still won't tell my kids).

But as I got to know Michael, there was another, completely foreign part of him I didn't understand. (It would take me another 30 years.) From the day I met him, he had a commitment to public service that was deep, heartfelt, profound, unshakable and to me, mysterious and completely unfathomable. Even as a freshman, Michael already knew that his calling was to help others and to do so he was determined to become a public service lawyer. It confused and unnerved me to know someone with so much certainty about the meaning and direction of his life. It couldn't have been more different from mine.

After our first year our lives took different paths. When they would touch again, it would be in ways neither of us could have predicted.

Different Paths

With the Vietnam War going full tilt, I left school and joined the Air Force, spending a year and a half in Southeast Asia. Michael and I kept in touch via letters—me telling him about adventures in the military, fighter planes, electronics, and foreign countries. His letters explained to me why I was an idiot, war was immoral, and that while he appreciated my dedication to national service, it was public service that was the higher calling. Each of his letters ended with him reminding me that I was destined for a different career.

When I got back from Thailand, the war was winding down and Michael was now in the University of Michigan Law School (having finished his undergraduate degree in three years). For my last year in the Air Force, I was stationed on a B-52 bomber base, 183 miles from Ann Arbor. I knew the exact mileage as I would drive it every weekend to see my girlfriend and hang out with Michael. Over dinner, we'd argue about politics, talk about how to best save the world, and he'd tell me what he was learning that week in his law school classes. I remember when he taught me the best way to understand an issue was to learn how to argue both sides of a case.

It didn't take long before he was loaning me his last quarter's law books to read during the week at the airbase where I was keeping the world safe for democracy. (While students in law school were hiding their Playboy magazines inside their law books, I'm probably the only guy who had to hide his law books from fellow airmen under a pile of Playboy magazines.)

Remove the Tag

In his last year in law school, the high point for Michael was arguing his first pro-bono case in Detroit for a tenant who claimed he was being illegally evicted. (In Michigan law, students could appear and practice in limited court settings under the supervision of an admitted attorney.) When I drove down to Ann Arbor that weekend, I was regaled with Michael's tale of his passionate defense of his first client as he stood in front of the judge waving his arms for effect in his first-ever sports coat. Michael said he was ecstatic that the judge ruled in his favor, but was a bit confused when the judge motioned him to approach the bench. In a low voice the judge said, "Son, that was a pretty good argument for a law student. However the next time you're in court, you may want to remove the price tag from the sleeve of your sports coat."

When I got out of the military and went back to school, Michael was finishing up law school, and a year later he and his new wife headed to the South to work for Georgia Legal Services in McIntosh County in Georgia. I moved to Silicon Valley, and we kept up a sporadic correspondence, me trying to explain startups and Michael telling me about the world of civil rights and equal justice for the poor. If possible it seemed like his excitement for what he was doing matched mine. I just didn't understand why he did it.

It's a Calling

For entrepreneurs, understanding why people dedicate their lives to working for nonprofits is hard to fathom. Why work for low pay, on something that wasn't going to deliver a product that would change the world?

Today, each time I see the staffs of those non-profits where I'm on the board, I get a glimpse of that same passion, commitment and sense of doing right that I first heard my freshman year decades ago. For the best of them, it's not a job, it's a life-long calling. The executive directors of the Coastal

Commission and POST remind me of what Michael might have become.

A Life Worth Living

One fine California April day in 1981, three years in Silicon Valley now into my second startup, I got a call from someone in Michigan who had been trying to track me down. Michael and his wife were bringing some kids to camp, and he was killed in a head-on car accident with a drunk driver. His wife and the kids survived.

It took me a long time, but as I got older I realized that life was more than just about work, technical innovation, and business. Michael and others worked to preserve and protect the values that made life worth living. And while we were making things, they were the ones who were who changing our society into a more just place to live.

There isn't a day that goes by on the Coastal Commission that I don't wonder what Michael Kryzs would do. To this day, he is my model as a human being who found his own compass.

I always hoped that mine would point in the same direction.

About The Author

Steve Blank

A retired eight-time serial entrepreneur-turned-educator and author, Steve Blank has changed how startups are built and how entrepreneurship is taught around the globe. He is author of the bestselling The Startup Owner's Manual, and his earlier seminal work, The Four Steps to the Epiphany, credited with launching the Lean Startup movement. His May 2013 Harvard Business Review article on the Lean Startup defined the movement.

Steve is widely recognized as a thought leader on startups and innovation. His books and blog have redefined how to build successful startups; his Lean LaunchPad class at Stanford, Berkeley, and Columbia has redefined how entrepreneurship is taught; and his Innovation Corps class for the National Science Foundation forever changed how the U.S. commercializes science. His articles regularly appear in The Wall Street Journal, Forbes, Fortune, The Atlantic, and Huffington Post.

Blank's first book, The Four Steps to the Epiphany (2003), offered the insight that startups are not small versions of large companies – large companies execute business models, but startups search for them – and led him to realize that startups need their own tools, different from those used to manage existing companies. The book described a Customer Development methodology to guide a startup's search for a scalable business model, launching the Lean Startup movement in the process.

His second book, The Startup Owner's Manual, published in March 2012, is a step-by-step guide to building a successful company that incorporates the best practices, lessons, and tips that have swept the startup world since The Four Steps was published.

His essays on his blog, www.steveblank.com, and his two books are considered required reading among entrepreneurs, investors, and established companies throughout the world.

In 2011, Blank developed the Lean LaunchPad, a hands-on class that integrates Business Model design and Customer Development into practice through rapid, real-world customer interaction and business model iteration. In 2011, the National Science Foundation adopted Blank's class for its Innovation Corps (I-Corps), training teams of the nation's top scientists and engineers to take their ideas out of the university lab and into the commercial marketplace. To date, more than 400 handpicked teams of scientists and engineers have participated in I-Corps.

Blank also offers a free online version of Lean LaunchPad through Udacity.com; more than 250,000 people have signed up for the class, which is also the centerpiece of Startup

Weekend NEXT, a global entrepreneurship training program launched in fall 2012.

Steve is a prolific writer, speaker and teacher. In 2009, he earned the Stanford University Undergraduate Teaching Award in Management Science and Engineering. In 2010, he earned the Earl F. Cheit Outstanding Teaching Award at U.C. Berkeley Haas School of Business. The San Jose Mercury News listed him as one of the 10 Influencers in Silicon Valley. Harvard Business Review named him one of 12 Masters of Innovation. Despite these accolades and many others, Steve says he might well have been voted "least likely to succeed" in his New York City high school class.

Eight Startups in 21 Years
After repairing fighter plane electronics in Thailand during the Vietnam War, Steve arrived in Silicon Valley in 1978, as boom times began. He joined his first of eight startups including two semiconductor companies, Zilog and MIPS Computers; Convergent Technologies; a consulting stint for Pixar; a supercomputer firm, Ardent; peripheral supplier, SuperMac; a military intelligence systems supplier, ESL; Rocket Science Games. Steve co-founded startup No. 8, E.piphany, in his living room in 1996. In sum: two significant craters, one massive "dot-com bubble" home run, several

"base hits," and immense learning that resulted in The Four Steps to the Epiphany.

An avid reader in history, technology, and entrepreneurship, Steve has followed his curiosity about why entrepreneurship blossomed in Silicon Valley while stillborn elsewhere. It has made him an unofficial expert and frequent speaker on "The Secret History of Silicon Valley."

Steve is a former Commissioner of the California Coastal Commission, the public body that regulates land use and public access on the California coast. Steve is on the board of the California League of Conservation Voters (CLCV). He is a past board member of Audubon California, the Peninsula Open Space Land Trust (POST), and was a trustee of U.C. Santa Cruz.

Steve's proudest startups are daughters Katie and Sarah, co-developed with wife Alison Elliott. They split their time between Pescadero and Silicon Valley.

Holding a Cat by the Tail

Printed in Great Britain
by Amazon